THE GAME ASSET
PIPELINE

THE GAME ASSET PIPELINE

BEN CARTER

DELMAR
CENGAGE Learning

Australia • Brazil • Japan • Korea • Mexico • Singapore • Spain • United Kingdom • United States

The Game Asset Pipeline
Ben Carter

Publisher: Jenifer Niles

Cover Design: The Printed Image

For product information and technology assistance, contact us at
Cengage Learning Customer & Sales Support, 1-800-354-9706
For permission to use material from this text or product,
submit all requests online at **www.cengage.com/permissions**
Further permissions questions can be emailed to
permissionrequest@cengage.com

Library of Congress Control Number: 2004014970

ISBN-13: 978-1-58450-342-2

ISBN-10: 1-58450-342-4

Delmar
Executive Woods
5 Maxwell Drive
Clifton Park, NY 12065
USA

Cengage Learning is a leading provider of customized learning solutions with office locations around the globe, including Singapore, the United Kingdom, Australia, Mexico, Brazil, and Japan. Locate your local office at **www.cengage.com/global**

Cengage Learning products are represented in Canada by Nelson Education, Ltd.

To learn more about Delmar, visit **www.cengage.com/delmar**

Purchase any of our products at your local bookstore or at our preferred online store **www.ichapters.com**

Printed in the United States of America
1 2 3 4 5   15 14 13 12 11

FD026

Acknowledgments

Many thanks to my friends, family, and all my colleagues, especially the team at Lost Toys (many of whom had the misfortune of using early attempts at developing the systems described herein).

Contents

Preface

The video games industry is currently growing at a terrific pace. This is not only seen in increased sales figures and the level of integration into popular culture, but also in the sheer amount of effort that goes into developing a top-selling game. Teams of more than 100 people work regularly on large-scale games projects and the demands for the creation of vast quantities of extremely high-quality content on incredibly tight schedules often defy belief. Yet somehow, these teams often succeed. Not always, certainly, but frequently enough that consumer expectations are consistently being raised by new games that push technology beyond its previous limits.

Despite the tremendous growth that the industry has undergone however, there are still many working practices that were developed when a typical game team comprised 5 or 10 people, and are rarely questioned, simply because they have become so ingrained. It is only recently that developers have begun to realize that the point has been reached where merely *creating* content is not necessarily the most pressing problem: managing the creation process and getting that content into the right place at the right time in the right format is often a far more difficult task. It is still a disturbingly frequent occurrence that hundreds of development hours are wasted dealing with asset and pipeline issues, even when just trying to get the game to *run*.

The solutions and ideas presented in this book are, in many ways, a work in progress. The industry is constantly evolving, and each new development brings with it a whole host of new data management problems. As I write this, the question of what the next generation of console technology will bring is looming large on the horizon. The one thing that most experts agree on is that without a doubt, the volume and quality of asset data required will take another order of magnitude leap. Despite this, we still have not got a firm grasp on the problems we face today, and although I believe that the systems and implementations described here represent a worthwhile attempt at that goal, there is still a long way to go.

There are three distinct facets to the topics covered in this book: constructing robust and usable asset management systems, building systems necessary to implement an entirely automated (or as close as reasonably possible) system for *managing* asset processing tasks, and the nuts and bolts of performing the most common tasks. As such, some areas will be of greater relevance than others to some readers.

Chapters 2, 3, 4, and 6 represent both design and implementation details for a comprehensive asset management and processing solution. These chapters will interest tools programmers and producers or managers who are interested in learning about how such a system works (or *could* work, for those who have yet to take the plunge to start building their own).

Meanwhile, Chapters 5, 7, and 8 focus largely on the low-level processing tasks a typical asset pipeline is likely to be called upon to perform. These chapters cover fairly technical topics and are likely to interest tools and engine programmers. (While pipeline tasks are strictly speaking outside the remit of most engine programmers, many of the more complex processes are closely tied to the core engine code, which leads to many engine programmers moonlighting as tools programmers to ensure those areas function as they desire!)

Chapter 9 covers the management of the processing pipeline, and in particular, how dependency maintenance tools such as *make* can be used to update files in an efficient manner. It also discusses the problems involved in building a robust and flexible framework that a variety of different processing tools can be built with, ensuring interoperability and the sharing of common functionality.

Finally, Chapter 10 describes the last stage in the pipeline, the production of assets that can be included on the final game media. Efficiently laying out the data is discussed, along with some uses and methods of data verification, encryption, and compression. The last section covers the tasks faced after the game has shipped: methods for supplying patches that update data in the game to add features or fix bugs, and archiving the pipeline and asset data for the future.

My hope is that this book will prove to be useful in demystifying this sometimes convoluted field, and that the concepts and algorithms presented will give a head start to anyone looking to develop his own asset management and processing solutions.

1 Introduction

In This Chapter

- Offline Processing
- Beating the RAM Barrier
- Other Factors
- The Asset Pipeline
- The Asset Feedback Loop
- The Structure of Game Assets
- Builds
- Version Control
- Asset Dependencies
- Data Validation
- Workflow

A modern video game is a massively complex construction, comprised of a vast number of interlocking parts that work together to form an interactive audio/visual experience for the player. As the power of both PC and console systems increases, players expect more immersive, detailed worlds and characters, fueling the demand for games to include more and more "content," in the form of high-quality 3D models, textures, artwork, sounds, and music, to name just a few of the hugely diverse range of resources that make up the average video game.

As the complexity of games increases, developers must rethink how to manage the development process to cope with the longer development schedules, larger teams, and the sheer volume of information created during the process. It is no longer possible or desirable for team members to have the entire structure or design "in their heads"—everything must be documented, planned, and carefully managed—otherwise chaos will result.

1

In the programming arena, techniques for managing the scaling of project complexity have been in place for many years, driven mainly by the needs of large, commercial developments in fields such as banking and manufacturing. As a result, there is a very good road map for projects scaling to virtually any size, and a large body of information on the steps necessary to ensure that larger projects can be handled in a structured manner. Techniques such as object-oriented programming, design-by-contract, and modular architectures are commonly used by developers to separate projects into manageable chunks. There are sophisticated tools such as source control and bug tracking systems to enable large numbers of programmers to work together (fairly) smoothly on a single piece of software.

However, there has been little similar development for resources other than program code. Here, games are often at the cutting edge in terms of the volume and quality of content required, and there is relatively little experience that can be brought in from outside the industry to assist in dealing with the challenges faced. Even just efficiently storing and cataloging artwork, sounds, video, maps, and other data (often collectively referred to as the game "assets") required for a game is a mammoth task. But the problem is even more complicated—the assets must somehow make their way into the game, in a form that the code can use.

OFFLINE PROCESSING

The obvious question to ask at this point is "why bother"? Why can't games simply be written to load the same formats that art programs and music packages do, thereby reducing the problem to a simpler one of mere file management?

In some cases, this is a perfectly valid approach. Particularly in the case of PC games, where extensibility may be a concern (so that third-party or user modifications, often called "mods," can be easily developed and distributed), "off-the-shelf" file formats provide many advantages. They usually allow a wide range of content creation packages to be used, and the "turnaround time" needed to update an asset in the game is negligible. It is also the case that PCs (and to a certain extent, PC users!) are more capable of handling the increases in disc space requirements and load-time processing that usually result from taking this approach.

Console games traditionally have had much more offline processing applied to their data, for a number of reasons. Until the advent of CD-based machines, console games typically had to fit into the small space afforded by ROM-based cartridges—first-generation consoles such as the Atari VCS™ had a meager 16 K of available space on their largest cartridges, and even the Super Nintendo® offered a maximum of 6 MB of total space (and only a handful of big budget games such as *Star Ocean* and *Tales of Phantasia* used these cartridges). While some cartridge systems featured substantially larger capacities (like SNK's Neo-Geo™ arcade system), these were expensive and not widely popular. Even worse, on all such systems, the cost of manufacturing larger cartridges was higher, and as this cost was borne by the publisher there was considerable pressure on developers to ensure that their games fitted into the smallest possible space. To achieve this, game assets had to be compressed and all unnecessary headers and information stripped from them, leaving only the raw data that was to be used by the game.

Even though the situation today has almost reversed, in that console games typically ship on DVDs with capacities of 4.5 GB or 9 GB, while PC games are still most frequently distributed on (a number of) 650 MB CDs, the practice of preprocessing as much data as possible for console versions of games remains. The disc space limitation may have been mostly removed, but in its place two more limiting factors have emerged—available RAM and disc access speed. With cartridge-based games, all the game assets were available at (relatively) high-speed to the game "on demand." With CDs or DVDs, it typically takes the drive several hundred milliseconds to "seek" to a specific part of the disc to retrieve data, and once it is there the data can only be retrieved at around 300 K/sec (for a double-speed CD drive as used on the original PlayStation™ and similar machines) or 6000 K/sec (for a double-speed DVD drive, as used on the PlayStation 2™).

Needless to say, with those access times, it is necessary for data to be loaded from the disc into memory before it can be used. Therefore, the "working set" of data that is required for the current area of the game must fit into the RAM available on the console. So while there is no longer the great impetus to pack data efficiently onto the disc itself (except, as we will see later, for speedy access), the packing problem has re-emerged as a byproduct of the heavily limited space available in memory. Current games consoles typically have approximately 32 MB of RAM available—the highest specification system on the market today is Microsoft's Xbox®, with a whopping 64 MB. This contrasts starkly with the PC market, where at the time of this writing 256 MB of RAM is often considered a practical minimum, and machines with 512 MB or more of memory are commonplace—no doubt this will rapidly increase in the future as RAM cost continues to tumble.

BEATING THE RAM BARRIER

So, are console games almost as limited on CD-based systems as they were on cartridge machines? In short, the answer is no. Consider the case of a game in which the player must explore a large environment—for example a castle. Loading all the geometry, textures, effects, and so on for the entire castle would require a prohibitively huge amount of memory. However, at any one moment, the player can only see (and interact with) a tiny fraction of the total area—essentially, the room in which he is currently standing. So, as the player moves around, the game can keep the current room in memory and load the next one whenever the player walks through a door.

At its simplest, this solution can be implemented by stopping the gameplay, loading the next room, and then starting again—the approach used by games such as the original *Resident Evil*. However, many developers and gamers considered this too intrusive because it broke up the flow of the gameplay and made the player wait each time he moved between rooms. So, the technique of *streaming* was born.

Streaming

Streaming is the process of loading into memory in the background while the game is being played, depending on what will be required next. The most common use for streaming is for in-game music—rather than storing the entire track in memory, only a small buffer (typically only a few seconds of music, occupying a very small amount of memory) is kept, and as the sound system is playing data from the start of the buffer, more data is being read in and added to the end. Since the disc can be read faster than the music is being played, the buffer always remains full (in fact, the buffer is unnecessary under theoretical "perfect" circumstances, but is required to prevent the music "skipping" if a scratch on the disc or another game task interrupts the reading process for a short time). For the majority of early CD-based games, music or in-game speech was the sole use of streaming technology.

More advanced uses of streaming are now commonplace, however. While early consoles had difficulty reading fast enough to handle more than one "stream" of data at a time (so, for example, using the disc to stream music would preclude using it for any other concurrent purpose), the DVD drives on modern machines are capable of reading and seeking fast enough that they can maintain several continuous streams of data at once. It is not uncommon for games to be reading a stream of music, a stream of in-game speech, and a stream of game data simultaneously.

This flexibility has enabled games to move beyond the "one room/stage/level at once" model and introduce "seamless" environments. The key to this is the ability to predict what the player is going (or is likely) to do next. It is rare for a game to be designed so that the player can move instantaneously to any point in the gameworld or encounter any of the games enemies at any time, for example—and in many games (such as scrolling shoot-'em-up games like *Ikagura* or *R-Type*, or racing games like *Ridge Racer*) the player's progression through the game is strictly linear.

In a game such as the castle example, enough memory is set aside that *two* rooms can be loaded simultaneously. One of these is always the room that the player is currently in, while the other is the room that the player is going to next. As the player explores one room, the game is loading the next—so that when the door is opened, there is no apparent loading or delay. The game simply switches to the data for the next area, throws away the data for the last one, and starts the loading process again.

Of course, depending on the nature of the gameplay the process can be much more complicated (if, for example, the player can choose one of a number of routes to follow, or the world is not broken up into convenient "room" segments). However, these problems can all be solved with some effort. Games like *Grand Theft Auto 3* and *Jak and Daxter* demonstrate huge, non-segmented, sprawling worlds that the player can explore freely.

OTHER FACTORS

RAM concerns are not the sole reason for wanting to preprocess assets into a form as compact and close as possible to what the target system will actually be using, however. Whether data is being streamed or not, the smaller the actual file size, the less time it will take to read from disc, which will either increase the efficiency of the game's streaming system or reduce the loading time, both of which are significant (especially when developing for consoles, where the machine manufacturers and licensors often impose strict "maximum loading time" limits on developers). It is also important that on consoles, the CPU has as little work to do as possible. Again, compared to PCs, console main CPUs typically lie somewhere between "somewhat underpowered" and "very underpowered." While on a PC a small amount of processing (for example, "swizzling" or rearranging the data in a texture for more efficient access) will usually be masked by the speed of the hard drive or disc the data is being read from, on a console processing can massively increase the time needed to load data, and if that data is being streamed the effect can be far worse as the extra processing will be directly competing for processor time with the game itself!

While the small processor hits associated with simple reformatting of data are serious factors when designing any sort of game, they are not "show-stoppers." It is still perfectly possible to ship a modern console or PC game that loads assets from source files in this way. Increasingly however, games use many more sophisticated processing steps that are not only inefficient to perform on the target platform during loading, but completely impossible.

One of the first games to demonstrate this was iD Software's classic *Doom*™, which used a high-level data structure called a "BSP tree" (Binary Space Partition tree) to perform visibility and rendering calculations. While *Doom's* levels were relatively simple and the 2D BSP process it used quite fast, it was still too slow to be used when loading the game—sometimes taking several minutes per level. When iD's subsequent game, *Quake*™ arrived, the more complex 3D BSP trees it used often necessitated several *hours* of processing on a fast PC to calculate for a reasonably-sized level!

The arrival of these very computationally expensive processes as a required step in preparing data for the game caused a sudden change in the game development process. Suddenly, the efficiency of offline processing became a major factor in the development of the game—as the time each asset took to process increased, it was no longer possible to simply "brute force" the processing by rebuilding all the assets for the game every time you wanted to burn a new disc. In addition, with designers having to wait significant amounts of time just to see what effect their changes had in the game, and a complete rebuild of all the game data taking many hours or even days, carefully managing the asset processing problem at every step of the development cycle became an absolute necessity.

THE ASSET PIPELINE

This is where the *asset pipeline* came into play. Quite simply, the term describes the sequence of processes that takes assets from their source form (usually the direct output of whatever package the artist created them in) to the final data that can be burned onto a disc or cartridge to form part of the finished game. The goal of a well-designed asset pipeline is to act as its name suggests: you put source data into one end of the pipe, and it comes out of the other end in a form the game can use, hopefully as fast and with as little human intervention as possible.

In many ways, the primary goal of the asset pipeline is not to construct data for the final game. It is comparatively rare that a fully working game disc with all the assets needs to be produced. It is certainly an event which happens more frequently as the game gets closer to being completed, but compared with the by-the-minute regularity with which *in progress* changes get made to the data, it falls into a distant second to the main objective—ensuring that the "feedback loop" for game assets is as short as possible.

THE ASSET FEEDBACK LOOP

The feedback loop can be described very simply. For any given asset (a texture, character model, map, etc.), the feedback loop is the process needed to take that asset from the editor in which it is being constructed or altered into the game so that it can be tested or examined (see Figure 1.1 for an example). This is the most critical path for the vast majority of the artists, designers, and programmers working on the game. Even with the best tools, there is no substitute for being able to view work in context in the game itself. And since the vast bulk of the asset creation process is an iterative process (a succession of alterations and "tweaks" until the desired result is achieved) the bounding factor in the time needed for this in a modern game is almost always the length of the feedback loop.

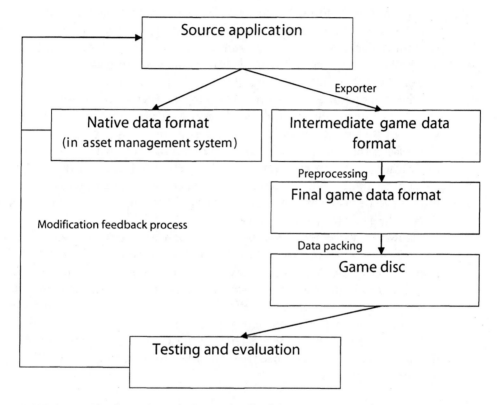

FIGURE 1.1 The flow of a typical asset feedback loop.

Consider the case of a simple texture map on an in-game model. When performing a simple process such as trying to match the texture color to that of the environment around it, an artist may easily spend only 5–10 seconds on each iteration of the feedback loop actually altering the texture, and another 5–10 seconds examining the results. If it takes 40 seconds for the texture to be converted into a form the game can read, and for the artist to re-run the game executable and load the necessary level, then twice as much time is spent waiting as actually doing useful work!

Forty seconds may seem like a long time, but for a game in development it is not uncommon for processing and game load times to be far longer, even for a "simple" asset like a texture map. Imagine how much time the designers working on *Quake* maps must have spent waiting as they tested minor alterations to their creations.

A common "solution" to this problem is to deliberately shortcut the feedback loop for often encountered situations. For example, the game could be made to load the majority of its resources from preprocessed files (for speed), but selected assets (those being currently edited) from source files instead, processing them as it loads them. Another common solution is the provision of "artist preview tools," standalone applications that provide a simple, efficient emulation of one of the game's functions, for example loading and displaying character models in a window with simple animation controls. This sort of lightweight tool is typically much faster than the game because it does not have to load or display any of the other assets, and since it is not part of the game itself, it can deliberately use less efficient techniques (which, for example, consume large quantities of RAM or are too slow to be viable on the target platforms) enabling it to produce the same results as the game with less preprocessing.

However, while such tools are undoubtedly an extremely useful solution to specific "worst case" instances of the feedback loop problem (and incidentally, can provide many other benefits, such as allowing assets that only appear occasionally during normal gameplay to be tested and examined easily), there are still many places where they cannot be used effectively. Level design and gameplay balancing, for example, are largely impossible to perform adequately without the game itself being used for testing. So the efficiency of the asset pipeline and minimization of the time the feedback loop needs are both key to increasing the efficiency of the development process.

THE STRUCTURE OF GAME ASSETS

The assets used in the construction of a game fall into many categories—sounds, artwork, music, maps, and so on, but they all share certain common features. In general, each asset forms an individual element of the game experience, and there is a hierarchy in which assets get combined to form one "gameplay unit" or a single scenario, level, or such, which constitutes a coherent chunk of the game experience.

For example, in a traditional platform game, a gameplay unit might be a level, consisting of a map containing some scenery, a number of creatures, and some puzzles. The level map itself is clearly an asset, which then in turn contains or references the 3D models for the scenery, the character models, and a background music track—all of which are assets in their own right. These in turn reference textures for the models, sound effects, behavior lists for the characters, and scripts for the puzzles—again, more assets. All of these individually created components must be combined to form a single level or "package," as each asset in the hierarchy is dependent on the assets beneath it to function correctly, and the assets above it to give it context.

Of course, in some cases it is not necessarily true that assets conform strictly to this hierarchical structure. For example, a character may appear in more than one level, in which case all of the assets associated with it need to be either included in every level it appears in separately, or made available in some common area. The central character might be another special case as it is present everywhere in the game. Hence, the hierarchy becomes more like a series of hierarchies or even a web for different subsections of the game, based on the dependencies between assets.

To take another example, in a racing game, a single asset hierarchy might form one track, creating a package derived from the layout, scenery meshes, and textures. But including car models in this package would be pointless, as every car will appear on every track. In this case, making each car or subset of cars an individual hierarchy makes more sense, as cars are in no way tied (or dependent on) a specific track, and vice versa.

Some games may have multiple concurrent "strands" with overlap between them. For example, an RPG may have different sets of assets for battle scenes and exploration sections, but with some characters shared between them. A set of these battle and exploration packages would then form the package for a particular section of the game-world, effectively forming yet another hierarchy on top of the base gameplay sections.

Of course, not all games break up neatly into separate chunks like this. In particular, games that offer a free roaming world without fixed levels often cannot be effectively divided into sections along "gameplay unit" boundaries. Instead the most commonly used approach is to break the game into functional units, separating assets by type, so for example all of the characters form one package, all of the vehicles another, and all of the scenery in a given section of the map another. In these cases, it is more often technical limitations that dictate how assets should be broken up than design constraints.

When deciding how to structure game assets, it is important to take into account both the final form the assets will take and the manner in which they will be created. In cases such as large continuous world games where the dividing lines are not immediately clear, the former problem is actually more easily solved algorithmically (and the assets moved into the necessary locations at some point in the asset pipeline itself). This is partly because the requirements of the engine and technology are likely to change over time, and partly because the layout required is unlikely to be well suited for the asset creation process (e.g., if it forces scenery to be broken up according to where it is positioned on an overall map).

Once a structure is decided upon, however, it is vital to ensure that it is adhered to. In some cases, the structure itself may actually be enforced by the use of file metadata or other "smart processing," but in any situation maintaining the standards and layout used will avoid many potential problems. In particular, should it prove necessary to change the structure of the assets at a later stage (this is not an infrequent occurrence during development), if the existing assets are correctly sorted the task will be much simpler and potentially automatically performed, because no actual examination of each asset to determine its role will be required.

BUILDS

Besides the day-to-day task of taking work-in-progress assets and converting them for testing and development work, the other major task that the asset tools must perform is the production of assets for specific "builds" of the game. A build generally differs from the development data in that it is intended to include a complete, coherent set of data for all (or a specific segment) of the game. All the assets should be "in sync" with each other and there should be (hopefully) no errors. The assets that are under development are constantly changing and therefore it is normal that at times there will be some that have been updated and others that have not—for the developers, this is not a problem as they are generally only interested in examining or testing the specific items they are currently working on. However, builds are typically used for demonstration purposes, more comprehensive testing, or as submissions to become the final version of the game; hence any inconsistencies or errors in them are a serious problem.

This problem can be tackled in many ways, ranging from having a separate processing pipeline (using the same tools, but isolated from the development systems) for producing the data for builds, to integrating the ability to tag and "freeze" data in the development pipeline to allow a consistent set to be extracted. Almost as important as being able to get the data out of the system, is the ability to record what data was used to construct each build. In cases where builds are used for external testing or review, it can often be weeks before any feedback reaches the development team, and they need to be able to look at a record of the old data to discover the cause of problems or determine which have subsequently been fixed.

VERSION CONTROL

For similar reasons, it is also often desirable for the asset management tools to keep track of the "history" of assets—the sequence of changes that have been made to them, who made them, when, and (in some cases) why. This ability, commonly known as "version control," has been a staple feature of code management tools like *Visual SourceSafe* or *Perforce* for many years, but until recently the high requirements (mainly in terms of storage space) of storing this information for large binary assets like textures and models has hampered its acceptance. With the radical drops in storage costs and the increased necessity for version control across all aspects of large projects, however, it is now coming into more and more widespread use.

Version control serves many purposes but it primarily enables assets to be "rolled back" to previous versions in the event that changes cause problems or are simply deemed to have a detrimental effect on quality. In this case, any version of a file can be retrieved for comparison. Some systems enable "branching" of sets of files or the creation of parallel sets of data that can be edited separately and then merged back into the main "tree" at a later time if necessary. For example, this could be used if an artist wanted to try out a new visual effect on a number of models, without affecting the rest of the project until it was fully tested. It also provides a useful audit trail, which can be invaluable in tracking down where problems were introduced, and by whom. This is key information in the process of ensuring that the problems do not reoccur. Most version control systems also incorporate the concept of file "check-outs" and "check-ins", which is a process by which a single developer can gain exclusive access to a file or asset while he modifies it, thereby ensuring that there is no risk that someone else will make changes that conflict with or overwrite his.

ASSET DEPENDENCIES

Another problem that arises with large projects is the issue of asset dependency. Dependencies arise where assets reference or use one another, for example, a model using various different textures, or a map which incorporates a number of characters, scenery and object models, scripts, textures, sounds, and so on. This can cause major problems in some cases, if an asset needs to be modified but it is not immediately obvious what consequences will occur. For example, a generic brick wall texture may have been used in many different items of scenery in a game by different artists, and changing the color of it to suit the lighting in one area may radically impact the look of other, unconnected parts of the game.

In cases like these, it is extremely useful for the game pipeline to be able to feed information to the artists about which assets are used, how often, and where. Dependency information can be maintained as a manual task, simply by keeping notes on where assets have been used, but this is prone to errors and can quickly be rendered useless by even one person's failure to update the information correctly. Hence it is much more useful if the information can be automatically generated each time the assets are fed through the pipeline, ensuring that the developers are always aware of what areas of the game need to be tested to guarantee that their changes do not cause further problems.

DATA VALIDATION

Another major task for the asset pipeline, closely related to the feedback loop problem, is to provide *validation* of data for the game. The scale and complexity of most games today means that exhaustive testing of every level, stage, or area of the game is not usually performed on a regular basis until quite late in the development cycle. As a result, if an invalid, corrupted, or otherwise broken asset is added to the game data, it may not be noticed for a significant amount of time, often not until the last few hours of intensive testing before an important deadline!

Catching errors late in the development process has several obvious disadvantages, including the obvious possibility that an error may *not* be caught! It is also desirable that errors be flagged as soon as possible for efficiency reasons. It is far simpler for a developer to correct a simple error in an asset if they are informed of it while they are still working on it (or have just "finished"), but if they are made aware of it days or weeks later, the effort required to find the original file, re-open it, then locate and fix the error is far greater. This is especially true in the case of complex assets such as skeletally animated 3D models, where the time needed for the artist to reacquaint himself with the structure of the skeleton and animation, and then determine how best to make the required change can easily run into hours!

Therefore, it is highly desirable that data errors be caught as early as possible. This is easier in some cases than others. Some types of errors are very obvious and easy to check for—for example, texture maps which are not a power of two in size (most hardware does not support textures of other sizes, or does so only at a great cost in efficiency), or models that have missing textures. Both of these can be easily confirmed with a handful of lines of code, and do not rely on knowledge of any part of the game outside the asset itself. They are also very common errors, and as such, they are good candidates to be included in the very first checks performed by the asset pipeline, which often take place during the export of the data from the source package (this also means that they can be conveniently reported to the artist responsible the moment he tries to save the file).

Other errors, unfortunately, are more subtle, and do not become apparent until much later in the pipeline. For example, a character may have been placed in a level in a position where there is not enough space for it to stand without its head being forced into the ceiling. Detecting this error requires knowledge of both the size of the model file and the geometry of the level it is being placed in. Even worse, it is not immediately apparent whether it is a problem with the map design or the model. It could be that the level designer had inadvertently placed the character in the wrong place, but it could equally be true that the designer had built the level and then the model artist made the character taller. It may even be that it is a change in the size of another model in the world (a piece of scenery, for example) that has caused the problem.

Error Handling

In circumstances like this, there are difficult decisions to be made as to what the asset pipeline tools should do. Assuming some sort of error reporting structure is in place to allow problems in the pipeline to be fed back to the team, should the error be reported to the map designer, the modeler, or both? Instead, should it be reported in-game to the person who next plays the level? The person who is actually running the pipeline? Or someone higher up the team structure (such as the lead artist) who can decide which of the conflicting assets should be changed?

Simply deciding to send an error message can be a major design headache, but there is a yet more complex problem associated with broken data in the pipeline— namely, *what to do with it*. Halting the process and reporting an error is one approach, but this is generally impractical. If a single badly sized texture can stop the game data being built, then the amount of time lost as other team members wait for the problem to be resolved (or, worse, simply give up on waiting and try to fix it themselves) will be incredible. The pipeline needs to be as robust as possible, even when faced with incorrect input data, it should be able to produce some sort of salvageable output. For example, missing or invalid textures can be replaced with a "default texture" which is usually a brightly colored, easily recognizable pattern so that it is quickly spotted in-game should the error go unnoticed elsewhere (that said, at least one game has shipped with an object still using a bright green and red default texture in it)!

Missing textures or models are easy to replace with placeholder items, but the problem is much more difficult when the problem actively "breaks" a level or section of the game. For example, a map might be missing a "the player starts here" marker, or the terrain for the level could be missing. In these cases, there are two choices: the asset processor can either simply output nothing (and prevent those levels or areas being played until the problem is fixed), or it can go back and use the "last known good" or valid set of data it had. This can either be achieved by the system itself keeping copies of the data, or by interfacing with an asset version control system, which enables the processing tools to retrieve past versions of any file it needs.

Both approaches have their advantages and disadvantages. Using the last known good data means that there is always a "complete" set of game data available with which to play the game, but equally old data may be out of sync with the rest of the game and cause more problems farther down the pipeline. Outputting nothing resolves any potential sync problems, but prevents any other testing or development on that section of the game until the problem is resolved, and can often cause bugs that take time to track down (for example, if the game crashes when a player walks into the room, it may not be obvious at first glance that this is because the room itself didn't export correctly and hence doesn't exist)!

WORKFLOW

Another area where the asset management system can have a significant impact is in the workflow for producing and integrating assets into the game. In most teams, there is a defined process (in theory, at least) for testing and approving assets. While adherence to this is not so necessary for small developers, with larger teams it becomes vital to ensure that consistent standards are being applied across all areas of the game.

Typically, the process for doing this involves one or more key people being required to sign off, or approve, every significant change to the assets. With a suitable asset management system, this protocol can actually be enforced, rather than simply relying on people remembering to go through the requisite steps. If the system keeps track of the approval status of each asset (resetting it as necessary when significant changes occur), then at any time a simple search will reveal which assets have yet to be reviewed.

Another very useful benefit of this involves selectively "releasing" assets to the pipeline depending on the intended purpose. For example, assets that have not yet been approved can be included in internal development builds, but until they have been signed off on they will not be used for release versions. This ensures that no unapproved elements can be seen by outside parties. This is a particularly important point when working with licensed material.

From a producer or manager's perspective, the asset management system can also be the source of a wealth of useful information about the status of the project—he can determine the number of assets in each area of the game (and the growth of those numbers over time), what sections have changed recently, and who is currently working on what. It is possible to build up a surprisingly detailed picture of the progress of development. While this is no substitute for actually receiving status updates from the lead responsible for each department, it can provide a useful overview and early pointers to potential trouble-spots.

Another area where the asset management system can assist in making the development process smoother is by providing a means to notify people when changes occur whether it be it on a large scale (e-mailing a list of all the assets changed during the previous day to the entire team each morning), or on a small scale (e-mailing individuals when a file they last edited is altered by someone else). This can be significant in streamlining areas of workflow that cannot be directly controlled by the asset system, by notifying the localization coordinator when the game text database is changed, he can collate the modified strings and send them for translation.

CONCLUSION

The rising complexity, team sizes, and quantity of "intensive" processing tasks such as BSP tree building involved in game development are rapidly pushing the development of efficient, robust, and user-friendly asset management and processing tools to the forefront of current game development projects. There are many obstacles, both technical and structural, to building a system that enables such large-scale development to proceed with the minimum of problems. But none of these problems are insurmountable, and many have already been effectively resolved in other areas of game development or computer science in general.

2 | Where Do Assets Come From?

In This Chapter

- Tool Integration
- Adding Features
- Custom Export Tools
- Data Formats
- Custom Intermediate File Formats

The first step in the asset pipeline is, predictably, the point where assets are actually created. This first step is the most important, and also in most circumstances, the most time-consuming. It is therefore a critically important but sometimes overlooked concern of any well-designed asset management system that it makes this initial step as streamlined and painless as possible, even if only a few seconds are saved each time an alteration is made to a source asset for the game, the total saving over the course of the entire development period will be quite significant.

The vast majority of all game asset creation tools fall into one of two categories. They are either one of a relatively small number of commonly-used commercial "off the shelf" tools such as 3ds max®, Maya®, and Photoshop™, or they are a custom tool, created in-house for a game-specific or platform-specific task. In some circumstances there may be more esoteric externally-developed tools in use (for example, when developing a game using a licensed engine such as the *Quake* or *Unreal*™ engines, it is often necessary to use the map editing tools that were developed by the original developer of that engine; however, these tools are generally supplied with a complete asset pipeline of their own for use with the engine.

From the asset management and processing perspective, these two groups of tools differ in a few small, but important respects. Well-known "industry standard" commercial tools are likely to already have integration with some of the existing asset management systems, and the ability to read and write at least a small number of the most common file formats for their particular data type. However, if support for the management system, file format, or any other tool required is not available, then adding support can be a tricky task as the source code to the application is not usually available, and modifications must be made through whatever "plug-in" API may be available. In some cases, it may simply be impossible to add the support required without the assistance of the company that produced the application.

On the other hand, in-house tools are unlikely, unless a significant amount of effort has been invested in developing and maintaining them, to support any external programs or file formats other than those that were required when the tool was originally developed. This can cause significant problems if there are a number of such tools, as retrofitting them with the necessary code to support a new or modified asset management or processing pipeline can be a time-consuming process, particularly if the code was not originally structured to allow such an addition. However, in virtually all circumstances, at least in-house tools will have source code and (with luck) support from the original developers, so it is reasonably certain that such tools can be modified to handle whatever new requirements arise, even if the time and effort needed to do so is significant in some cases.

TOOL INTEGRATION

Whether the tools in use are commercial packages, developed in-house, or a combination of both, ensuring tight integration with the rest of the pipeline is the key factor in making the whole process more efficient. The users of the tool (artists, designers, etc.) should spend as much of their time as possible *in that tool*. Every time they have to switch to another application to perform some task, or copy a file to a new location, or simply see what name they are supposed to use for a component, they are losing time and potentially, breaking their concentration.

Of course, while in an ideal world everything would be integrated into the primary asset source tools so that the artists could manage, export, preview, and integrate their work into the game without ever leaving one package, in reality this is rarely an achievable goal. There are too many different tools to support, and only a handful of them support the necessary levels of integration with third-party code to allow this sort of interaction. Even for those that do, the costs, in terms of programmer time, to implement this are usually prohibitive.

However, relatively small levels of integration can radically improve the usefulness of tools by providing often-used functionality in the environment, or streamlining frequent processes. For example, consider the case where a conversion tool must be used to process the output from a 3D modeling package into the form required by the game. The vast majority of the time the user will want to save a file and process it immediately. So, even simply adding a feature whereby on startup the conversion tool will automatically select the last file saved (by, for example, reading the file modified dates in the source directory) will save a great deal of time that would otherwise be spent hunting through a list of files for the required one. Going a step further, it would not be difficult to allow the converter to check for newly-modified files and automatically convert them while it is running. Suddenly, from the user's perspective, the conversion tool has become invisible—he starts it running, and from then on, any file saved is automatically converted. As far as the user is concerned, the conversion step no longer exists.

Even without using any direct interface to the original 3D package, it is possible to achieve this degree of "integration," and do so in a way that will easily interoperate with any other package the artists wish to use. Most packages offer many other opportunities for such low-cost integration too. For example, it is common for complex tools like 3D packages to have built-in "macro" or scripting languages, which can often be used to invoke external executables and feed them information. By linking a button o hotkey in the interface to a script that writes out some information, calls a standalone tool to perform some work, and reports the result, users can get the impression that tools have been built into the package. Again, since the bulk of the work is still taking place in the (package-independent) executable, this approach can be easily scaled to support many different programs, as it is only the small macro script that needs to be rewritten in each case.

ADDING FEATURES

While in many cases the tools for asset management and processing build on the existing feature-set of the content creation packages (after all, that is the reason such packages are used), it is almost inevitable that during the course of development it will become necessary to actually add new features to the content creation tools.

For example, it is common for advanced game graphics engines to support features that are not available in some 3D packages, such as programmable shaders or displacement mapping. In these cases it is necessary for the artists to be able to supply additional information (shader name, parameters, etc.) for the surfaces they create outside of what the package itself supports. This is typically achieved in one of three ways: naming conventions, additional data fields, or plug-in objects.

Naming Conventions

Probably the most common mechanism for extracting additional information from tools is the use of naming conventions. This is the very simple practice of taking advantage of the fact that the filing system and most content creation packages allow the use of (usually quite long) names for elements they create. By altering these names, it is possible to provide extra information which the content creation package itself preserves (but otherwise ignores) and passes on to the rest of the pipeline.

Naming conventions can be quite complex, and encode a surprising amount of information. For example, it might be the case that all self-illuminating surfaces in a game are given a name that ends in "_lit" so the artists can still use a meaningful (to them) name, such as "tinroof" followed by the additional information required to form "tinroof_lit." This can be extended further by using multiple naming conventions at the same time, and there is no reason to restrict the system to simply adding static text. Numeric values, names of other objects, anything that can be represented as a textual string can be inserted.

Of course, there is an obvious downside to the use of naming conventions. If multiple systems are in use, names can quickly get unwieldy (surfaces called "tinroof_lit_noshadows_reflective50%_walkable_hitsound=metal,"), and potentially even run into the maximum limit on name length. It is necessary for everyone to remember (or refer to a list of) the different conventions in use, because even a small typing error can potentially introduce a difficult to track bug by breaking part of the expected functionality. It is also impossible to use naming conventions to specify extra information for objects that do not have a name or similarly redundant field that can be used.

Additional Data Fields

Some asset creation packages support the concept of adding user-defined fields to the data they store, or have a single field (usually storing text) which can be used to include comments or additional parameters for an object. In either case, this approach is much like the naming convention strategy, except relatively neater. It is, however, still usually necessary for artists to remember the names of the fields required, and the format in which data should be entered into them.

In the cases of both this and the naming convention approach, however, many of the disadvantages can be overcome by writing some simple additional tools for the packages in use (possibly using the built-in scripting language, if one exists) which encode the necessary information into the name and/or user data fields. By presenting the user with a simple dialog box or other edit tools for the necessary parameters, and validating input on the spot, the number of potential errors can be massively reduced, saving time for everyone involved in the process.

Many tools structure the "user data" field as a simple block of text. This can be effectively used in combination with a small external tool to provide a more intuitive user interface to the edited properties without needing to actually integrate support into the tool itself. The trick is to develop a simple program which allows the various values to be adjusted, possibly with some sort of simple preview functionality, and then get it to construct the required data in the form of a string which can be copied directly into the main tool (or from it) using the OSs "clipboard" functionality. This way, human errors can be kept to a minimum, and only a minimal amount of extra effort is required to insert the data into the content creation tool.

Plug-in Objects

The third, and by far the most complicated, solution to this problem is to make use of the package's plug-in interface to construct a custom object type, or extend an existing one to add the necessary information.

This approach is by far the "neatest," and provides a higher level of control over the behavior of and information stored by the object than the other approaches mentioned. It is possible to provide advanced features such as a real-time preview of what effects the editable parameters will have directly on the content that is being edited. It is also often more efficient to perform more complex calculations (such as precomputing reflection maps for surfaces, or compressing textures "on-the-fly" and displaying the results of using different formats in a paint package) by making use of services the main tool provides for such purposes.

The downside of using plug-ins to perform this task, however, is the additional development time and maintenance required. It is not a trivial task to write a plug-in that adds significant functionality to a large existing package, especially since the interfaces for doing so are frequently quite arcane and may not be well-documented in some areas. Plug-ins are almost always completely tied to the package they are written for, and it will be necessary to expend almost as much effort again to "port," or convert, one to another package. In some cases, it will also be necessary to modify or even rewrite sections of plug-in code when moving between different versions of the same package! In addition, while the other two techniques can be trivially extended with almost no effort when a new piece of information is required, a new version of a plug-in module will need to be developed and distributed to the users of the package before they can utilize any new features.

Using plug-in objects almost always goes hand-in-hand with writing a plug-in to export data from the package to a custom format, since the standard file formats used by most packages will not support the data the plug-in is producing.

CUSTOM EXPORT TOOLS

Custom export tools are by far the most common use of custom plug-ins. Writing exporters which allow the tool to directly write to a format the game or next stage in the asset pipeline can read, allows a lot more flexibility in selecting which information will be exported and in what format, and can be extremely useful in improving the integration with other tools.

In general, an export plug-in must use the *API*, or Application/Programmer Interface, provided to query the data the package holds about the current scene, and then write that data to a file, performing any conversion tasks as required. For packages that are working with complex data (especially 3D modeling programs), this can be a very complex task, which requires quite a detailed understanding of how the host program stores and manipulates information. Fortunately, in the case of most packages, the plug-in API is supplied with a number of sample plug-ins that can be modified and extended, and there is almost always a simple export plug-in included with these that can form the basis for a custom exporter.

Export plug-ins are not, of course, limited to simply writing data from their host package. It is quite common, and indeed desirable in many circumstances, for the exporter to perform additional processing on the source data, saving effort and potentially a lot of time later on in the pipeline. For example, many 3D packages allow the use of higher-order primitives such as curved surfaces in scenes, but it is very rare for these to actually be supported by game engines. While it would be possible to export such surfaces "as is" and then tessellate them into triangles at a later stage in the pipeline, it is far more efficient to perform this step while exporting, when the data is both readily available and the host package probably provides functions for performing the bulk of the tessellation work.

It can also be very useful to perform some data validation at "export time," as it means that any errors detected can be reported to the user (and therefore hopefully fixed) immediately, rather than only being flagged later in the processing. Minimizing the turnaround time for this type of feedback loop, where the resource pipeline will report errors or other changes that need to be made to the user, is a major factor in improving efficiency. The majority of such errors are relatively simple to fix (for example, a missing texture or badly-named object), but if they are not reported until after the user has saved the file and closed the application, the amount of time required to make the necessary modifications is massively increased. The time required to relocate the file, reopen it, make the changes, and resave it could actually exceed the time to make the change.

DATA FORMATS

For virtually any common type of asset data, there are a number of file formats that are frequently used for interchange between programs and exporting to other tools. These are usually fairly well-documented, although in some areas the formats are more stable than others (2D bitmap images, for example, have a very well-defined set of common formats, while 3D scenes formats are much less mature). The following are a sample of some of the most widely-used formats for various data types—there are many others, including some emerging formats designed to handle features which are still under development or not currently used.

2D Bitmap Data

The staple "lowest common denominator" formats that are widely used in games development are Targa (TGA) and Windows Bitmap (BMP) files. Both of these formats can store compressed data, but are normally used in their uncompressed forms, which results in the image being stored simply as a block of raw binary data, prefaced with a short header containing information on the dimensions, bit depth, etc. of the file. As with most of the common 2D bitmap formats, the data is stored either in RGB format at 8 bits per channel per pixel (with an optional 8 bit alpha channel), or as an 8 bit indexed color image with an associated 24 or 32 bit palette (in the case of BMP files). Until recently, the idea of needing more color resolution than this for games development work was unheard of, so it is still very rare for formats that support more than 24 or 32 bits per pixel (bpp) to be used. TGA and BMP files only store a single image, with no animation or layer information.

In recent years, the Portable Network Graphic (PNG) format has grown in popularity, partly due to the increasing number of open source libraries and tools that are available for manipulating files in it. PNG was designed to be a highly flexible file format, and it supports up to 16 bit per channel bit depths, as well as indexed color images, and a range of extra information such as color correction data, and progressive image data (allowing lower resolution versions of the image to be constructed from a partial PNG file). While PNG itself is a quite complex format, employing a chunk based file structure and compression, the existence of freely usable libraries makes it relatively straightforward to integrate into existing tools. There is also another format known as Multi-image Network Graphics (MNG), which builds on many of the same techniques as PNG to provide a similar format that supports storing multiple images for animation purposes, with an animation orientated compression system added.

All of these formats, with the exception of some of the compression modes MNG can employ, are lossless. In other words, the image that they store is not modified in any way. This is a highly desirable trait for use in a processing pipeline, as images may go through many stages of editing and conversion, and each time a file is saved in a "lossy" format like JPEG, a small amount of quality is lost. Even over a handful of iterations, this degradation will build up until the image is unusable because of the quality loss, as can been seen in Figures 2.1 and 2.2.

FIGURE 2.1   The original source image (magnified).

FIGURE 2.2 The same image after heavy compression using the JPEG algorithm (magnified).

Audio Data

The most frequently used formats for audio data are Wave (WAV) files, and Audio Interchange File Format (AIFF) files. Both formats are based on the Information Interchange Format (IFF) system, which is a chunked file format designed to allow easy extension and backwards compatibility for data. AIFF and WAV store fundamentally the same data—the audio is a sequence of samples, often in 16 bit uncompressed format, along with a header that gives details of the number of channels, the precise sample format, and the sample rate. AIFF files can only store uncompressed audio data (although there are some AIFF-derivative formats that can handle compression), while WAV files can store data compressed with any one of a large number of windows *codecs* (COder/DECoder modules, each of which implements a particular audio or video compression system).

Both AIFF and WAV files are relatively easy to read, and there are a large number of freely available libraries that perform this task. Compressed WAV files can be tricky to deal with in some circumstances, as it is necessary to have the appropriate decompression codec available to handle the file. Fortunately, on Windows™ the OS provides a number of APIs for handling WAV files that transparently perform the necessary decompression or compression tasks, assuming the relevant codec is installed on the machine.

It is becoming increasingly common for games to use highly compressed audio formats such as ADPCM, MPEG Layer 3 audio (MP3) or Ogg Vorbis for playing back sound and music. These formats use a number of advanced lossy compression techniques based on psychoacoustic models which strip out elements of the source audio that cannot normally be heard. As with image data, however, when manipulating audio data it is important that an uncompressed, or lossless compressed format is used, otherwise each iteration of the processing will result in a degradation in audio quality. It is also especially important not to convert from one of the highly-compressed lossy audio formats (such as MP3) to another, if at all possible, as these typically employ sophisticated "psycho-acoustic" techniques that strip and/or regenerate elements of the sound which cannot be heard. These inaudible artifacts will often confuse audio encoders, causing them to produce output that is badly compressed or is of poor audio quality.

Video Data

Unlike most of the other assets that are used in modern games, video data presents many unique problems simply due to the sheer size of the files involved. Even a relatively small amount of video can quickly overshadow the size of every other asset in a game put together, especially in the uncompressed state usually needed for processing—for example, at a standard NTSC TV resolution (640×448×24 bit) at 30 frames per second, one minute of video will take up a massive 1476 MB of space!

Video file formats are also unique in that they are very complex, particularly when dealing with compressed video in any form. It is largely impractical to try to write tools that deal directly with anything other than the most basic uncompressed video files unless a custom compression/decompression layer is required. Even when writing an entirely new codec (a very rare occurrence given the complexity of the task) this approach is of dubious value. It is usually much more efficient to write a module conforming to the host OS standard for codecs, which can then be used with any application. Therefore, the vast majority of video processing applications function by using either the APIs supplied by the operating system or an external library, which provide a relatively easy way to access such files, automatically loading the required codecs and performing compressing and decompression on demand as frames are requested by the application.

By far the two most common file formats for video processing are Audio/Video Interchange (AVI) files, and the various flavors of Motion Picture Experts Group (MPEG) files. The AVI file format was originally designed by Microsoft for use with Windows, but implementations of AVI readers and writers have since been developed for most popular operating systems. AVI files are effectively wrappers around the codec-specific compressed audio and video data, with some header information to allow applications to locate the required codecs for playback.

The MPEG designation covers quite a range of actual encoding techniques, all based on broadly the same principles and wrapped in a common file format, but targeted at different applications. The most commonly encountered video formats are MPEG-1 and MPEG-2, which are used in the Video CD and DVD disc formats respectively. MPEG-2, in particular, is supported by custom decoder hardware in some console systems and many PCs, and is very well-suited to handling relatively large quantities of very high quality video. While MPEG-2 playback is designed to be relatively fast and easy to accelerate with dedicated hardware, making it ideal for console applications, high quality MPEG-2 encoding is still a fairly slow process, even on modern high-end PCs.

The MPEG formats are generally used only as output formats, however, since as with audio, working with compressed video files is generally not a good idea, the quality degradation issue quickly becomes insurmountable, and the overheads of decompressing and recompressing the data for each processing step can be significant.

Video File Sizes

An important point to note when working with video files, particularly on older operating systems and applications, is that many have difficulty handling large files, particularly those notably over 2 GB or 4 GB. This may seem like a ridiculous limit, but using the same uncompressed NTSC video as described above, these limits equate to approximately 1 minute 20 seconds and 2 minutes 45 seconds of video respectively!

Versions of Windows using the FAT or FAT32 filing systems in particular cannot support files larger than 4 GB on those drives, and in particular the AVI format has a limitation that prevents files larger than 2 GB from functioning correctly. There is a newer revision of the format, known as AVI 2.0 or "OpenDML extensions," which removes this limitation, but as of yet many tools still do not support it. Is it not uncommon for tools to split large videos into 2 GB or 4 GB chunks and then recombine them at the final compression stage to avoid this limitation.

Another format worth mentioning is Apple's QuickTime (MOV) format, which is broadly based on the same principles as the AVI format. However, the lack of good format documentation or compatibility with the standard video APIs on operating systems other than Apple's own MacOS have lead to its being mostly ignored by developers. It is still very popular for distributing video to end-users, however, and some specialist packages such as *Avid* make use of it. For manipulation of QuickTime data, Apple provides an API for Windows and MacOS which can be used.

As a result of the general difficulty in building tools to deal effectively with video streams in AVI or MPEG files, it is also not unusual for developers to simply sidestep the problem entirely, and store video as a large number of individual image files in TGA or a similar lossless format, and only convert these into an actual video file at the final compression stage of processing. This approach has disadvantages as it makes managing the volume of files generated more difficult, but it does simplify tool development and reduce the potential problems caused by file size limits, etc.

3D Object Data

Unlike all the other data types mentioned so far, 3D objects and scenes are very much at the "cutting edge" of format design. There is little consensus among developers on what elements a 3D format should include, let alone actual concrete standards for such formats.

As a result, virtually every 3D content package has its own (often proprietary) file format, and there are a number of competing "standard" formats, none of which cover the full range of possible data which might be required in such files. It seems unlikely that this situation will be resolved in the foreseeable future, as 3D graphics technology tends to advance faster than new standards can be set.

To make matters worse, some of the common file formats are almost completely impossible for applications other than the original content creation program to read. One of the most common examples of this is 3D Studio Max's .MAX file format, which is structured in such a way that in order to be able to read it you would have to rewrite a fairly large chunk of 3D Studio Max itself!

The most common "standard" 3D file format is Virtual Reality Markup Language (VRML), originally intended to be a 3D counterpart to HTML, the markup language used by Web pages, however, it should be noted that "common" is a relative term here, and VRML use is still fairly rare outside of academic circles. As with HTML, there are various different flavors of VRML, with changes made as technology has evolved. VRML is a relatively complex format, although well-designed and structured, which makes it quite easy to parse. However, VRML is quite unwieldy for use in games, with the format allowing vast quantities of useless information, such as navigation and behavior data for the "virtual worlds" it was original designed to support, while omitting other fairly commonly used information such as bone information for skinned meshes.

Due to the lack of widely supported standard formats, most developers either use one of the basic formats their chosen 3D package supports directly (often the package's native format), or write their own exporter and custom format. The latter approach has the distinct advantage of allowing any custom data that is required from the package to be included easily in the file, and if necessary further exporters/ importers can be (relatively) easily written to allow other third party packages to operate on the files.

CUSTOM INTERMEDIATE FILE FORMATS

Particularly with 3D object files, therefore, and also with game-specific data such as level maps, object descriptions, and so on, it is usually necessary to design a custom file format to hold the data. While in simple cases this format may be what appears on the final game disc and is read by the code (a "single stage" resource pipeline), more often than not it is more appropriate for such data to be held in an intermediate format which is then converted again before being included on the game disc.

There are several reasons for this apparently redundant extra step. First, for the maximum efficiency (in terms of loading time, processing required during game or level startup, and memory usage), the ideal final data format should be as close as possible to what will actually be contained in memory while the game is running. By storing data this way, the loading process becomes a simple case of reading in the file and (possibly) adjusting some pointer values. This is not only important for speed, but it is vital if the game requires data to be read in the background during gameplay, or "streamed." In this case, any processing that must be done on the data after or during loading must be carried out while the game is playing, potentially causing a significant impact on performance.

So, it is highly desirable to perform as much preprocessing as possible to ensure that the minimum of work needs to be carried out at runtime. However, storing data in "in-memory" formats has one major disadvantage—compatibility. The closer the data format gets to being what the game will actually use, the more likely it is that format will change if an alteration is made to the code or data structures. This is obviously not a problem once the game is completed, but during the development cycle it is likely that both major and minor changes will alter the required data formats on a regular basis. Since adding additional processing to handle older file formats or special cases would defeat the purpose of using such a system, the only solution is to recreate the data files if a change has been made that renders them incompatible with the current code.

This is where the intermediate files come in. If every change required (for example) all of the game models to be re-exported from the 3D package they were created in, it would generate a huge amount of tedious, time consuming and error prone work for the artists. If, however, the exported models are stored in an intermediate format that is not tied to the specifics of the game code, then it is a relatively simple task to change the converter that produces "game-ready" assets and reprocess all of the affected files. This task can certainly have the potential to become as time consuming and awkward as the manual method if large numbers of files are involved, but since it can be relatively easily automated and optimized it is much easier to keep the required time and effort (both human and machine) under control.

Another advantage of splitting the processing into two passes is that it allows for multiple output files to be generated easily (for example, to produce a separate compiled asset for each target platform the game will run on). With an intermediate file format, it is not only easier to produce these output files, but the cost of the initial export only has to be borne once, no matter how many different platforms are supported.

It is also the case that many of the outputs of the asset building process are likely to be composites formed from two or more of the source input files or processing. For example, a compiled model might contain both geometry and textures (from external files), or a map might be split into chunks, and then each chunk processed to produce shadow information for light-mapping. A single stage pipeline would require these steps to be performed either in an editor or exporter, or at game load time, neither of which is an ideal solution. In particular, this becomes very important when considering the problems that arise from outputs which are dependent on many inputs. If, for example, the textures for a model are included with the model file, that means that changes to the textures then require the model to be re-exported from the package that created it in order for the textures stored with the file to be updated as well. This type of interdependency between files can be very hard to manage effectively in a single-stage pipeline, especially as changes may have impacts in files which are not obviously related, or even edited with entirely different packages!

Obviously, the design of an intermediate file format is going to be driven by different factors to that of a format that is intended for use in the game itself. Factors such as disc space required and load-time parsing required are secondary to those like extensibility, ease of use, and backwards compatibility.

Text or Binary?

One of the most obvious questions for a file specification such as this is whether the data should be stored (as with virtually all game data) in binary form, or as an ASCII (or similar encoding) text document. This question pertains more to the tools that the files will be used with than the format itself. There are some straightforward advantages and disadvantages to each file format, however:

Text File Advantages

- Human readable and editable—while it is possible to read most binary formats in a hex editor with the aid of a copy of the specification, it is a very time consuming and error prone task, suitable only for the most trivial of debugging procedures in the majority of cases
- Many existing tools are available, particularly for Unix systems
- No problems with different processor byte orders or type sizes
- If well-designed, they are effectively "self-documenting" so reading a sample file explains the format

Text File Disadvantages

- Generally several times larger than equivalent binary data
- Parsing time for large files is significant, even in the context of offline processing tools
- Code to load and save files can become large and unwieldy

Binary File Advantages

- Significantly more compact than text files
- Less likely to become accidentally corrupted by user editing or unexpected character codes used in non-English text or encoded data
- Much more efficient in terms of disc space, reading, and writing speed

Binary File Disadvantages

- Not easily readable or editable without custom tools
- Requires explicit documentation so it is necessary to maintain a fairly complete set of format specifications or some form of loading/saving code library for tools to use
- Different file format versions, or even the same file format saved by code on different processors or compilers are likely to be incompatible unless explicit steps are taken to ensure compatibility

Possibly the biggest difference between binary and text files, however, is not related to the actual technical composition of the files, but more to the attitudes of developers toward them. If file formats are based on text files, then in general most programmers, even without a formal specification, will tend toward parsing the files in a relatively extensible way, ignoring data that is unnecessary or unrecognized, and adding fields with human readable names and sensible data types. With binary files, however, there is a strong temptation to simply write out data "as-is" from memory, and to assume that it will be the same length and layout when reading it in again. This approach leads to file formats that are hard to extend without adding special cases or code for backwards compatibility, and data may not be stored in the most appropriate format. For example, on some compilers, multiple Boolean flags may be automatically packed into a single integer value, which makes reading them back in from a program built with a different compiler very difficult without knowing the details of the original compiler's packing scheme!

File Structure

There are effectively three types of file format: formats where the structure itself is contained in the file, formats where the file is "raw" data without any structure, and formats where the structure is in a separate file. The difference between the first two types of format is simple.

Files Containing Implicit Structure

Take, for example, a text file format containing information as follows:

```
CharacterName=Fred
CharacterType=Soldier
AIType=Aggressive
HitPoints=1000
```

This is an example of the first type of format where the structure is explicitly contained in the file. In this case, even without any further documentation, it is very clear what the different items of data in this file are. Furthermore, when parsing this file in code, it is possible to extract any of the values without knowing anything about the rest of the information. To read the HitPoints value to determine how many hit points the character should have, the code simply has to be read each line until it reaches the one that starts with HitPoints=. This process will still work perfectly whether the lines are rearranged in the file, data is removed, or new data is added.

Files with No Included Structure

Now, consider the following version of the same file:

```
Fred
Soldier
Aggressive
1000
```

As you can see, this file format holds exactly the same information as in the first example. However, the structure of the file is no longer expressed in the file itself. In order to understand the file (either as a human or from code), it is necessary to have external knowledge about (or at least guess at!) the order in which the data appears in the file. Because of this, the file format is a lot more fragile than in the previous example. If a pair of entries are swapped, then any tool that does not know about the change will end up reading the wrong data.

Separate Data and Structure Files

This is an example of the final type of format. There are two separate files, a structure file, which contains details of how the information is laid out, and the data file, which contains the actual information:

```
Data file :

AICharacter
{
    Fred,
    Soldier,
    Aggressive,
    1000
}

Structure file :

Structure AICharacter
{
    String  CharacterName;
    String  CharacterType;
    String  AIType;
    Integer HitPoints;
}
```

It is important to note that typically there is only one structure file for each type of file, but many data files. In this case, the structure file also contains basic type information for the values stored in the data file, specifying some values as text strings and one as an integer number (HitPoints).

Split structure/data files are mostly useful in cases where it is necessary for tools to operate on data in formats they may not have explicit knowledge of, or where the same data can be represented in a number of different formats. The structure files provide a very good means of documenting and altering the file format, without having to make any code changes at all, and it is possible for non-programmers to easily add extensions to such files with minimal effort. It is also sometimes very useful to have textual structure files and binary data files, thereby providing a halfway house that allows the efficiencies of binary files for the bulk of the data but keeps the structural information in an easy to read and modify format.

However, the big disadvantage of this type of file is that if the structure and data files are ever separated or get out of sync with each other due to changes in one not being reflected in the other, then attempts to read the affected files will most likely go seriously wrong. This is a major problem especially when dealing with intermediate game data files, where it is not uncommon for old files to remain unchanged through many updates to the format and tools they are used with. In this case, it almost becomes necessary to keep a single structure file for each data file, at which point many of the disadvantages of the split format are negated.

Some of these problems can be alleviated by allowing the structure file to be added to, but not for existing entries to be changed or removed. In this way, older data files are still valid (assuming the parser knows to stop when it runs out of input data), but extensions can be safely used in more recent files. Another commonly used solution to this problem is to provide an "upgrade" tool, which can take two structure descriptions and map from one to the other, moving the data around in the source file as necessary to match the new structure, and adding default values to new fields. This can be very useful in automatically keeping data up-to-date without needing to re-process or re-export files, although the logistical overhead of ensuring that all the necessary data files are upgraded when the format changes can sometimes be a prohibitive factor.

Wrapper Formats

For many projects, it is desirable to have a single "wrapper" format, or "container" format, in which all data is stored. The advantages of this are twofold. First, having a standard wrapper format means that the basic file reading/writing libraries for this format can be written and reused by all the various tools. Second, a standard, well-designed format can make development much simpler by providing a known basis for the structure of further data carrying formats, and enshrining desired properties (such as backwards compatibility) into the design of every further format specification by including them at the base level.

Fundamentally, the overlying structure of virtually any non-trivial data file can be considered to be a layout similar to that of a database. There are a number of *records*, each of which has a fixed structure containing a number of *fields* that hold data (often with type information). In the simplest form, a data file is simply a linear list of records. However, this is often very limiting, as items of data which may appear frequently (for example, vectors containing X, Y, and Z coordinates) must either be hard coded into the system as basic field types, or expressed longhand every time they are required.

One of the most elegant solutions to this problem is to follow the pattern already commonly used within programs, and to allow records to be *contained within* fields. In other words, a field can either contain data from one of the fundamental types (an integer value, or a text string, for example), or it can contain another entire record. This approach has two very useful benefits. First, it allows the creation at a file-level of new compound data types, such as a vector of three floating point numbers) which can be reused anywhere without needing to add them to the fundamental types supported by the file format. For example, consider the following structure:

```
Structure Vector
{
    Float X,Y,Z;
}
```

As can be seen, this represents our vector as a structure called "vector." This can then be used in other structures as follows:

```
Structure CharacterObject
{
    String  Name;
    Vector  Position;
    Integer HitPoints;
}
```

As can be seen, the Vector structure can be used in exactly the same way as the built-in data-types Integer and String. The actual layout of the data in a CharacterObject record in the data file (remember that now CharacterObject can be used as a sub-record itself too, if necessary):

```
Record Character1
{
    String Name="Fred"
    Record Position
    {
        Float X=10.0
        Float Y=20.0
        Float Z=0.0
    }
    Integer HitPoints=100
}
```

The second advantage of allowing this type of structure is that it makes encapsulation possible. Encapsulation of data is, quite simply, the process by which the actual structure (or, in some cases, contents) of some of the data being stored is hidden from the code which is operating on it. To take the example of our vector type again, by wrapping it up into a sub-record, it becomes easy to simply write a pair of `ReadVectorFromFile()` and `WriteVectorToFile()` functions which perform this task without the overall code's needing to know anything about the storage of the data. This is also important for backwards compatibility, because with the vector encapsulated like this it is very easy for the code to skip reading it if it does not want or know how to, it simply skips the entire sub-record. If the vector was not encapsulated, then the code would need some knowledge about how it was laid out (specifically, how much data it contained) in order to skip it.

Actually achieving this type of file layout is surprisingly straightforward. All that is needed is for each field in the file to store a name or identifier of some form, its type, and the length of data it stores (or a suitable end marker, such as the curly brackets in the previous example). If one of the integral types the format supports is "record," indicating that the field contains a sub-record rather than explicit data, then it is a relatively simple matter for the reading and writing code to keep a stack of all the current blocks and move into and out of them as the code requires.

References

Another consideration which may be worth thinking about when designing a wrapper format is the problem of how to handle resources that need to reference each other, but are not embedded together (or even, in some cases, in the same file). For example, a 3D model file might contain references to external texture maps, or a skinned mesh within the file might need to refer to bone objects elsewhere in the object hierarchy.

In many cases, especially for external files, the obvious solution of simply recording the filename of the required resource is the simplest and most reliable means of storing this information. However, in some cases, particularly with data that is stored in the same file (or in a specific place in another file), and is not generated from a source with a convenient identifier, then it can be useful to have a source of *UIDs*, or Unique IDentifiers.

At the simplest level, UIDs can simply be created by having a counter that is set to zero upon starting to write out a data file. Each time a UID is requested, this counter is incremented by one and the value returned. Objects that need to be referred to can then request a UID for themselves, which can later be used to reference them elsewhere. By making UIDs a built-in type for the format, this creation and resolution process can be automated, and with a little trickery (pre-reserving

UIDs or storing them after the rest of the file has been written), forward references (to data which has not yet been written to the file) can be handled. While this makes them more complex to develop initially, the benefits of being able to refer to any suitable piece of data without having to go through the time consuming and error prone process of developing a different indexing scheme for each case are significant. There are many more complex schemes for UIDs, including using different UID ranges for different files or types of data, and having a central repository of registered UIDs, which ensures that they are genuinely "unique" across all the project data files.

XML

In recent years, one of the most pervasive buzzwords in all aspects of the computer industry has been "XML." XML stands for Extensible Markup Language, and it is a standard for building documents or files containing structured information; a universal form of wrapper format, in a sense. XML is actually a subset of a language called SGML (Standard Generalized Markup Language), which is itself specified by ISO 8879. SGML is a generic model for building complex interdependent document layouts and structures, and is generally regarded as being fairly unwieldy and hard to implement for more simple cases, hence, XML was created.

XML is a text-based format, which looks very similar to HTML at first glance. XML files are generally designed to be human readable, and can be edited with relative ease in a text editor, even by non-programmers. An example XML file might look like this:

```
<?xml version="1.0"?>

<AICharacter>
    <Character>
        <Name>Fred</Name>
        <Type>Soldier</Type>
    </Character>
    <AIType>Aggressive</AIType>
    <HitPoints>1000</HitPoints>
</AICharacter>
```

Note that the indenting in this example is purely for clarity because XML files ignore whitespace characters in nearly all circumstances. As can be seen, the file consists of a series of *elements* (to use the XML terminology), each of which is designated by a *tag* surrounded with triangular brackets. In a very similar hierarchical structure to the sub-records discussed earlier, elements can appear within other elements, producing the nested sections of the file. The data itself appears between pairs of element tags, with the *closing tag* denoted by the / (forward slash) character at the front of the name.

XML is inherently extensible so named elements can be easily ignored by the parser or higher level code if they are not understood or required, and with a little effort it is even possible to include elements with version tags which are selectively processed depending on what the program is expecting.

In this form, XML is relatively straightforward. There are many other features, such as standards for specifying arbitrary text and raw binary data, *attributes* (optional values that can be specified inside element tags), and standards for including references to other data, but the basic principles are all quite simple. This is how a large number of applications use XML, simply adding their own element structures as required. However, XML's real strength lies in the system it has for handling document structures formally.

XML DTD Structure Files

The way this is achieved is through *DTDs* (Document Type Declarations). DTDs are files that describe the expected structure of a particular type of XML document, in a manner that can be parsed by software and used to perform logical operations on documents (for example, checking them for consistency or performing format translations). A DTD for the example XML file above might appear like this:

```
<!ELEMENT AICharacter (Character, AIType?, HitPoints)>
<!ELEMENT Character (Name?,Type)>
<!ELEMENT Name (#PCDATA)>
<!ELEMENT Type (#PCDATA)>
<!ELEMENT AIType (#PCDATA)>
<!ELEMENT HitPoints (#PCDATA)>
```

This DTD expresses the structure of each element in the file in turn so AICharacter is composed of a Character element, then, optionally an AIType element (the ? indicates that this element is optional), followed by a HitPoints element. In turn, Character is composed of an optional Name element and Type. Each of the remaining elements contains PCDATA, which stands for "Parseable Character Data." In other words, the actual information the code is interested in.

With this information, an XML parser can examine the original file and determine if it conforms to this structure, as well as making inferences about the data from it. There are many uses for this capability, but one of the most interesting is file conversion. Given two DTDs and some simple information about mapping elements between them, it is possible for a program to take XML files in one format and convert them into another entirely without human intervention, and without the program itself needing any foreknowledge of the formats it is working with.

This is an incredibly powerful tool and if every XML-based format has an appropriate DTD, then it is possible to convert from any format to another without writing a single line of code! One of the most common tools for performing this is XSLT (XML Stylesheet Language Transformations), which was designed and is commonly used for converting XSL (XML Stylesheet Language) documents from one form to another, but can perform simple translation operations on XML documents.

This provides another interesting solution to the backwards compatibility problem—as described previously, as a format with separated data and structure files, XML is one of the few common file formats where structural changes can be easily propagated to existing files, making it possible to update all the old data to use the new format rather than having to accommodate the older variants until they "naturally" fall out of use due to files being manually updated or re-saved.

There are also many other existing XML tools, including dedicated XML editors, some of which are able to parse XML DTDs and use them to ensure file validity when editing and present more sophisticated interfaces onto the data. Even without a suitable DTD, simple syntax checks can still be performed on XML files by many tools, including Microsoft's *Internet Explorer*. An XML parser is a relatively simple piece of software to write (albeit not quite as simple as many of the wrapper systems previously discussed), and there are many freely available libraries for XML parsing and file writing. Using XML for data files does incur certain penalties—most notably the time required to implement or integrate a parser and file writer and develop DTDs (if required) for file formats, and increased processing overheads from the more verbose file format. But there are numerous advantages, mainly in the vast libraries of existing software for manipulating XML files and the inherent extensibility of the format.

CONCLUSION

Whichever approach is used, the initial export process from the content creation tools and the file formats used for it is one of the most vital, and most difficult to change once implemented, steps in the asset pipeline. It is worth considering the problem carefully, both in terms of current and likely future requirements, before deciding on solutions to these problems. Advances in technology mean that the goalposts are constantly moving in this area, and even the best designed systems will almost inevitably run into problems that could not have been foreseen when they were originally conceived. The real test, therefore, is how both the software and the people using it can adapt to handle such issues. There is no simple "one size fits all" answer, and to make matters worse, in the majority of circumstances, there will be additional limitations on the design of these systems imposed by existing code or workflow practices.

3 A High-Level View of Asset Management

In This Chapter

- Why Asset Management Is Not Source Control
- Asset Identification
- Broken Data
- Local Changes
- Synchronizing Code and Data
- Building a Distribution Package
- Automated Testing

So, having looked at the processes through which assets are created and exported from their source tools, we now come to the point where *asset management* becomes part of the pipeline. Asset management systems are designed to provide a centralized repository in which all of the game data is stored, often in both source and game-ready forms. This repository is the focal point for the efforts of the entire asset creation (as opposed to programming) team. It provides a single location where all of the data required for the game can be found, and in addition most asset management systems also support a degree of work-flow management as well, tracking changes, managing data updates, sign-off checklists and similar.

The vast majority of asset management systems are designed so that their basic structure is a hierarchical tree, mirroring the layout of the assets on disc. Because of this, the latest (or, for that matter, any given stored version) of either the entire repository or a sub-tree thereof can be replicated to a directory structure on a client machine. This is the mechanism normally used when editing or utilizing the assets from the repository: the files are copied onto the local client machine, the required processing performed, and then the altered versions of assets are *committed*, or copied back, to the server.

WHY ASSET MANAGEMENT IS NOT SOURCE CONTROL

In many respects, asset management is very similar to the source control systems used for managing game code. However, there are a number of small but vitally important distinctions that make using the same system for both code and data potentially problematic.

First, typically source code is in the form of human readable text files. On most projects, even if the game systems are clearly delineated and kept separate, there are almost always a number of key source files that are shared among many different subsystems and edited frequently by a large number of different programmers. Hence, source control systems are designed to support this behavior by allowing "multiple checkouts," where several users can edit the same file simultaneously, and then their changes are merged (either automatically or manually) as they are committed back to the repository.

This automatic merging behavior is only possible because of the nature of source code files. With a little knowledge about the programming language being used, it is possible for the merging utility to separate changes made by different users to unrelated parts of the same file and apply them simultaneously to the "master" copy. Even when conflicts do occur because two users have made changes to the same part of a file, they can usually be resolved with little effort by allowing the user to select which changes should be applied. The rigid syntactic rules and structure of most programming languages ensures that when "merge errors" do occur due to changes being misapplied, they are usually easy to spot as the offending section of code will not compile cleanly.

None of these useful properties, however, applies to most of the other assets used in a game. The majority of other assets are binary files, which are not easy to parse or merge without detailed information about their format and contents. In addition, it is very hard for a machine to separate the areas affected by individual edits to an asset and apply them separately. For example, what would happen if two artists painted on the same texture? Even if the system was capable of isolating the changes made by both and applying them in a sensible fashion to the master copy, chances are the result would be nothing like what is actually desired!

Fortunately, artwork and most other areas of game asset creation are generally much more rigidly structured and controlled than programming. While a single logical change to the game code may easily require small changes to a large number of files (adding prototypes to header files, for example, or replacing references to one variable with another), asset changes are generally much more localized, affecting only one specific file or a small number of related files (for instance, the textures for a specific model). Broad changes that affect a large number of files are usually restricted to similarly broad changes in the assets themselves, for example, giving all the sounds in the game more bass or altering the color balance of an entire level.

As a result, it is both difficult and usually unnecessary for asset control systems to implement "multiple-checkout" and merge functionality, so most either provide very basic support, or simply none at all.

Differences in Data

The second major difference between source control and asset management systems is also related to the nature of the files that they manipulate—specifically, the size of them. The source code for a typical game often easily fits in 5–10 MB of disc space, possibly less depending on the size of the game, libraries used, and other factors. Individual files are usually only at most a few tens of kilobytes in size, and while there are many of them, unless the project is very poorly designed they will be in a relatively rigid structure, with functionally similar or interdependent files grouped together.

The small size of the source code files, combined with the fact that it is often necessary to examine or roll back to older versions of files when fixing bugs or testing different revisions of the game means that most source control systems simply store every single version of every file that has ever been committed, along with the change notes and other useful information such as the date, version number, and name of the user who made the change. Even all this data, over the course of a medium-sized 1–2 year project, will still probably only amount to a few hundred megabytes of information, especially if compression is used. In addition, since it is relatively straightforward for a source control system to identify relevant changes between files, if repository size does become a problem the data required can be dramatically reduced by storing only those changes, rather than complete versions of files for every revision.

Unfortunately, the files typically stored in asset management systems are much larger. Even the smallest texture or model is usually at least 32 KB, larger than the vast majority of source code files! Especially when music or video files are involved, file sizes can quickly increase massively (it is not uncommon to encounter single files that are 200–300 MB) as large as the complete source repository for some projects! This immediately creates storage problems in the repository, which can quickly become unmanageably large, especially if multiple revisions of binary files are kept. Another side effect of the nature of most asset files is that since it is very difficult to determine changes between versions of files effectively, it is usually necessary to store complete copies of each required revision in the repository.

This size problem is a major issue, both in terms of online storage and backup strategies. With the source assets for a typical game often totaling well over 50 GB once items like uncompressed audio and video streams have been taken into account, providing enough space for even a handful of revisions of each file can be a challenge, let alone the complete version history that source control systems usually provide. Backups are equally problematic, especially because current increases in hard drive capacities are far outpacing increases in suitably reliable offline storage media.

The size of asset data does not just affect the repository itself, though there are major implications for how clients access and store the data as well. In the case of source code, it is almost always necessary for every programmer to have a complete copy of the source code in order to compile the game. As the source code is fairly small, this is not a major problem, and the hard drive space and network bandwidth required to distribute updates is negligible. This is sadly not the case with asset data, however. While the storage requirements for a complete set of data for an average game are not completely ridiculous, the space used on every client machine does represent a significant "wasted" resource. Ideally the game and asset system should be designed so that it is not necessary for every team member to have all the data. After all, if only the audio designers and programmers need the several gigabytes of uncompressed audio files that comprise the unprocessed form of the in-game speech banks, why should everyone on the team have to deal with them occupying valuable disc space?

Handling Very Large Files

One interesting storage problem that arises when files get very large is that many programs and in some cases the OS itself can fail when dealing with them. The two most typical boundaries are 2 GB and 4 GB, the maximum size that can be addressed (in bytes) by 32 bit signed and unsigned numbers, respectively. It is not at all uncommon for unexpected failures to result from trying to manipulate files above the 2-GB size marker (for example, although it was able to read large files, the I/O library on one popular console system could not seek to a point beyond 2 GB in a file in "one jump" so a number of smaller incremental seek operations had to be used instead). Of particular note is the fact that the still-popular FAT filing system (and variants thereof) used by many machines cannot store a single file larger than 4 GB. For these reasons, many asset management systems and tools store large files as a number of smaller files which are read sequentially to extract the required information, sidestepping the problem but potentially introducing others as the segmented files must now be carefully managed as a group.

More of a problem than the storage, however, is the server load and network bandwidth that is occupied distributing updates containing large volumes of data to all of the members of the development team. With increasing team sizes, this is a problem that will only become more significant. For example, a team of 10 people simultaneously retrieving a 100-MB file from one server over a 100-Mbit LAN will take just over a minute and a half to complete the operation, with 50 people, the time required becomes just over 8 minutes! Even worse, that calculation is based on network bandwidth usage alone—even in the best case it is more likely that the server itself will be the bottleneck, not the network. Game development in particular has a habit of generating worst case loads on server applications, such as when a major change is made and suddenly everyone wants to make sure they are current before doing any more work with the older assets.

Some systems attempt to minimize the storage and bandwidth requirements by using compression or file deltas (sending only the differences between files). However, as previously mentioned, the effectiveness of these on asset binary files can vary widely depending on the exact format of the data being stored. It is generally the case that these techniques can achieve an incremental improvement in the overheads of storage and transmission (at the expense of additional CPU overheads on the server and client), but to achieve large gains requires careful selection of the strategy for organizing and working with asset files.

One approach is to split the assets in the repository into sections, for example, for models, textures, audio, and video. This has the advantage that each individual team member can retrieve only the data that he is interested in, and exclude the rest. Of course, it is likely that some people or automated systems will need complete or near-complete sets of data (for example, for asset processing or build construction), but the problem has been greatly reduced in scope. The difficulty with this approach is that it requires some discipline to avoid cross contamination where assets get placed in the wrong section, or common processes use data from many sections. It is also possible for the sections to become unbalanced such that all the large assets are in a widely used section (for example, if video sequences are placed in a common "art" section shared with textures and models), which will also render the benefits ineffective.

Another technique is to change the workflow associated with the asset editing process to remove the dependency on files being stored locally. In this case, the process of "checking out" a file for editing will also copy it to the local hard drive, and (in some cases) "checking in" that file will remove it again. This significantly reduces the storage and bandwidth overheads to almost the bare minimum required, but adds extra complexity and room for error, especially when "composite" assets made up of many files (such as a model and its associated textures) are being modified. It also means that a regularly updated separate set of data is required for developers who need to run the game to test their changes, or have some easy means of integrating the individual files they have updated into an existing version.

Zombie Files

A particular danger of this technique, but one which occurs often in every asset management system is that of dealing with "zombie" files. Zombie files are those that no longer have use in the project, but have not been deleted from the asset management system, often because by the time they are noticed no one is sure if they are being used any more or not! Zombie files can be the source of all sorts of problems, as they not only consume disc space, but also clutter up the project workspace. It is not at all uncommon during the late stages of a project for many hours to be wasted figuring out which of the many versions, often duplicates of one file that were created as the result of files being copied or renamed during testing of various ideas, is actually being used in the game! Even worse, it is often the case that significant work is done on a zombie file before this problem is even realized.

Asset management systems can help avoid the problem of zombie files by providing tools to easily track them down (for example, by quickly checking which of a group of files was last updated, or highlighting duplicate files). The processing pipeline can also assist in some cases, too, by providing dependency information that indicates which files are being used in the game. It is possible in some cases, though, for asset management systems to make the problem worse, not better. In particular, when checking in files or directories recursively, some systems make it very easy to accidentally add new files they find on the client to the repository. While this makes it easier to add new assets to the database, if it's not carefully controlled it can also lead to test versions, work-in-progress, and even temporary files being imported as well!

Another problem that arises when using centralized asset management is that of zombie files on users' machines. These are files that are no longer in the asset management server, but for some reason still exist on some machines. This can occur because the files were not deleted when the server version were (some asset management software does not do this automatically), or because at some point a user copied them in from outside the system. These files simply serve to consume disc space unnecessarily, and potentially, confuse the user. It is also the case that occasionally, "anti-zombie" files appear: files that are being used by the game, but for some reason have not been added to the asset control system. Most of the time these files are noticed almost immediately by team members who do not have them. However, sometimes they go unnoticed as the majority of the team already has the files (left over files from an earlier project is a common reason). These files are especially dangerous as they can differ among machines and cause the game to fail unexpectedly when run on a "clean" machine that does not have them.

ASSET IDENTIFICATION

The sheer number of assets that an asset management system must handle is astounding, and while there are certainly technical challenges in manipulating that volume of data, by far the most significant hurdle is a purely human one: organizing and identifying the data so that it is actually possible to find assets when they are required!

For technical reasons, it is sometimes necessary to stick rigidly to naming conventions for assets, but even then these are often meaningless for many purposes—for example, "`wld1_sec2_bridge.tga`" may well tell you that the file in question is the texture for a bridge in world one, sector two, but without looking at the texture there is no way to tell what it actually *looks* like, or what part it plays in the bridge as a whole. Even worse, the majority of games are not even this organized—naming conventions are ad hoc or ignored altogether in some circumstances, and after even only a few months in development the asset database is flooded with assets named "`building1.mesh`" or "`temp_test.wav`"!

Metadata

Since in many cases examining the assets themselves to see what they are or to locate the desired one will be difficult or nearly impossible (imagine trying to locate one sound effect among hundreds with unhelpful filenames!), it is extremely useful for the asset management system to support the storage of additional *metadata*. Metadata is extra information that is not part of the file itself but relates to it, for example, a description of the contents, or the name of the person who created it. By using metadata, it becomes possible to easily locate and identify assets even without knowing what their actual contents are.

Much of the useful metadata must be entered manually by those working on the assets; however, some extremely useful information can be automatically generated by the export tools or resource pipeline and fed back into the asset management system for storage. The prime example of this is data on the dependencies between assets—for example, which textures a model uses, and in turn which models a particular texture is used on. In a fully functional asset pipeline that handles all assets, it is possible to construct an entire dependency tree for the entire game, showing exactly how and where each asset is used. This information can be invaluable when making changes—for example, if a model needs to be changed, the artist responsible can get a list of every level that model appears on and check that it fits into the environment correctly in each instance. Unused assets can also be simply "weeded out," as well as temporary or experimental data which has been inadvertently included.

Change Tracking and History

A vital part of any asset management system is the ability to store multiple versions, or revisions, of each file in the repository. This functionality makes it possible to examine the history of the file, usually along with such information as who made each change, when, and what other modifications it was related to (which is particularly useful in the case of wide ranging changes or alterations to interdependent files). While it is uncommon for asset management systems to have the more complex "understanding" of the context of changes that source control systems enjoy, it is still possible for them to provide many useful tools for humans to analyze the differences between versions of the same file, for example, by displaying pairs of revisions side by side in an asset viewer.

While examining the changes that have occurred on a given file (or complete project) is by far the most commonly used feature of asset management systems, the most sought after functionality and arguably the driving force behind the development of such systems in the first place, is the ability to "rollback" or retrieve previous versions of files. This enables mistakes to be undone, even after considerable time has elapsed since the changes were made, tests to be performed with older assets if necessary (for example, to check for changes in performance characteristics), and generally provides a safety net for experimentation. There is no danger in making radical changes to assets to see what the effect is, as they can be easily restored afterwards if the experiment fails.

As mentioned before, unlike source code control systems, asset management servers typically have to work with limited space for storing past versions of files. However, even a few previous revisions can be invaluable, and most systems still maintain the history information for changes even if the files have been removed, providing a useful audit trail of which modifications occurred when. In addition, with a little more information, the asset management system can be more intelligent in its selection of which files to discard.

Repository Labels

The key to achieving this is the addition of labels to the asset management database. A label is quite simply, a tag (usually given a name) attached to a particular set of file versions. While labels can sometimes be applied to subsections of the database, their most common use is to mark versions of the entire asset set at particular moments in time, for example, the set of assets used for a milestone build, or before a major series of alterations were made. Labels provide a quick way to refer to these precise data sets even after further modifications have been made to the files. As an example, it will be possible to retrieve the exact files that were burned onto the alpha submission discs later on in the development process should it become necessary to recreate that build for some reason. As well as providing useful markers for humans accessing the database, labels give hints to the asset management system that particular versions of files are important, and should be kept longer than others. This can radically improve the efficiency with which the system uses its available storage resources.

Branches

Another feature that arises from labels is "branches." Branching is a system whereby the asset database can be split into two separate branches, both containing the same files, with changes being applied to one or both. Most commonly, one of these branches will be the "main branch," where work continues as normal, while the second branch is used to perform testing or minor development. A common use of this occurs when producing milestone builds: prior to the build being created, a branch is created for it in the asset management system. Development can then continue on the main branch as normal, without affecting the milestone version branch; in turn, milestone specific changes can be committed to the milestone branch without affecting the rest of development. If it proves necessary, it is usually possible to merge branches or subsets of branches, incorporating changes from one into another (for example, to add fixes from the milestone build back into the main tree).

Changelists and Atomic Operations

One of the most useful features in version tracking is the ability for a number of linked changes to be committed to the repository at the same time, with a common change description, in a sense, extending labels to cover all modifications. In many asset management and source control systems, this is known as a "changelist," a list of related modifications. By separating changes to many files into a single logical unit like this, it is much easier to identify which alterations "belong together," and to access a meaningful list of modifications to browse.

Taking this a step further is the idea of "atomic check-ins." Atomic check-ins are based on the concept of "transactions," which is used by almost all modern database systems. A transaction is a set of operations that performs a single logical operation, for example, in the case of a financial database, moving funds from one account to another. This might be achieved by debiting the money from one account and then crediting it to another, which are two separate actions. The problem is that if the operation fails halfway through (for example, if a server fails), then the database is left in an inconsistent state: the money has been removed from one account, but has effectively now "disappeared" because it has not been added to the other.

This is exactly the sort of problem transactions were originally designed to solve. A transaction bundles all the actions together in such a way that either all the actions succeed, or they all fail. A transaction cannot be half completed, even if the server running it crashes in the middle, in that case, the database is rolled back to the state it was in before the transaction started. This is known as an atomic operation, because, as the name suggests, it cannot be split in two.

Atomic check-ins use transactions to perform the check-in process on a group of files. This way, if one of the files cannot be modified (for example, if it has subsequently been changed by another user, generating a merge conflict), then none of the files are checked in and the user is prompted to resolve the problem before trying again. This can be very useful in avoiding the problem of broken data in the asset repository. The most common cause of invalid data being placed on the server is when a user gets half way through checking in changes, and then has to stop to resolve a problem. Until he finishes, there remains a half completed set of modifications on the server.

BROKEN DATA

One of the biggest problems in asset processing is dealing with broken data. Of course, "broken" is a very vague term as assets can be broken in several ways. In general, these various faulty data files can be categorized as "missing assets," "out-of-date assets," "artistically broken assets," "technically broken assets," and "corrupt assets."

Missing Assets

Data can simply be missing entirely. This is most frequently a problem when the asset in question is referred to either by another asset or directly by the game code. Generally this is the easiest fault to detect in code, although the direct cause (misnamed files, data not added to the asset repository, and miscommunication among team members are all common culprits) can be harder to discern.

Out-of-Date Assets

These are assets whose contents are simply too old, either relative to the game code or other assets. Strictly speaking, they aren't a problem in themselves, but they tend to be a common cause for other data problems (particularly if atomic check-ins are not available), and the mechanisms for detecting and fixing them are unique. These are usually relatively easy to detect if the checking is done sufficiently early in the asset pipeline or when another problem is discovered.

Artistically Broken Assets

Simultaneously the easiest and the hardest problem to deal with, artistically broken assets are those that simply don't look, sound, or feel right. On one hand, this type of asset does not affect the technical side of the asset management and processing pipeline at all, but on the other, it is the only fault that absolutely cannot be detected automatically!

Technically Broken Assets

Technically broken assets are those that break some criteria imposed by the asset processing system or game engine. Typical examples include textures that are invalid sizes (most engines only support power-of-two texture dimensions), models with misnamed animations, or old file formats. Detecting these problems is usually fairly straightforward, although to do so early enough in the pipeline to fix them effectively often requires a lot of "domain knowledge" about the specifics of the game and engine.

Corrupt Assets

It is sometimes the case that assets are, for one reason or another, simply unreadable. This can occur because of actual file corruption (something that most good asset management tools should try to guard against and detect internally wherever possible), invalid file formats, newer or older versions of tools, or simply hardware or software failures. Generally speaking, detecting this problem is relatively straightforward, providing the file formats in use are well designed and have appropriate measures to test file integrity (or at least that the basic format is as expected).

Dealing with Broken Assets

The response of the asset pipeline to broken data largely depends on the stage at which it detects them. In general, the earlier, the better, although many problems (most notably technical problems relating to the game or engine and missing assets) can be very hard to detect until the later stages of processing, or even in some cases, at runtime. For example, if data can be checked before being committed to the asset repository, then not only is it easily possible to inform the user of the problem, but also the broken data is contained and prevented from causing trouble for other users.

The ideal situation is one where it is impossible to create broken data in the first place: while in most cases this is virtually impossible, wherever it is possible it should be attempted. Careful design of plug-ins and package tools can reduce the possibility of user error by, for example, providing drop-down lists of object names to eliminate the inevitable typing errors that would otherwise arise.

After the data has entered the pipeline, however, there are a few possible responses that the system can have to detecting an error. First, it can simply ignore it and continue. This may be desirable in cases where the error is minor (a missing animation, for example), and the game will be able to function without it. However, for more serious errors, ignoring the problem is generally not an option, as the result will be that the game simply doesn't run or, even worse, fails unexpectedly.

The system can try to fix the error itself. This is often possible with cases such as badly sized textures, where the image can be reduced or enlarged to the next suitable resolution. However, it is not generally desirable to have these changes applied to the original source file; instead they should propagate down the pipeline only as required.

Another response that may be possible if a problem is detected at a sufficiently early stage is to roll back or retrieve the previous working revision of the file (the "last known good" version) from the asset management system. This ensures that processing can continue, but can also cause a cascading failure if the asset that is rolled back has different dependent assets between the two versions.

Providing Feedback on Failures

Whatever response the pipeline takes when it detects an error, the most important action that needs to be taken is to inform the user (or users, potentially) of the problem. In the case of an interactive asset building tool or export plug-in, this is relatively straightforward, as a simple error message or dialog box can be displayed. For offline tools, however, particularly those that may be running on a server somewhere, this is not a workable solution.

In this case, the actual mechanical process of providing feedback can usually be performed in a fairly straightforward manner, the obvious system to use for error reporting being e-mail. A much trickier problem, however, is developing a strategy to determine who should be informed about problems. For this, the revision history kept by the asset management system can be vital. By examining the changes that have taken place since the last error free version of the asset in question, a list of those who may have been responsible for introducing (and hence are most likely to be able to fix) the problem can be produced. In many cases it will also be desirable to have a fixed list of people who are informed of every problem in specific areas of the pipeline, such as team leads. In addition, if a bug tracking or change tracking system is being employed, then asset problems could be logged there for assignment and resolution.

Of course, no system is infallible and in particular, automated error reporting can run into problems in the case where a single problem causes cascading failures throughout the pipeline. In particular, code changes, and some types of data changes involving highly interdependent assets can sometimes introduce errors in processing entire sets of assets that are actually unrelated to the broken assets themselves, which is a situation not dissimilar to that caused by missing braces in C code. Sadly, it is extremely difficult (if not sometimes impossible) to detect or rectify this situation. Rolling back the "broken" data to a working version will have no effect (as the error is elsewhere), and if left unchecked the system may easily end up reporting hundreds of errors to a huge number of people! To avoid this, it is obviously desirable to limit the number of failures that will be tolerated before the processing is aborted entirely, and to handle these cases differently for reporting purposes.

LOCAL CHANGES

While much of the focus in an asset management system is on the centralized control and automated processing it can provide for assets which are ready for inclusion in the game (or at least for wider testing), an equally important consideration is the handling of the hundreds of incremental changes that assets undergo during their initial construction. If the central server is the only path through which assets can reach the game engine, then it is almost inevitable that the sheer volume of revisions will surely swamp the system. In addition, forcing every asset through this path for testing will significantly lengthen one of the most critical feedback loops in the development process—the cycle of tweaking, exporting, and in-game testing used when building new game content.

There are two side effects to lengthening this process, both of them undesirable. First, it increases the amount of time required to make and test any change, reducing overall productivity significantly. Second, a lengthy feedback loop will discourage developers from testing frequently, leading to more broken data, and lower quality assets as the (usually fairly unrepresentative) preview functionality provided by external packages is used in preference to viewing in place using the real game engine and environment.

Asset Building Shortcuts

The most common solution to this is to allow the normal build process to be "short-circuited," performing only the steps necessary to process the single asset currently being edited, and keeping the resulting test data confined to the machine that it is being viewed on. This can be achieved with a server-based build process, but under most circumstances it is easier and ultimately more productive to build the system so that each developer can run a "mini asset pipeline" on his own machine, with simple controls to enable specified data to be processed as required.

It can also be useful for this deliberately shortened pipeline to have different characteristics to the "full" pipeline in some respects. For example, if the process for compiling a world map includes a computationally expensive lighting pass, then it will save a significant amount of time if this can be disabled in situations where aspects of the level other than the overall visual appearance are being previewed. Similarly, there are often optimization steps (such as visibility tree construction and triangle stripification) which are necessary to achieve the required performance in the final game, but which are completely redundant for testing purposes. Of course, it is not necessary to disable such processes entirely; particularly with algorithms such as lighting, simplified versions of the algorithms can produce an acceptable (for previewing) approximation of the results in a fraction of the time.

There is a danger to this, however, if the preview versions of the game are not representative of the final quality, then it is very important that everyone working on the game understands this and knows how the final data will differ from the preview. Otherwise, time may easily be wasted trying to fix problems that appear only in the locally-processed data or worse, real problems may be ignored because they are assumed to be an artifact of the reduced quality processing. Another reason for tightly controlling the local build process is that unless measures are taken to ensure the integrity of data on every machine, it is very easy for some machines to have assets that others do not, leading to situations where the master version of the game on the server does not actually contain all the required data, but the developers responsible do not notice because they have the required data locally: a variant on the "zombie file" effect which can happen when files are not removed from asset management systems correctly.

There is a tricky balance to be struck here. On one hand, it is desirable to allow developers the freedom to process and view assets locally, but on the other, it is best if these temporary files do not remain in existence long enough to cause consistency problems among machines. In many circumstances, clearing the local data from each machine whenever new data is retrieved from the network can be a reasonable compromise, although this can still cause problems in situations where developers are working on assets over long periods of time (more than a day or so), as they will almost inevitably want to update the rest of their data during that time. Many asset management systems take the approach that any file in the data hierarchy that was not explicitly checked out but has been modified on the client is a potential error and flag it as such, providing a useful safeguard against unwanted data accumulating on local machines.

Unrepresentative Previews

Another issue indirectly linked to the local data processing problem is the situation where a significant number of team members are not testing their work on the actual target platform for the game, either due to a lack of suitable hardware (often due to the relative expense of console test stations), or because the process for previewing data on the target is more complicated than simply using PC-side tools. In this case where a large percentage of the testing and editing is being done on what are usually high performance PCs, serious problems can often be masked simply by the relatively high power of the platform. In particular, the available memory and CPU/GPU speed are often vastly disproportionate to what the final game will have available. There can also be more subtle problems, for example, PC 3D graphics cards often perform anisotropic filtering which vastly improves the appearance of high-contrast textures under some circumstances, but is not available on the majority of current console hardware.

This is mostly a problem for console games, although PC games can suffer from the problem as it is fairly common for the development systems to be of a significantly higher specification than the desired minimum required to run the final game. In either case, however, the net result of this issue can be disastrous. Assets that perform and look or sound fine when previewed, can be radically different on the actual target platform, and in some cases completely unworkable.

To prevent this, there are two measures that can be taken: either making the preview tools and pipeline capable of emulating the limitations of the final system (for example, by rejecting at the processing stage any assets that exceed set memory footprint limits), or, in the case of console development, by supporting target preview, allowing the local system to perform the necessary processing to package up assets so that they can be used with the game running on real console hardware.

Due to the extensive data packing, compression and optimization for loading processes normally used on console games, the process of doing this can often require the pipeline and engine to be modified to support the use of assets that are not in their absolutely final forms or packages. While it is reasonable for the master build pipeline to pack all files efficiently when it completes a build, this process is generally much too slow to be viable during iterative editing of a single file. For development versions of the game, the easiest way to implement this is generally to allow two possible sources for assets: either from the compressed package files that the final game disc will contain, or from individual files on the host PC that the console is connected to. This allows the bulk of the assets to be provided from efficient, packed files, while those currently under development are in an easily updatable form.

Runtime Editing

In some cases, it may be desirable to go further and give the pipeline the ability to "inject" assets directly into the game as it is running. If it takes a significant amount of time to re-run the game and progressing to the point where the asset being edited is actually used, to be able to edit a file and immediately see the results in-game is a huge time-saver. In general, this can be achieved relatively simply as long as the game engine supports some mechanism for forcing the reloading of a given asset, with the increasing prevalence of streaming systems and other dynamic loading techniques in games, this is often a very straightforward task. With that in place, the asset processing system can check for a running instance of the game (usually either using normal TCP/IP network communication with the target, or a dedicated debugging interface and API) and send it a command which triggers the reloading of the assets it has modified. In this fashion, the system becomes almost transparent in use—once the game is running, the developer simply needs to reprocess the assets they are working on and the new versions immediately appear in the game.

In some cases, it can be advantageous to allow this system to operate in the opposite direction, too. While the vast majority of assets are only editable in the appropriate packages on a host PC, there are certain types that may be more conveniently edited directly on the target itself, for example, the positioning and tuning of lighting may only be possible there, or the alteration of game balancing parameters and scripts. In these cases, the host PC can either be used as a direct editing interface (with parameter changes being sent in real time to the target platform), or edits can be performed entirely on the target and the resulting changes written back to the host. In these cases, the asset data from the target must be inserted back into the asset management database, either manually by the user or by the pipeline system in some way. Which approach is more appropriate will largely depend on the quantity of such target edited assets in the game, and how frequently they need to be edited.

In addition, especially during the later stages of development when the emphasis is on tweaking or improving existing content rather than creating new assets, it is not uncommon for significant amounts of time to be spent simply locating the assets which correspond to a particular location or effect in the game. This is particularly true in the case of assets such as textures, where there is a very large number of them, and even if descriptions or other metadata are available simply knowing what to search for can be a major problem. Therefore, to make this process as quick as possible, an in-game toolkit can be provided which essentially allows any asset to be selected (in the case of visual elements, a simple cursor suffices: for other types of data different approaches may be necessary, such as a textual list of the currently playing sound effects). Once an asset is selected in the game, the name can be sent back to the host PC, which can then open either the asset itself or the appropriate entry in the asset database.

With a system of this nature in place, it becomes possible to construct an end-to-end asset pipeline that runs on the local machine of each developer but is (almost) completely transparent in operation. If the export tools are able to inform the processing system when a new file is saved (or the processing system simply monitors the source directories for updated files), then the processing can be performed automatically, and the results injected into the game when it completes. This minimizes the amount of time and effort required to preview assets, the user simply has to hit "save," and in (hopefully) a very short time their changes are reflected in the game they are playing. This low overhead, low turnaround time approach can yield huge gains in productivity and quality simply by leveraging many of the features of the "full size" central asset pipeline on local machines and adding a small amount of extra functionality.

SYNCHRONIZING CODE AND DATA

Sadly, it is not the case that all game development is done with an already completed engine, and it is highly likely that at least during the early stages of the development process, there will be many significant changes made to the structure of the various engine components and the file formats they use. Designing a pipeline that can cope with these alterations is a significant challenge, because by their very nature they are unpredictable and unlike most other data changes, can affect huge numbers of assets at once, forcing large chunks of the project to be rebuilt. Even worse, during development it is often necessary to support two different versions of the code, the "development branch," where new engine features are being implemented and the appropriate updated asset formats are required, and the "stable branch," which is in use by the rest of the team. The transition that occurs whenever a major update is moved from the development branch to the stable branch is often very difficult to manage, as any user who does not have the right combination of code and data will most likely find that they cannot run the game at all or worse, that assets break in unexpected ways, leading to time wasted debugging problems caused by mismatched file formats.

These two different branches can often be handled by the asset system by allowing two separate pipelines to run concurrently, using different versions of the processing code. The source data for both pipelines is the same, but the outputs are kept separate. In this way, the latest versions of all the assets are always available to the entire team no matter which version of the code they are using, but the two do not interfere with each other. This is particularly important as code changes to the processing system may easily introduce bugs that break the "development branch" pipeline completely, preventing any asset processing from occurring until the problem is resolved. If this happens to the main pipeline, it will prevent any game data from being built at all and likely reduce progress to a virtual standstill quite quickly.

In many cases, minor changes can be handled by allowing for backwards compatibility in the game code. When loading files, if files using the newer format are found they will be used, otherwise the system will fall back on the older ones. This can also be applied at lower levels, by ensuring that individual blocks of data can be extended without interfering with the existing information, and by implementing version checking (and potentially multiple paths for loading data). With these in place, updates can be staggered, with either the updated code or data pipelines being put into production use first, and then the others following a short time later once the updates have filtered through to everyone.

However, there are always cases where this is not possible, either due to the large-scale nature of the changes or because a feature or bug fix is required immediately in the main stable code branch. For these, a robust system for deploying changes is a highly desirable addition to the asset management system. The most obvious mechanism for doing this is to provide a way to switch the development and stable pipelines over quickly, bringing all the processed data along so that it is not necessary for the entire game dataset to be rebuilt. If the game executables used by non-programming team members to run the game are also included in the asset database, then it is possible for this switch to be entirely transparent to the majority of the team. The next time they use the asset system to retrieve data, they will get both the updated assets and the new executables required, bringing their whole system up-to-date in one operation. Disk space and processor time permitting, it may also be useful to keep the previous stable version of the pipeline in operation for some time after it has been superseded, so it is possible to switch back to it in the event that major problems are discovered in the new version.

Integrating Code into the Asset Pipeline

While the asset pipeline is usually only thought of as being a mechanism for processing data, it can sometimes be worthwhile to build some aspects of the code building process into the system as well. By making the central asset server able to fetch source code from the source control database and build game executables as well, a significant additional workload can be removed from programmers by ensuring that appropriate builds for development and testing are always available to other team members and for the process of constructing working game discs. There are numerous ways in which this can be achieved, but the most straightforward is to make use of the labeling system that almost all source control software provides—by labeling certain revisions of the code as "stable," "testing," etc., the asset server can simply retrieve a number of different sets and recompile them each time a change is detected. In this way, builds are always available when they are required, and in addition the asset pipeline can keep itself updated with the latest processing tools and data formats. When the programming team is confident that a given revision of the code works, all they have to do is update the labels, and the rest happens automatically.

Allowing the asset pipeline to update itself from the relevant code revisions can save a lot of time, but it does raise an interesting problem: unlike asset changes, for which a dependency tree of the required updates can be relatively easily constructed, code changes can have wide reaching and often unpredictable consequences, sometimes even altering the actual structure of the asset dependency tree! Handling this in such a way that ensures that all the required data is updated can be a very complicated task, and in some cases it may be simpler just to manually flag the required changes when the build label is updated, or have the asset pipeline simply assume that any code changes invalidate the entire asset output and start again from scratch.

Code Constructed from Data

Giving the asset pipeline access to the source control database and the ability to build game code has one other advantage, in that it allows the pipeline to cope with data assets that are actually incorporated into the game code somehow. While this is something that most game developers avoid as much as possible, there are some cases in which it is unavoidable. Two examples are initial loading screens, which are often incorporated into the game executable so that they are available immediately on start-up (as often required on console systems), and graphics "shaders," which are often constructed from code fragments assembled together to achieve certain effects in an artist specified manner. In most of these cases, where the output files from the build process are actually then compiled into the game itself as code, it is possible to construct a data path so that the source art generates the required source code files in the pipeline, which are then placed in an intermediate file storage area from which they are included in the executable rebuilding process. In some cases they can also be placed back in the source control database, so that programmers will also have the updated data the next time they build an executable.

BUILDING A DISTRIBUTION PACKAGE

If the asset pipeline is capable of building both the data and the executable for the game, then it is only one more small step to enable it to use these to construct a distribution package, essentially a set of matching code and data, packaged together in a suitable format for use (for example, a ZIP file or a CD/DVD image ready for burning). This can usually be achieved very simply—the process of packaging the data as required on the final media can be added to the end of the pipeline as another step, invoking suitable tools to perform the compressed file or image construction as necessary.

Only a small amount of effort is required to implement this, however, the resulting savings in time and effort can be significant, especially toward the end of the development process when it is often necessary to produce new builds of the game for testing on a daily basis. By shifting this task onto the resource system, no additional time beyond that needed to copy or burn the output file to a disc is wasted, and the ever-present possibility of human error affecting the (often long winded and tedious) process is removed.

Incorporating the distribution packaging system into the asset pipeline also means that this stage in the process gains the benefits the asset system brings to the rest of the game asset building process. The latest version of the game is always available when it is needed, and past "known good" versions can be archived in the asset management database for retrieval if necessary. The asset management system can also keep track of which exact versions of the code and data were used to build each CD, adding unique build labels to the code and asset databases so that if necessary the process can be repeated at a later date or changes made since a given build was examined.

AUTOMATED TESTING

While the topic of automated testing is outside the scope of this book, it is worth noting that an asset management system with a full end-to-end pipeline (that is, source art and code through to final media) can be a vital resource in running such a testing process. The testing system can grab completed builds of the game at regular intervals (or when prompted by the asset system that a change has occurred), and then perform the test suite on that build. Any errors can be reported back and logged alongside the build data in the asset management system, providing both an immediate indication when retrieving a build for further testing or other use of what may be broken, and which builds are "known good" and should be kept in case a demonstrable version of the game is needed on short notice.

Automated testing can provide valuable information on the progress being made in development and the current status of the game, too. By providing statistics on how many failures there are in each test run and where these occur, over time, the general trends as to which areas are ahead or behind schedule, and which ones are causing the most problems can be determined. In particular, this can be extremely useful in detecting patterns in the failures. If there are a lot of errors caused by one type of asset, for example, it may indicate that there is insufficient verification being performed in the export or creation tools, or simply that the procedures for handling that particular data type are too complicated.

CONCLUSION

While there are many facets of the asset management problem that are unique to it, many existing techniques from related fields such as source control systems and database management can be effectively used to tackle the difficulties encountered. The volume of asset data generated during game development can be a significant hurdle, however, especially when multiple revisions of assets are stored simultaneously.

The asset processing pipeline is a complex system, and must serve several purposes—primarily, the generation of data both for complete builds of the game, and intermediate data for development and testing purposes. The most vital aspect of the pipeline's role is that it must ensure a rapid turnaround time for assets—otherwise, the time required to build and test assets quickly becomes prohibitive, slowing development and reducing overall quality. In addition, the pipeline must be robust, and handle errors in a sensible manner, otherwise it runs the risk of stalling development while major problems are resolved, and allowing more subtle errors to make their way into released builds.

4 Building an Asset Management System

In This Chapter

- Storage Systems
- Transactions and Locking
- Client/Server Architecture
- Client Tools
- Managing the Local Repository
- Client Tool UI and Functionality Considerations
- Access Controls and Security
- Providing an External API
- Scripting Support
- Archiving and Purging Data

A full asset management and processing system is a very complex beast, comprised of a relatively large set of interlocking components. There are many existing asset and pipeline management programs, but the functionality typically required from the system as a whole usually extends into other areas. The build processes themselves are often heavily tied to the game's target engine and platform and must be custom built for the task at hand. Even in areas where this is not the case, the sheer range of possible requirements makes providing an all-in-one system that can handle every case virtually impossible. In addition to the core processing requirements, it is often desirable to have a wide range of ancillary tasks (for example, automatically packaging and transferring data across a wide-area network, or e-mailing reports of build problems to team members) handled automatically as part of the build process, usually by custom or externally produced helper applications. As such, implementing all but the most basic form of a useful asset system almost inevitably involves writing a significant amount of custom code, both to implement functionality not provided by existing components and to interface with the other libraries and tools already in use. However, carefully selecting and adapting where necessary, the best of the existing modules and utilities for the specifics of the system required can greatly reduce the implementation effort required and make the resulting pipeline much more robust.

STORAGE SYSTEMS

The basic foundation of any asset management system is simple: you need somewhere to store the data. In many ways, the choice of storage system is the single most important decision that needs to be taken when developing such a system, as it will determine to a large degree how much effort is required to implement the more advanced functionality that sets asset management solutions aside from traditional filing systems.

Native Filing Systems

The simplest and most obvious choice for a storage system is just that, to use the filing system built into the host OS the system will run on: most commonly NTFS in the case of Windows-based systems, and EXT2, EXT3, or ReiserFS on Linux derivatives (the FAT and FAT32 systems used by DOS, Windows 95, 98, and ME are not really worth considering for this role, as they were not designed for high load server tasks, and have been superseded by the more robust and higher performance NTFS). The advantages of this approach are fairly clear: the storage layer is very thin, introduces few potential performance penalties, is well-understood, tested, straightforward to develop for, and compatible with virtually every existing tool. However, there is one major disadvantage, too—the functionality most filing systems provide is very limited, leaving the implementation of revision storage, changelists, and virtually every other feature in the hands of the system developer.

One of the most significant problems faced when developing an asset based on the native filing system is that of version control. There are a few OS-native filing systems that support file versioning (that is, storing multiple revisions of the same file), VMS (the OS used on VAX mainframes) handles this, as does SCO's OpenServer system. Despite early pioneers like VMS adopting this approach, however, it was mostly ignored during subsequent filing system development, largely due to the increased disc space requirements and management overhead (both for the OS itself and the user). As a result, virtually none of the filing systems found in common use among games developers natively support storing multiple revisions of the same file, so in most cases in order to implement this it is necessary to add a layer of abstraction, which generates multiple physical files for each asset in the database, one for each version. While this itself is not a huge problem, the management of these files can soon become unwieldy. The naming conventions and storage structure the system uses must be carefully chosen so that there is no possibility of a collision between user-created and system-created filenames (for example, if revisions are marked by adding ".001," ".002," and so on to the filename, what happens if the user manually creates one asset called "texture.tga" and another called "texture.tga.001"?).

Unique IDs as Filenames

One solution to this is to discard user-specified asset names altogether for storage purposes and simply refer to each asset with a unique identifier number. This avoids many of the potential problems, but does require a layer somewhere in software that can perform the mapping to and from the user asset names. In addition, renaming assets in this way introduces a major single point of failure for the software—if the database containing the asset name list becomes corrupted, then the assets on disc are next to useless as their names are now meaningless. Modern filing systems attempt to alleviate this problem by using fairly sophisticated mechanisms to protect the integrity of the data in the File Allocation Table (FAT), such as keeping two copies of it at all times and performing updates to each in turn (so that if a system crash occurs, one copy of the FAT is always intact). If using a scheme where critical asset information is stripped from the files, it would be wise to implement a similar system to protect the key databases and ensure that they are backed up frequently to guard against other failures.

In addition, as mentioned previously, storing entire copies of every revision of assets can soon prove to be a large burden on the system—it may well be necessary to implement some form of compression or differencing algorithm, and it will certainly be a requirement that the system can either extract for archival or purge altogether asset revisions that are considered too old to be worth storing. In the case of compression, some filing systems provide support for this already—NTFS, for example, can have optional (transparent) compression enabled for any directory or drive.

There are many systems that provide a layer on top of the filing system and implement much of the functionality required for an asset management system. Using one of these can significantly reduce the amount of effort required to implement a full system by providing all the basic services in a form that is both well tested and straightforward to interface to other systems if necessary. (Never underestimate how much time will be required with a custom system simply writing tools to view and edit the contents of the asset database manually for debugging or supporting external tools!)

CVS

CVS, or the Concurrent Versions System, is worthy of special mention simply because it is so widely used, and is considered by many the baseline for source code management systems. CVS is an open-source client/server system that is primarily designed for source control but can be successfully used for binary data as well. CVS is used by a vast number of developers worldwide, and is exceptionally stable and well tested under most circumstances. CVS itself is based on an older version control system called RCS (the Revision Control System), which was in turn a replacement for SCCS (the Source Code Control System). Being open-source, CVS is easily modified and there are ports to virtually every operating system in existence. Although the client software is purely command-line driven, it is very easy to interface to other tools, and if required there are a large number of existing graphical repository viewers and other utilities that can be used with it. A good starting point for information on CVS is the CVS home Web site at *http://www.cvshome.org.*

CVS implements a traditional repository database on top of the native filing system of the OS it is running on, using separate files for each revision and storing metadata separately. The repository management is quite good, although the evolution of CVS over time has led to some features being implemented in a somewhat unintuitive manner, which can be a problem, particularly for developers new to the system, for example, moving or renaming a file is nearly impossible without removing and re-adding it (losing any past revisions in the process), and the version tagging mechanism is very idiosyncratic. The CVS feature set is mature, but some of the more advanced features common in more recently developed systems, such as atomic check-ins and advanced branch/merge support are not present. The first of these is the most concerning, from an asset management perspective, as it means the contents of the repository may be in an inconsistent state at any given moment in time due to a half-completed operation which is in progress. There is also no support for automatically rolling back operations that have only been partially completed as these tasks must be done "by hand" or implemented by the higher-level system using CVS if they are required. The lack of atomic check-ins also means that the associated metadata (comments and such) is stored with every file that the operation affected, which can make reconstructing a view of the order in which changelists were submitted and what files were affected very difficult.

One of the key differences to most version control systems is that CVS does not track check-out operations by default. Exclusive check outs can be "fudged" by setting a flag in the repository, but in general there is no information on who is editing a specific file. This is not an insurmountable problem for source control, as code merging is reasonably straightforward and non-exclusive check-out systems are the most common used, but for asset management it is a feature that will almost certainly need to be implemented at a higher level.

This is the single most significant problem that CVS poses for asset management systems. It is primarily designed for handling source code, not binary files, and this has influenced many of the design decisions. Although binary files are supported, many of the features of the system such as file differencing are not implemented (or simply not applicable) for them, and the CVS server itself can become unstable when used with very large databases. Large files can also pose a problem where network bandwidth is limited as some operations will transfer the entire file across the network, rather than only updating those sections that have changed. Operations such as trimming the repository to remove older revisions of files can be performed, but again are not supported automatically by the software.

Due to these limitations and others, there are numerous projects that have started with the goal of creating "a better CVS." Two of the most advanced are Subversion and Bitkeeper, open-source and commercial packages respectively which offer replacements with cleaner interfaces and more features, including better handling of binary files and atomic operations support.

Subversion

Subversion, like CVS, is an open-source project, which at the time of this writing had just reached its v1.0 milestone. Unlike many projects, this v1.0 release is not an initial version, but rather the point at which the project maintainers felt the system had proven itself to be sufficiently stable (and functional) to be used in a full production environment. Even before this point, however, many projects (including Subversion itself) were hosted successfully on the pre-1.0 releases. Subversion can be found online at *http://subversion.tigris.org.*

Subversion implements operations on the repository in an atomic fashion and also supports branching and tagging of revisions. Unlike CVS, all repository operations are tracked and can be easily rolled back if necessary, and individual committed changelists are stored as a single revision, with a single set of metadata associated with them.

Subversion is implemented as a set of libraries, with various tools that make use of them. Thus, it is relatively straightforward to build new tools that interface directly with it, either using the libraries directly or simply by invoking the included command-line utilities. Even the server is implemented in this fashion, making the construction of a custom server system (if, for whatever reason, it was required) fairly simple. The standard Subversion server is implemented as an Apache module, using a subset of the WebDAV protocol, which allows for remote access to files stored on an HTTP server. If this is employed, then it also becomes possible to access the repository at a fairly low level by communicating directly with the server using another tool that supports WebDAV. The DeltaV protocol (an extension of WebDAV) is used to provide the necessary support for file versioning and change tracking.

In addition to the Apache module version of the server, Subversion also provides a standalone server that can be run independently, and uses a custom protocol. This may be useful in circumstances where deploying a full Apache installation is too much of an overhead (in terms of maintenance or setup time, the runtime performance of the various servers is fairly similar) for the asset server.

Subversion has also made a point of adding features that are useful for operating with repositories containing data other than text or source code, most notably, it supports differencing binary files (this is not particularly useful for merging files in most cases, but by storing and transmitting only the differences between files the storage space and network bandwidth required for certain types of assets can be reduced quite significantly), and the repository database has been structured so as to support large binary files where necessary.

Although Subversion does not have quite as long a development history as some of the existing version control solutions (most notably CVS), it has a very comprehensive feature set and is well suited in general to being employed in asset management solutions.

Bitkeeper

The most significant other CVS replacement system currently in development is Bitkeeper, a commercial product developed by BitMover Inc (*http://www.bitkeeper. com*). The Bitkeeper feature-set is very extensive, although (as with all of the source-control packages, understandably enough) biased heavily toward handling text files.

In common with Subversion, Bitkeeper supports atomic operations, and also makes managing changelists and their metadata very straightforward. All repository operations are tracked and handled in the same way, so structural changes such as renaming or deleting files are visible in the revision histories and can be manipulated in the same way as content modifications.

The most significant unique feature that Bitkeeper provides is that of "staging areas," or hierarchical repositories. This feature allows multiple repositories to be set up that are linked together in a tree structure, giving each group of users their own "private" repository to work in which in turn can be synchronized to the master repository (or another intermediate one) as required. In this way, changes can be made and tested among the group working on them (a team constructing an individual level, for example) before being released to the rest of the team.

The functionality provided by multiple repositories can be emulated to some extent in other systems using branches for individual development areas, but Bitkeeper's implementation of the system makes this much simpler to maintain and massively reduces the possibility of human error adding changes to the wrong branch. In addition, by distributing repositories across multiple servers, overloading problems can be alleviated and development across multiple (physical) sites becomes much simpler without the need for very high bandwidth connections.

Bitkeeper is commercial software; therefore, it is not possible to modify the source code to suit your requirements. There is also no support for writing external tools to interface with Bitkeeper servers directly, the Bitkeeper client-side tools are necessary to do this. However, these are all primary command-line based (the graphical tools provided are wrappers around the command-line versions), and hence are fairly straightforward to integrate into most applications.

Another feature that Bitkeeper provides which is very useful for binary data is an extremely comprehensive set of automatic repository integrity checks. Checksums are calculated for all of the stored data and errors in the repository can be quickly detected. This can be quite important as in many other systems (such as CVS) errors in older revisions of assets will not usually be noticed until they are specifically retrieved from the repository, by which time it may be difficult or impossible to retrieve backup copies of the affected files.

Bitkeeper is in fairly wide use among a fair number of projects, although the commercial nature of the software has largely prevented the mass-scale adoption that CVS enjoys and Subversion is beginning to see (there is a free version of Bitkeeper available for open-source development use, although the license terms are quite restrictive). It has, however, proved itself to be capable of handling large projects very effectively, and the current Linux kernel sources are hosted in a Bitkeeper repository.

Perforce

While firmly designed and pitched as a source control system, Perforce, a commercial product developed by Perforce Software Inc. (*http://www.perforce.com/*), has established itself not only as a highly successful source code management solution, but also as a very capable product for managing binary asset data. Many large game projects have successfully used Perforce for storing both source code and assets.

Perforce operates on a changelist-based model, with all repository operations being handled as atomic transactions. There is support for merging and resolving conflicts in text files, and although there is no built-in support for the same functionality for binary file types, binary files are correctly handled by the underlying system and support for invoking external merge tools is included.

There is also support for a limited form of "views," which enables sections of the repository to be selectively remapped to different locations on the client filing system. This can be useful in circumstances where only specific subsets of the repository are required on each client, or where the game data is required to conform to a different layout than the repository. Unfortunately, Perforce only allows a very limited amount of metadata to be attached to files, and it is not possible to define views based on metadata as criteria.

Perforce runs on a vast array of operating systems, and has several different client applications, ranging from a "lowest common denominator" command line tool that functions on every supported system to specifically tailored GUI tools for Windows, Mac OS, and Linux, and integration with a number of common packages (mostly programming IDEs, though). There is also a direct API for integrating Perforce connectivity into other applications, which is quite straightforward to use.

One of Perforce's main standout features is the sheer speed and efficiency of both the underlying technology and the interface. Although certain lesser used actions (such as switching between repositories) can be somewhat clumsy, all of the day-to-day activities performed in the Perforce GUI are highly streamlined and the client/server communications are very efficient. In addition, Perforce supports adding caching servers to reduce the load on the main repository and allow users connected over slow links faster access to data.

As well as being fast, Perforce's underlying database technology is extremely stable, and uses journaling and on-the-fly checkpointing to help maintain data integrity and uptime. It also copes admirably with large files, although aimed at handling source code, there is little control offered over the archival and purging of old revisions: this must either be performed manually or handled by a higher-level system.

While Perforce is not designed with binary asset management in mind and is lacking many of the features that might be desired in such a package, the performance and stability it offers make it a very suitable choice for forming the base storage layer for a more advanced system.

Alienbrain

NxN Software's Alienbrain (*http://www.alienbrain.com*) is almost the only commercial asset management product aimed at and suitable for large-scale use in games development. The repository functionality of Alienbrain is reasonably well featured, although it is designed to store individual file histories only, the current version does not support atomic operations or grouped changelists, and structural changes are not handled by the revision control system.

At the time of writing, these features are planned to appear in the soon to be released Version 7. In addition, because of the file-based nature of the repository, the current version can be very slow at performing some operations, for example, fetching the latest contents of a folder involves the client individually checking every file for changes, rather than simply retrieving a list of those files that have been altered since the last synchronization. This situation is made worse by the lack of file differencing algorithms to reduce the required network bandwidth for updates.

One of the focuses of Alienbrain's development, however, and by far the most impressive feature of the package, is the sheer number of other tools that it can interface to. Plug-ins that provide integrated file check-in and check-out support for most of the commonly used content creation packages exist, and the graphical repository client can intelligently preview many common types of assets.

A comprehensive (if a little quirky) set of APIs also exist for interfacing custom code to the repository database and GUI if necessary. Most operations can be carried out using the included command-line tools, which provide a straightforward route for simpler integration tasks. The functionality these provide can be somewhat unreliable at times, however, as the communication between the tools and the main Alienbrain client relies on several external components. Once it is working correctly on a machine it is generally stable, but getting it to that state can be tricky. In addition, the command-line tools keep a significant amount of state stored between invocations, meaning that if two applications or scripts attempt to use them at the same time they can interfere with each other. Custom preview plug-ins can also be written to enable new file formats to be handled by the Alienbrain GUI.

The GUI itself is very straightforward, and easy for non-technical users to grasp, although it can be slow and cumbersome in many cases, especially for users more used to the streamlined interface provided by source control packages. The GUI can be reconfigured to a degree by the user or repository manager, which may be useful in some circumstances, especially because by default, some common operations are also inexplicably hidden or only available after performing several steps. For example, the process of determining which files are currently checked out is needlessly complicated for such a frequently used function. Another extremely useful feature of the GUI is the ability to view past revisions of assets quickly, and perform comparisons between them on-screen. This can be extremely useful since for most types of assets automatic differencing algorithms are virtually useless.

Unlike the other tools examined here, Alienbrain also provides functionality for managing workflow, the procedures required for creating, approving, and integrating assets into a game. The repository maintainer (or other users with the appropriate Alienbrain client software) can set up the necessary steps that must be followed, and these will be enforced by the asset server as required. The tools integrate a fair amount of functionality for this purpose, including an integrated mail system for notifying users of changes to assets, and the ability to maintain metadata describing the state of each file in the repository and its progress through the workflow.

Alienbrain also provides tools for maintaining the repository at a sensible size: past revisions of files can be automatically deleted or archived to other media, which makes restoring them at a later date possible. Repository backups can also be easily set up, and one very useful feature is the ability to easily perform backups of a selected set of files or revisions, thereby removing the need for regular backups to include large quantities of redundant historical data.

In general, Alienbrain goes a long way toward providing a complete "drop-in" solution for asset management, with suitable hooks provided to handle the interactions with the rest of the asset pipeline. Unlike all of the other systems discussed here, the functionality for handling binary assets is built in and much of the package is structured around providing solutions specifically for games development. While in terms of technology Alienbrain is much less sophisticated than many of the alternative packages available, in many cases the tradeoff in low-level features may well be worthwhile in view of the additional higher-level functionality (such as the extensive set of previewing and plug-in tools), and the myriad of smaller advantages inherent in having a solution tailored to the specifics of the problem at hand.

Databases

Another option that can be used for asset management is to base the system on an existing database system, such as the popular open-source system MySQL (*http://www.mysql.com*), or a commercial offering such as Oracle® (*http://www.oracle.com*) or Microsoft SQL Server (*http://www.microsoft.com/sql*). There are numerous advantages to this approach: an existing database will already provide very robust and well-defined functionality for performing atomic transactions and managing many simultaneous client connections, and the problems of storing and searching metadata for files can be eliminated almost completely simply by adding this information to the database records.

Existing databases also tend to have very well-defined interfaces (often using the industry standard SQL, or Structured Query Language), and there are many tools available for them.

The disadvantage of this approach, however, is simple yet almost always renders it useless. Existing database packages are all structured around the idea that the data being stored is quite small, text records, typically, generally not amounting to more than a few KB each at most. Certainly, there are many database solutions that can scale to handle huge volumes of information, but almost always in the form of thousands or millions of these small records. In comparison, an asset management system will only use a comparatively small number of records, but will store large quantities of data, sometimes many tens of megabytes, in each. Sadly, forcing this much data into a system not designed to cope with it will (if possible at all) almost always reduce performance to completely unacceptable levels. Although database technology is improving as developers increasingly discover the need to store large quantities of binary data in their systems, at present using an off-the-shelf database server for asset management is virtually impossible for all but the smallest tasks.

That said, however, there is considerable mileage in hybrid approaches. While traditional database systems are not designed to handle the quantities of binary data the files in an asset management system represent, they are perfectly positioned to store the metadata associated with those files. This can have very significant advantages, as the metadata is by far the most frequently accessed and modified part of the asset database, and by removing the unique problems associated with handling it (such as allowing for rapid searching and transactional updates) the remaining problems (those related to the storage of the mostly unchanging binary data in the asset files themselves) are made significantly simpler.

TRANSACTIONS AND LOCKING

One of the major problems that can arise (primarily when using a traditional filing system as the base storage system, but sometimes in other situations depending on the software being used) is that of file or record *locking*. This is the process through which a program can acquire exclusive access to a set of files in order to modify them—the files are effectively "locked" and therefore inaccessible to the rest of the system until the program has finished with them. Support for locking varies wildly between different OSs and filing systems, but virtually none implement the level of fine-grained control required for an asset management system—it will almost inevitably be necessary to implement some form of access arbitration system on top of the support provided by the filing system.

Again, the database system concepts of transactions and atomic operations play a major role in defining the locking and access semantics for an asset management system. The goals of a perfect system should be that only the minimal amount of locking needed to ensure correct operation is done (as locking large numbers of files will impair performance as tasks must wait for access to the data they need), but at the same time be able to provide guarantees about the integrity of the data at all times.

Operation Queues

At the most basic level, access arbitration can be achieved simply by having a single queue of operations for the asset management system to perform. Each operation is a single transaction, and they are processed in the order they are received. In this way, each transaction is able to have full access to the database, and there is no danger that the state of a file will be changed by any other operation until it has completed (the assumption is made here that the transactions are structured in such a way that it is logically impossible for a transaction to interfere with its own operation, even in complex systems, this is relatively easy to guarantee simply by checking the transaction beforehand).

This approach works perfectly, with one small, but fatal flaw. The system can only execute one transaction at a time, and in order to ensure consistency, large operations must be submitted as a single transaction. So if a client requests a copy of the entire current set of data, then no other client will be able to do anything until that process completes! Clearly, this is unacceptable for even a small-scale system.

Therefore, the system must be capable of executing multiple transactions simultaneously, but still retaining the integrity of each. There are two approaches to achieving this—traditional locking of sections of the database, and pre-screening transactions to ensure that conflicts do not occur. The second approach works well in databases where very large numbers of small transactions are taking place, by choosing which transactions can be executed concurrently based on which assets they access, no further checks are required to ensure the integrity of the data. However, in the context of an asset management system, there are several very common operations (such as retrieving a complete update of all data) which touch a very large number of assets in the database, and therefore would effectively be nearly impossible to schedule alongside any other transaction.

Record Locking

This means that locking individual files or records as they are accessed is a much more attractive solution in the case of an asset management system. In most systems, there are two types of locks that can be held on a file: exclusive and non-exclusive. As the names suggest, an exclusive lock can only be held by a single process at a time, while multiple non-exclusive locks can be held. Typically, these map onto write and read operations, respectively, any number of tasks can read from a file simultaneously, but only one may write to it (and during that time, no others may read). If you consider the usage of a typical asset management system, it is clear that the majority of the locks will be read locks. It is a comparatively rare operation to perform an update to a file.

It is important at this point to consider the distinction between the different revisions of an individual file, and the metadata associated with that file. If all these were treated as a single unit for locking purposes, then the efficiency of the system would be vastly reduced. The reason for this is simple—there is a large disparity between the access patterns for files and metadata. There are a large number of operations that alter the metadata for files (checking out, checking in, labeling, rolling back), but as the metadata is small and these operations typically only involve changing a few bytes, they can be completed very quickly. Equally, the metadata for files is read on a very regular basis. However, the file data itself is only written to by one operation (checking in), and read more infrequently, but these can take a significant amount of time, as the file size may be very large. If locking the file for checking in had the effect of locking the metadata for the entire duration of the transaction as well, then it would make any operation on that file, even just checking the name, block until the check in was complete!

Separating Metadata and File Locks

An interesting point that differentiates the usage patterns of the database in an asset management system from that which appears in more traditional database applications is caused by the version control system. In an asset management system, it is very rare (in some cases impossible) for a write operation to alter an existing file. In virtually all cases, the write will create a new revision of the file instead. It is only the metadata that gets updated in the same manner that a traditional database record would. By considering the different revisions of files as separate entities for locking purposes, this can be exploited to greatly improve efficiency in the system.

Consider the case where user A is fetching a copy of the current revision of the asset database from the server. During this time, user B checks in a new revision of "mytexture.tga." The first thing that the fetch task does is to lock for reading the metadata for every file in the database, and read the latest revision numbers into an internal buffer. It can then unlock these, allowing normal operations to continue on the metadata, and acquire a read lock on the files it wishes to fetch instead. Under a locking scheme where file revisions are considered as one, the check in transaction will not be able to acquire a write lock on mytexture.tga to update it until the fetch operation has completed (or, at least, has copied that file and unlocked it, assuming that it releases the lock on files as it finishes with them).

However, if the individual revisions can be locked independently, then the fetch task can lock just the revisions it is actually going to read. When the check in transaction occurs, it must wait for the lock on the file metadata to be released (although this should only take a very small amount of time), and can then lock that and create the new revision of the file. It can then immediately lock that without interfering with the lock the fetch task holds on the older file, and write to it. The updated file is thus committed to the repository during the fetch operation, but the fetch will still retrieve the older file that it has locked. This ensures the transactional integrity of the fetch, as far as it is concerned, the database state has not changed during the time it was operating, and the set of files it has retrieved corresponds to the set that existed when it started. There is no danger of the fetch retrieving an inconsistent set with some old revisions and some newer ones.

It should be noted that with a looser locking scheme such as this, the internal behavior of transactions needs to be carefully considered to avoid the possibility of inconsistencies arising from "race conditions" where another transaction is trying to access the same data at the same time. For example, the check in operation must lock the metadata for the file it is going to update, create (and lock) the new revision file, and then unlock the metadata. Then it can copy the data into the revision file at leisure, as the metadata indicates the presence of this revision (meaning that another check in operation will not try to overwrite the file), but the lock it holds on the file prevents any other task from actually retrieving data from it. A good rule of thumb is that any operation that locks and unlocks a file or record more than once needs to be closely examined for possible failure cases, as there is no guarantee that the data has not been changed between the time of the first and second locks.

CLIENT/SERVER ARCHITECTURE

Any asset management system must be comprised of two sections: a server that stores the data, and a client that accesses and utilizes it. However, it is not immediately obvious where the dividing line between the client and the server should be drawn in terms of software architecture. For example, it is actually an entirely valid approach to have no dedicated server software at all! Microsoft's SourceSafe source control system is based on exactly this principle and operates solely using the network file sharing functionality built into Windows. Of course, there are many potential problems with this approach, most of which are demonstrated superbly by SourceSafe itself—most notably in that the lack of a server means that arbitration of access between the clients must be carried out using little more than basic file locking, and in the event of contention over resources there is no central authority to resolve the problem. Features such as atomic operations are nearly impossible to implement in such an environment as well.

Clientless Architectures

Equally, it would be entirely possible to build a system that operated without a dedicated client program, for example, by interfacing to the server through a standard Web browser. There are many problems with this as an approach, however: Web-based clients tend to be very slow at complex tasks (as virtually every user operation requires the data to be sent to the server and a new page retrieved), and the level of access to the local filing system needed is not generally supported for security reasons. Asset preview would also be very difficult to implement, and functionality for launching external programs to view assets is generally fairly limited (again, due to security concerns). Many of these problems could be circumvented by providing a trusted Java applet or ActiveX control that can run embedded into a Web browser, but at that point the applet has effectively become a dedicated client application itself, simply running in a browser window rather than separately on the desktop.

Some existing revision control solutions provide the ability for limited Web access, for example, Bitkeeper has an HTTP server that allows browsing and downloading files from a repository, and Subversion's use of the WebDAV protocol means that its repositories can be accessed from suitable enabled browsers on some machines. However, in both of these cases this functionality is provided in addition to a standard client application, mainly as a way of providing "casual" repository access to users who simply want to examine a specific file and do not have the necessary tools installed.

The Client/Server Boundary

The main factor that will influence the choice of which functionality should be handled by the client and which by the server is that of the balance between CPU usage and network bandwidth. In general, the more processing is done server-side, the slower the server itself will become. But in turn, moving processing over to the client will often require the client to request more data from the server, thereby increasing the network bandwidth required for each operation. In many cases, the structure of transactions will determine where the dividing line is drawn, as it is extremely desirable for the server to be able to complete an entire transaction without any communication with the client being required during it, as additional communication increases both the time required for the transaction (and hence the interval during which files or records may be locked) and the likelihood of the transaction's failure if a communication or client error occurs.

The communication between the client and server can take place over a number of different channels, but by far the most commonly used are the Internet TCP/IP protocol, and the various file sharing systems (such as SMB and NFS). TCP/IP is the de facto standard for network applications, and has the advantage that it is very robust, portable, and will operate (or can be made to operate) over virtually any combination of physical network layers. The downside, however, is that TCP/IP does not provide any explicit functionality for transferring or examining files. It is up to the application to implement a structure for requesting a file, and the process of reading it from disc, transmitting the contents and storing it again on the target system. The same must be done for any other required operations such as reading directory structures or filesystem metadata. Several existing protocols exist for doing this, the most commonly used is HTTP, and the more recent HTTP extensions WebDAV and DeltaV.

Using File Sharing Protocols

As an alternative, using an existing file sharing system to perform the binary asset file transfers (while, in many cases, using TCP/IP to transmit control information and metadata) is an attractive solution. Network file sharing is very simple to use—in virtually all cases, the built-in OS functions for copying files can be used with no changes, and all of the associated operations such as reading directory structures, file sizes, etc. will work with no need to re-implement them. Modern operating systems generally support accessing network file stores as an extension of the existing filing system namespace (or, in the case of Unix systems, by mapping the shared data directly into the main filing system). Therefore, all that is required to retrieve a file from the network is to determine the appropriate path with which to access it.

Unfortunately, in some cases, network file sharing protocols can be unreliable, and it is often the case that bridging or tunneling them between networks or across VPNs can be something of a "black art" and very hard to achieve acceptable performance or stability with. Another potential problem that can be hard to work around is that in some cases the OS will cache accesses to network files, sometimes leading to inconsistent states between machines on the network if files change rapidly, a very tricky state of affairs to detect and cope with.

Also, the nature of communication between the client and server will be determined by the desired usage patterns. If the system is only to be used on an internal high-speed LAN, then compressing data for transmission is almost certainly a pointless exercise, which may actually *reduce* the overall speed of the system (by increasing the CPU load on client and server). On the other hand, if the system is to be used over the Internet or a bandwidth-limited VPN, then compression will almost certainly be essential to make it usable.

Intelligent File Updating

Above all else, the vast majority of the bandwidth used by an asset management system is consumed by the process of transferring files to the client machines. In many cases, no matter if it is based on TCP/IP or another custom protocol, the usability of the system can be improved dramatically by making a few relatively simple optimizations. When transferring files, the client and server can first compute CRCs or hashes of the file contents (preferably with the server caching these in the metadata for each revision to reduce CPU overheads) and compare these, immediately eliminating the need to transfer any file that has not changed. In some cases where very large files are being transferred, it may also be advantageous to perform CRC checks on individual chunks of the file, and only transfer those chunks that have changed. The usefulness of this trick will depend largely on the nature of the file, as some formats (particularly those using compressed data) will cause the contents to change completely even if only a small alteration has been made.

Another potentially useful approach, depending on the exact network protocol in use, is to use *multicast* or broadcast functionality to transmit files as they are changed. Multicast is the process through which a single packet can be sent to multiple recipients simultaneously, although it is largely unused in current applications, it could potentially be used to distribute updated versions of assets to multiple clients simultaneously. In this case, it will probably be necessary for clients to implement a caching structure for new data, as in many situations the user will not actually *want* the updated files immediately, but if they are available locally the transfer overheads can be saved when the user later requests the update. The benefits of this approach largely depend on the nature of the data in use and the frequency of changes. If several asset revisions occur between user updates, then it may not be worth caching changes as many of them will never actually be used.

Another means of speeding up asset distribution in cases where (as is normally the case) the server CPU time and bandwidth are the limiting factors is to allow clients to share assets among themselves, in a manner not unlike that used by peer-to-peer file sharing networks. In this case, the server could maintain a list of which clients have already received a particular file, and redirect new clients to those machines instead, if the load on the server is high. In this situation, every client would need to have the ability to act as a file server (this may already be the case if an existing file sharing protocol is being used to transfer asset data), and when a transfer is initiated the requesting client simply connects to the address given by the server (which will be that of another client machine) and transfers the file as normal. If this technique is employed, then checksums or hashes for the files is almost essential as even with server-side checking there is more possibility for errors where the client being used to serve the file has a modified version or simply is not able to provide a complete copy. In any case if the file is unavailable or corrupt, the requesting client can then ask the server to provide another source for it and repeat the procedure.

CLIENT TOOLS

The layout and structure of the client-side tools for any asset management system will determine a lot about how they can be used. Many systems build the actual core functionality into a set of command-line tools (or one command-line tool), which can then be invoked by other tools to perform operations on the repository. Others provide a general purpose library on top of which tools can be built. In general though, it is desirable to build at least two user-accessible layers into the system. A GUI tool of some description which can be used to examine and perform "tweaks" to the repository (less commonly used operations such as reverting or examining past revisions of files) as well as the basic functions such as checking in and updating sets of files, and a collection of command-line tools that can do the most commonly needed functions without user intervention.

GUI Tools

GUI tools are very useful for several reasons: foremost and most obviously, because they provide a friendly interface to the system that can be used with little instruction or training (a vitally important factor when working with large content-creation teams). Additionally, because they give a high-level overview of the contents of the asset database in a form that is relatively easy to integrate with other graphical tools such as preview displays. The time and effort savings afforded by having even basic preview functionality built into the main repository view cannot be underestimated, even with comprehensive metadata, there are always cases where the only way to understand changes that have been made (or even to know what the exact asset that is being examined is) is to see them visually.

Command-Line Tools

Equally, having command-line driven tools (which can run without user prompting) is vital to allowing the automation of often-repeated tasks. While a full library API may be more appropriate for integration into significant tools such as the asset pipeline manager, there are numerous small tasks in game development that do not warrant writing a dedicated program to perform them, but could be usefully automated nonetheless. For example, if a user has to edit a specific set of files that are spread across the database frequently for some reason, then a pair of batch files that check out and check in those files can save a surprising amount of time over having to locate all the required files in the GUI tools.

Shell Integration

Another client tool that can be exceptionally useful in many circumstances, albeit one which is somewhat harder to develop than many others, is a shell integration plug-in. Shell integration is the term (originally coined to refer to applications that extend the Windows Explorer "shell") for writing a plug-in that extends the system's basic file browser application to support new features. In the case of asset control, by writing a shell extension it is possible to add the ability for users to perform all the operations they would normally do from the GUI tool from within their normal file browser. This in itself is fairly useful, but where the functionality really comes into its own is on operating systems (such as Windows) where the common file dialogs such as the "Open File" and "Save As" windows are handled by the main file browser. In this case, a shell extension becomes a cheap way to extend integration to every application on the system, as it becomes possible to perform asset control operations from within any file selector!

MANAGING THE LOCAL REPOSITORY

In virtually all cases (the main exception being when a lazy caching system and virtual filing system are in use, which is covered later in the section on caching strategies), it is necessary for each client machine to have a copy of at least a subsection of the repository on their local machine. These are the files that they work from, most in a read-only capacity (for running the game, for example), but others in a read-write fashion as they are updated. These changes are then either committed back to the repository or discarded (and the altered files overwritten with the latest repository version).

The process of synchronizing the local repository with the server is the single most frequently performed asset management operation. If the user's local repository is not up to date, then he is not able to see the latest changes that have been made, and, even worse, any changes he makes himself run the risk of being based on outdated assets. Hence, under normal circumstances, most users update their local repositories at least once a day.

However, it is vitally important that this synchronization operation is a manual task, the user should never be forced to retrieve the latest data in order to perform an operation, or have it done "behind his back" by the system. The reason for this is simple: in a perfect world, everyone wants to use the latest data, but the world of games development is rarely perfect! There are always moments when the latest data is broken in some way, or when a developer is working on a complex set of changes or tests that will be disrupted if the files suddenly change. As such, it is critical to give users control over when to update their local repositories.

Preventing Unwanted File Modifications

In most asset management systems, the files in the local repository are always set to be read-only by default. This way, it is nearly impossible for the user to accidentally modify a file that they have not checked out from the repository first. The check out process (optionally) retrieves the latest version of the file, and then marks it as writable, allowing edits. In turn, the check in procedure marks the file as read only again. This way, the asset management client always has a clear idea of which files the user has checked out and modified at any time.

However, this system is far from ideal. In some circumstances, the user may be forced to modify files manually by removing the read-only flag himself (for example, if the asset management system is unavailable due to a network problem, or if he has copied a new version of the data directly onto his machine). To handle these cases, the client should provide some function which enables files to be checked out without altering their local state, so the current local versions can then be checked in. It is also extremely useful to have a system whereby the entire local repository (or a subsection of it) can be scanned for files that have been modified, added, or deleted without being checked out, to handle large modifications, or simply if the user has forgotten which files they have changed! Once a list of such files has been compiled, files can then be individually selected to be checked out, removed, or overwritten with the latest server version. It is worthwhile being a little wary of bulk adding files found with this operation, though, as often there are many temporary files or test versions of assets in the local repository in addition to the "real" files.

When an asset is deleted from the repository, its stored files and metadata should not be deleted, but instead a flag set to say that the file has been removed. This is partly because it provides a way to "undelete" files if required, but mainly because it allows clients to remove the local copy of the file as well when the files are next synchronized to the server. If this is not done, then clients will slowly get cluttered up with deleted files, some of which may even get inadvertently added back into the repository by users! This is often the cause of very subtle and annoying problems, usually only discovered when a new "clean" machine is set up and tested without any of the extraneous files.

Handling Temporary Files

Although asset management systems in general have far fewer problems in this regard than source control solutions, it is useful to have some system for automatically excluding temporary files from all asset management operations. Many applications automatically create temporary files, backups, or other extraneous data in the directories they save data to, and it is almost inevitable that without some sort of control some of these files will find their way into the repository. This isn't necessarily a problem, as such, but it adds additional unnecessary clutter and can sometimes confuse the applications at a later date when they find the temporary files again (especially if the asset manager has made them read-only)! For many cases, a simple set of wildcard filters will keep these from being considered by the client: the vast majority of temporary files have extensions like ".tmp" or filenames with special characters such as "~" or "_" at the beginning.

CLIENT TOOL UI AND FUNCTIONALITY CONSIDERATIONS

One fact about asset management systems that should never be forgotten is that no matter what their technical basis, from a user perspective the system is essentially a database. A specialized type of database, certainly, but a database nonetheless, and so many of the usability issues commonly encountered and conventions employed by database packages apply. One of the single most key requirements of any database system is that the user must be able to find and retrieve data quickly. Virtually every operation that is likely to be performed (the usual exception being new data entry) starts with one or more records being located for viewing, editing, or analysis.

Hierarchies and Views

Unlike a conventional database, however, virtually all asset management systems have an additional constraint which can be both a help and a hindrance, their database actually consists of a selection of files (some containing a number of revisions), which in general must map directly onto a traditional hierarchical file structure. This hierarchical paradigm is not often employed in traditional databases, but it can provide an extremely useful way of setting out the basic structure of the project.

However, that structure can also become a serious limitation if it is not understood and maintained correctly. Setting out the initial structure for the database is very important, as changes later will most likely be both difficult to implement and confusing to the team working with it. However, at the start of a project it is often difficult to see how the final game structure will fit together; predicting the volume and distribution of assets across the entire game in advance is a very inexact process at the best of times. In particular, it is very easy for the tree to become unbalanced, with assets accumulating in a relatively small number of the branches, for example, in the case where they are broken up by game level, but there is a global "common" area in which everything that is used by more than one level resides. This may be a suitable structure when the game has a small number of very distinct levels, but as more content is added there is generally more repetition of themes or styles. In this case, as assets are reused during construction of levels, more and more files will move into "common," or even worse, will simply be left in the level-specific sections of the hierarchy, effectively masking the additional dependencies that they create.

In addition to the task of simply maintaining discipline with regard to the asset layout, strict hierarchical filing systems almost always impose the restriction that there is only one canonical view of the hierarchy. While this is by far the simplest approach, both in terms of implementation and for users, it does restrict categorization. For example, while it may be logical to break assets up by level for processing or level design purposes, those editing the assets themselves may find it simpler to work with a structure that separates out characters, buildings, weapons, and so on. In some cases it may be possible to shoehorn both classifications into one hierarchy (for, by example, placing a sub-tree under each level, which breaks up the assets by type), this is far from ideal as it adds significant extra complexity, and all but the top level of the hierarchy is now duplicated across a number of sections.

Using Multiple Hierarchies

Ideally, the layout of the hierarchy would differ depending on the task at hand: separated by level, for example, for level designers searching for materials, separated by visual style for the art team, separated by type for processing purposes, and so on. If all of these were maintained manually, however, it would require major effort to ensure all of the assets were in the correct places, most game developers have trouble keeping even one file hierarchy up-to-date! Fortunately, one common element in virtually all of these layouts is that while the macro-level structure (that is, the top level or two of the hierarchy, for example, the list of asset categories or level names) is unique and would probably need to be defined by hand, the micro-level structure (which files go where) can be defined in terms of attributes from the asset's metadata, such as the file type and what dependencies to other assets it has. Much of this can be automatically generated either by the asset management system or the export tools, eliminating the time required to keep it up-to-date and the possibility of user error. If the metadata is augmented with even a small amount of user-provided context information (such as the visual style of the asset), then it becomes possible to define the entire structure in terms of what are effectively database queries, "this sub-tree contains assets where the style field contains 'Ice worlds'" for example. In this way, the hierarchy becomes self-updating, as long as the assets are tagged appropriately, they will appear in the right place, and defining new hierarchies is trivial as no manual sorting of assets is required as long as the necessary metadata exists.

Potentially all of these separate hierarchies could actually map into the on-disc layout of the files, although in the vast majority of cases it would almost certainly be more useful to have a single base layout on disc, which is then remapped by the GUI into the user's desired form (remapping the physical files to match the hierarchy could be useful for some processing systems, however). Doing this not only reduces overheads, but also makes it possible for the user to switch between different hierarchies with minimal overhead, effectively, each hierarchy has become a different "view" in traditional database terms, all referring to the same physical data on disc. With the flexibility this brings, users can quickly switch between views depending on the task they are performing, without ever needing to refer to the physical layout of the files on disc.

In addition, individual views do not necessarily need to contain the entire contents of the repository. For example, a view could consist of only the files of one type (or a selection of types), enabling an artist to filter out all of the audio, level, and scripting files from the repository and see only assets which are relevant to them. Another view could filter out all of the files that were altered since the last major build, giving an instant indication of what has been changed in the intervening time. This selective inclusion of files can also be useful when users (or automated tasks, for that matter) are in a situation where they need to retrieve a complete section of the repository for processing or offline editing, by restricting the view to only the broad selection of files they are interested in, the process can be made significantly more efficient.

Separating Projects

Clearly, the functionality provided by repository views, or even a small subset thereof, can be used to separate projects from each other. It can also in some circumstances be useful to separate data for individual target platforms, in cases where different versions of assets are being used. In these circumstances, it is useful to extend the filtering action to include areas such as changelists and history displays, so that while using a view on a specific project all of the other project's entries are filtered out. Ideally, each individual project view should behave as though nothing in the repository outside its scope actually exists, thereby removing the maximum possible amount of extraneous information. In practice, this may not be possible (for example, when asset dependencies extend outside the view) but the closer the system gets the more efficient it is, both in terms of providing relevant information to the user and in terms of the amount of data each client has to monitor.

Sharing Files between Projects

Strangely, there are also some circumstances in which the opposite is desired, where it is necessary to share a file or files among a number of projects. In this case, the most straightforward way to implement this is to allow a single logical asset to exist in multiple places in the hierarchy, effectively giving it several names or project affiliations. Depending on exactly how flexible the hierarchy/view structure in use is, this may be possible without any changes whatsoever. This assumes that all of the projects in question wish to share *updates* to the file as well, though, which is often not the case, particularly in the late stages of development. (Particular care must be taken when handling file deletion in this case, otherwise one project may remove a file another is still using!) To deal with these cases, it is sometimes more useful to implement file sharing as a branch operation, so each project gets an independent copy of the file, but with the ability to merge changes at a later date if desired.

Searching

While browsing the hierarchy for assets is the obvious method for finding things, and a relatively efficient way to do so assuming that the hierarchy is well-defined, there are still many situations in which search functionality is essential to being able to locate the required file quickly. A traditional filename search is useful, certainly, but the real power of search tools is only exposed when, again, suitable metadata is available for the files in the database. With this, the value of search tools is massively increased as it becomes possible to perform tasks such as finding all the assets that a particular person created, or assets that are used in more than three different levels. In most cases, the search functionality can be implemented using the same query system as the hierarchy views mentioned earlier, effectively significantly reducing the required development effort.

A feature that often goes hand in hand with searching is sorting. Being able to sort the results of a query by any element is a very useful feature, as it easily enables a user-driven form of "fuzzy searches," for example, in the case where the name of an asset is not exactly known, it is much easier to glance through an alphabetical list of all files of the appropriate type than to perform multiple searches for each possible variation on the name. Equally, when looking for "which assets are taking up the most space," sorting a list by size and scanning down is significantly faster (and, arguably more useful, as it shows the distribution of sizes across all files) than constructing a query that returns all the files bigger than a certain size.

In addition, search functionality like this can be invaluable in interfacing asset processing systems to the asset database, in most cases, it is necessary to specify groups of files (usually of specific types) to submit for processing together, and a flexible query system makes it extremely straightforward to generate lists of the required file sets from the database.

Unique Identifiers

One of the most significant problems with an asset management database that allows for multiple views of data and advanced searching functionality is that it becomes very hard to uniquely identify an asset from a user's perspective: there is no longer a single canonical file path that can be used to locate it (or, more likely, it is hidden by the GUI in most views). It is also the case that many external tools may need a straightforward way to reference an asset from the database in a manner that will not change depending on the view or file structure the user has selected, and possibly will even be able to track that specific asset if it is renamed or moved.

The obvious solution to this is also the simplest: assign every asset a unique identifier of some form, typically a numeric value. In all probability, the database system will have to keep an identifier of this form available internally anyway, so exposing it is a simple change. As long as this identifier is unique across the entire database, it can be used from anywhere to reference the asset.

It may also be useful to extend the identifier system so that assets have multiple unique IDs, one which references the asset itself (or, more specifically, the latest version of the asset), and one for each specific revision of the asset. This way, it is possible for users and tools to manipulate individual revisions with ease.

Another trick which can be useful is to structure the unique identifiers so that they can be made to resemble filenames, for example, a 32-bit value can be represented in hexadecimal as an eight character case-insensitive sequence such as "43D187A0", which conveniently works on just about every filing system in common use today. By adding an appropriate extension (in cases where file types are identified by extension), it becomes a filename that can hold the asset itself, which can be useful both within the asset management system and with external tools. With genuinely unique identifiers, the entire asset database can potentially be stored in a single directory on the main OS filing system if required! While in itself this is not necessarily useful, by naming temporary files this way during processing, it can be guaranteed that two assets will never inadvertently overwrite each other, even if the temporary files are being written to the same directory.

The one major downside of this approach is that as the filenames no longer bear any relationship to the actual contents of the file, working manually with the data in the repository is virtually impossible. Doing any useful operation requires the original filename to be looked up in the metadata database or unique ID index to determine what the file will actually be called on disc. While under normal operation this is not much of a problem, if a fault occurs and the metadata becomes corrupted then reconstructing the repository can be a huge problem, every single file revision would need to be manually examined and renamed! Therefore, protecting the integrity of the metadata is critically important under these circumstances. If a database or similar system is in use, then the built-in integrity and backup strategies may be sufficient protection, but it is wise to ensure that this is the case (and, for the truly cautious, install some suitably simple and failure-resistant backup such as a text file auto-generated nightly that contains all of the IDs and asset names). When working with a custom system, it is highly advisable to use the same techniques used by OS filing systems to protect their file allocation tables, such as keeping two copies of the index and only updating one at any given moment, and journaling individual updates so that erroneous changes can be rolled back.

Linking Files

A small enhancement to this functionality that can have a dramatic impact on the usability of the asset management GUI is the addition of a specific format for handling links between files, by using the unique ID as a reference. This can take many forms, for example, a specific field type, or a URI-style format such as `assetmanager://<unique ID>` which can be embedded in any field. The latter style is more flexible (especially as it allows references to assets to be included in documents outside the asset management database, such as e-mails), but can be slightly trickier to implement as it requires registration of the new URI tags with the OS or browser for the links to be usable from external applications. If it is used, however, then simply adding a "copy URI to clipboard" or similar option to the asset browser will enable users to insert references to specific assets or asset revisions in other documents quickly.

Whichever system is used, it enables users to quickly jump from one asset to another which it references, for example, from a 3D model to any of the textures the model uses, assuming this information is inserted into the database by the exporter or another tool. While the time savings over simply locating the required asset by name may seem minimal, it quickly adds up in cases where there are lots of inter-dependencies between assets, and there is no risk of confusion if multiple similarly-named assets exist or users with differently mapped views want to reference the same asset.

Metadata

The key to many of the features described here is providing appropriate metadata for all of the assets in the database. Typically, much of this can be automatically generated: with a little effort, fields such as the asset creation and modification date/username, size, file type, and even which other assets it depends on can be set by the asset management tool or exporter. The key to ensuring that user entered metadata is provided, however, is to make it as easy as possible to specify, and possibly compulsory. If the metadata fields are simply provided in the asset management UI, then no matter how many times developers are reminded about them, they will forget to fill them in. Since going through the database and retrospectively adding metadata is an exceptionally thankless task, it is best to avoid this situation, as most likely it will snowball until the majority of assets are missing crucial metadata, and the system becomes useless.

The main trick to confirming that the data is completed is to ensure that the user is prompted for it every time they add or export a new asset. This approach can be seen in many source-control packages, where comments on each check in operation are requested in the confirmation dialog. Unfortunately, all users tend to develop a resistance to pop-up windows that appear to serve no purpose—unless they are very disciplined, it is likely that many people will instinctively press "OK" as soon as they see the window after a short time (especially if it appears when they are trying to test data, or in other cases where the metadata "doesn't matter" as far as they are concerned)! By refusing to allow the user to continue without entering at least *something*, the system prevents this reaction, and in most cases the required information will be filled out. Beyond this, by far the most effective way of ensuring that the data is actually correct is to *use* it. If the metadata is part of the asset pipeline as well (and hence incorrectly tagged assets will not be correctly processed), then there is an ongoing system of checks to ensure that at least the most critical data is valid.

After technical measures, the second most important consideration when defining metadata is to make sure that everyone on the team understands what each field represents, and how to classify assets appropriately. For example, if weapon assets are broken up into "swords," "daggers," and "bows," make sure that there is agreement on the difference between a "sword" and a "dagger"! It is also highly desirable to attempt to provide lists of suitable values (in drop-down lists in the metadata entry form, for example) to avoid the inevitable misspellings and inadvertent extensions of the classification system (the sudden unexpected appearance of a "blade" type, for example).

Metadata Revisions

Unlike a traditional database, an asset management system also stores historical data—previous revisions of files. As such, it may also be advantageous to store revision data for the metadata associated with a file as well. Doing so ensures that if, for example, a file was re-classified at some point in the past, and then if the state of the repository at a point in time prior to that was retrieved, the file would have the correct classification for that revision. This also ensures that information such as the file dependencies are correct if the file is rolled back or a past revision is examined.

Metadata can either have an independent revision history, or be stored per revision against the asset file itself. The distinction is subtle, but important. If the metadata is stored against the asset file revisions, then there will be no record of changes to the metadata that were not accompanied by a corresponding update to the asset itself. Storing metadata revisions separately resolves this problem, but introduces an extra layer of complexity as metadata revisions must be mapped to file revisions, and the revision history of an asset must contain a record of both file and metadata changes. How significant this distinction is depends on the exact nature of the metadata in use, and the process for making modifications.

Using Metadata to Track File States

One significant advantage of allowing metadata revisions to be stored is that with a few small modifications the system can be used to enforce certain workflows and provide state information for assets. Consider the case of a system that allows modifications to be made to selected metadata fields on *past* revisions, as well as the current one, without affecting the revision history (that is, without creating a new revision of the metadata as a result of the change). If the system also allows for search queries to return past revisions of a file based on metadata criteria, then it becomes possible to use the metadata as a state tracking system.

This can be done simply by creating a field called "state." This can have a number of different values, for example, "In development," "Testing," "Stable," and "Broken." This represents this asset's position in the development workflow: new revisions of assets are created with their state as "In development" (when the creator is still experimenting with them), before progressing through "Testing" (when they are finished and ready for the rest of the team to use) to "Stable" (when they have been signed off and can be included in builds for external use). The "Broken" state is used for assets which are not usable, either for artistic reasons or due to a technical problem with their processing (in which case this state could be set automatically by the asset pipeline tools).

The key to using this is that queries can then be constructed to allow the processing pipeline (and users) to retrieve the latest version of an asset with a specific state. So, for example, the processing pipeline would retrieve all the assets with a state of "Testing" or "Stable" when compiling data for internal use, but restrict itself to only assets marked as "Stable" when working on a build for wider testing. In the case where the latest revision of an asset is not suitable, it will work back through the revision history until it finds the last one which is (or there are no revisions left), essentially locating the "last known good" revision. So, if a new version of an asset is being developed, while it is in the "Testing" phase internal builds will include the new revision, but external builds will have the older (but signed-off) "Stable" one.

This also means that failures in the asset processing pipeline can be handled automatically. Any asset that cannot be processed is marked as "Broken," and all future processing operations will ignore it and use the last valid version instead. A user can then simply query the asset database for all assets where the most recent revision is marked as "Broken," and immediately see where the problems to be fixed are.

Workflow Control

This system effectively implements a basic form of workflow control that is integrated into the asset management system. In order for assets to proceed past the "Testing" phase and appear in builds for external use, it is necessary for them to be moved to the "Stable" state, which can be when they are checked and signed-off by the appropriate team member. This can be a very useful way of enforcing the correct practices and ensuring that no unchecked artwork ever gets included by accident, without unduly impacting the normal working processes, as untested assets can still be used in internal builds. It is also trivial for a check of the database to be made for all assets awaiting sign-off (i.e., in the "Testing" state), streamlining the process further.

This principle can be extended if necessary, by adding additional states and potentially by adding more complex criteria to the determination of what assets are processed or made available to users, for example, a designer working on a specific level could ask the system for the "Testing" versions of all assets used in that level, but the "Stable" versions of assets everywhere else in the game, thus minimizing the number of unnecessary changes to the data he is working from. This type of partial data retrieval requires support from the build pipeline itself as well as the asset management system, but the advantages it brings are not inconsiderable.

As mentioned previously, by enabling searches to be performed using this metadata, it becomes possible to monitor the status of the assets in the project with relative ease. This can be useful both on a very specific level (retrieving a list of all the assets awaiting sign-off, for example), and on a more general basis. By collecting statistics about the distribution of assets in the repository over time, a clearer picture of how work is progressing can be formed.

Asset Statistics

There are many ways in which this can be achieved, the simplest being through a manual process of interrogating the database each day and charting the results. However, as the asset database stores information on the different versions of files and their metadata, it is possible to retrieve historical information at any time as it is required. This means that any particular statistic can be tracked since the beginning of the project, even if the necessity to do this was not realized until later on in the development cycle.

Many of the most useful statistics from a management perspective involve not the actual states or transitions between states for assets, but the times spent in each stage of the workflow. This gives an indication of how long that stage of the process took, or how much it was delayed by other factors. Assets spending a long time in the "awaiting approval" state may indicate that the art director responsible for approving them is indecisive, overworked, or simply on vacation! No amount of statistics from the asset database will help answer the questions arising from this, but they can at least act as guidance regarding *which* questions to ask.

In addition, by doing this it is possible not only to identify the causes of problems that have already occurred (for example, a missed milestone due to large numbers of assets needing reworking after being rejected from the approval process), but also to predict (to a limited extent, obviously) potential future difficulties. For example, rather than simply picking a number based on intuition or a broad average across the project, the average time needed to create one particular type of asset for a specific level can be determined very easily. This can be highly significant, as every game inevitably has some areas that require more effort than others. Examining the variance of these figures across the project can even reveal where these are, and if one section stands out as being disproportionately out-of-line with the others, then that may indicate an underlying problem in that area to be addressed.

Of course, statistics are only of value if the source data is chosen carefully—a measure of the time taken between creation and final sign-off for every texture beginning with the letter "a" is unlikely to be a useful measure of anything. Fortunately, many of the useful partitioning schemes for the data are likely to already exist in the asset database for other reasons, for example, as a result of the assets being split up by level, or character models being separated from static props. As a result, creating a few simple search criteria based on the existing metadata can very quickly produce fairly high-quality data for analysis.

If a sufficiently powerful metadata and searching system is present, in some cases it may even be possible to replace the traditional systems of spreadsheets and whiteboards for tracking and assigning asset creation and modification tasks with a suitable set of fields in the asset database itself. This has many benefits: all the data is available in one consistent location and can be easily analyzed. In addition, by automatically updating, or prompting the user to update, information as changes are made to assets, the details stored can be more easily kept in sync with the reality of the situation.

Preview Functionality

One piece of functionality that can greatly improve the productivity of users working with an asset management system is the ability to preview assets "in-place," in other words, without leaving the asset manager window. This is a huge boon because it enables easy identification of assets without having to fetch the revision in question and open it into the appropriate tool. Even if there is extensive metadata for each item in the database, there will still be many cases where the only way to determine if a given asset is actually the one that is wanted is to actually examine it.

There are two distinct approaches to providing this functionality—using stored preview information (usually held by the system as metadata), and using runtime previewing. There are advantages and disadvantages to both, and the choice of which to use is largely a trade-off between additional programming time and program complexity against preview quality.

Stored Preview Data

The stored preview approach works by generating the preview information for each asset as it is added or updated in the database, typically by relying on the exporter for the content creation tool to provide it. In this scenario, there are two or three different "base" preview formats, such as "bitmap image," "text file," and "sound." For each of these, the preview interface supports only one specific variation of the format, for instance, "bitmap image" previews must be a 100×100 uncompressed TGA format file, or "sound" previews must be 10 seconds or less of raw 16-bit unsigned sample data. This makes the preview code itself very simple, and the previewing process extremely quick and robust as all that it has to do is display (or play) the data as required. It is already in the correct format.

Obviously, this does add to the complexity of the export tools, but in general the overhead is relatively minimal, as the exporter is already doing a format conversion on the file, and it usually has access to most of the functionality of the host program so (for example) it is trivial to take a snapshot of a 3D model as displayed by the 3D package it was created in. As an alternative (or in addition) to this, the asset management system may be able to invoke preview building tools for file formats that are imported directly rather than via an export plug-in, for example by executing the original content creation tool with a script that generates the preview data. This can either be done on the client machine when the file is first added or checked in to the database, or periodically on the server.

The major disadvantage of this approach is that the preview is a relatively low-fidelity reproduction of the original asset, and it is not possible to interact with it in any way, for example, by rotating a 3D model to examine it from another angle. It can also be hard to see the differences between two revisions of some types of assets in this way, unless the changes are large enough to show up in the preview or the preview itself shows the area of interest: consider, for example, the case of a 3D model where changes have been made to the side of the object facing away from the viewer! However, for simple asset identification and observing more significant changes, this simple preview is more than enough, and in the remaining cases where a more extensive examination of the asset is required, the original content creation tool can be loaded instead.

Runtime Previewing

Runtime previewing, on the other hand, does not require any pre-generated information, but instead relies on the asset manager client GUI being able to either display the asset itself, or invoke an embedded instance of the original creation tool to do so. For example, it is possible on Windows systems to launch some applications using the OLE (Object Linking and Embedding) or ActiveX interfaces in such a way that the application GUI appears within another program. This approach means that the preview is always perfectly representative of the asset in question and the user can do any examination he requires from inside the tool.

On the other hand, the programming effort required to set up this system is not inconsiderable, especially because many programs do not support OLE or similar systems, and adding internal viewers for each file format required is a fairly major task. It can also cause serious performance problems if the asset management system has to invoke large applications (such as 3D modeling packages) to preview files, in this case, it is definitely desirable to have previewing disabled by default and make users manually confirm that they wish to preview a file. Another potential problem is that in many cases certain users will not have the required applications installed, particularly in the case of expensive packages where purchasing licenses for team members who do not use the program frequently is not an option.

Of course, it is not necessary to exclusively use one system or another. Stored preview data can be provided for all files, but an option to switch to runtime preview provided for file types where the viewer can be embedded (and another option again to launch a separate previewing process for file types where that is required). This would mean that a basic preview is always accessible, with more advanced options enabled for users who need them (and have the necessary support software).

Showing Asset Modifications

One of the most powerful tools that asset management systems offer is the ability to see at a glance the history of modifications made to a specific asset, and the effect these had. With source control solutions, the traditional mechanism for displaying the differences between two revisions of a file is to perform a textual analysis of the file and highlight added, removed, and modified lines individually. However, only a tiny proportion of the files in the typical asset repository are text files, and very few file formats are easily amenable to this type of analysis.

Therefore, the simplest and most effective mechanism for viewing asset modifications that can be used on any type of file (well, any type of file for which some sort of preview functionality is available) is just to display both versions of the file side-by-side. This way, it is relatively easy for the user to determine what, if anything, has been changed. This is very straightforward to implement if stored previews are being used, as the viewer code is entirely internal to the client. In this case, it may even be possible to implement slightly more sophisticated differencing tools, for example, a bitmap preview that can be faded between the two versions of the asset, or highlighted pixels which have changed in value. In the case of assets where two revisions cannot be usefully "displayed" simultaneously (such as audio data), often the simplest approach is to provide an option to "flip" between the two revisions of the file quickly, previewing one at a time.

In the case of runtime preview, this is generally impossible (unless the content creation package being used provides some form of native differencing tool), as the client has no knowledge of the data being displayed. In addition, some packages are not capable of running two instances simultaneously, which can make even simply displaying the two revisions alongside each other impossible. Unfortunately, there is little that can be done in these cases, except for disabling modification viewing or relying on stored preview functionality instead.

ACCESS CONTROLS AND SECURITY

In some circumstances, it may be desirable to limit the actions that users can perform on the asset database, for example, to allow only team leads to move assets into a "stable" state after sign-off, or simply to prevent users accidentally altering assets outside their working area.

It is important to remember that the purpose of access control in an asset management system is quite radically different from that in most other databases. In a commercial database system, access control is used to prevent users viewing or altering data, often because it is commercially sensitive or private: consider the case of a shop database, which contains customer records, credit card details, and invoices (typically, while viewing of invoices is unrestricted, alteration must be very carefully controlled to avoid the possibility of fraud). In these cases, access controls are there to protect the system against potentially malicious action by the people who use it.

In the case of games development, fortunately, it is very rare to have a situation where this is the case. In general, if you are worried about your asset database being used maliciously by authorized users, then you have far bigger worries than the technical details of the access control system! For games development purposes, access controls are usually there to avoid accidental changes being made to data, and to enforce workflow protocols and such which otherwise users may be tempted to skip when working under tight deadlines.

Because of this, in most cases the level of control required is relatively coarse-grained. For example, it is not usually necessary to restrict control on a per-asset basis, or even a per-type basis, but more on a broad set of categories, such as "audio assets," "art assets," "level maps," and so on. For this, marking subsections of the asset tree or even just classifying assets by file type will suffice as a mechanism for controlling access.

Users can be most easily identified by a simple username/password combination (or simply a username) for the purposes of both access control and tracking changes. With the extensive use of external tools, plug-ins, and scripts that most asset managements feature, it may well be desirable to store this authentication information in a shared location on the user's machine, as re-entering it every time they perform an action on the database will quickly become a chore (particularly if automated procedures must do this as well).

Using Views to Control Access

Another approach to access control that may be useful if the asset management system supports multiple data views, is to implement the controls as restrictions on the views themselves. Since there is no necessity for views to contain a complete representation of the repository, by restricting the views available to a user access can be effectively limited to only those files that are included in the views selected. In addition, by marking views as "read only," they can be given access to other parts of the repository without being able to alter them.

It is also extremely useful to restrict the access users have to alter metadata, even on assets that they can make changes to. This can take the form of a restriction on setting certain values (in the case of the workflow enforcement mentioned above), or a simple prohibition on altering the contents of a field. The latter is most useful in preventing accidental changes to automatically-generated information, such as creation/modification dates or dependency lists. This can often be made read-only to all users, although it may well be the case that a few people (such as the programmer responsible for maintaining the asset pipeline) will occasionally need some mechanism to modify them to correct errors.

Making provision for this type of "emergency access" is a vital part of building a robust system. Even if only one "super user" system administrator account is actually able to do it, having some mechanism whereby *any* data in the system can be modified (even, for example, past revisions of assets or "internal" system fields such as the UID of stored files) is essential for dealing with cases where failures (either human or machine) occur and it is necessary to "patch" the data to work around the problem.

External Security

Of course, the other aspect of access control is that of preventing unauthorized access to the system from outside, for example if the asset server is made available to developers working from home over the Internet. In this case, however, the best advice is simply not to even try to secure the system. Unless you are an expert in cryptography and secure coding practices, it is extremely foolish to try and implement a security system for such a critical resource. The chance of developing a system that can withstand exposure to the extremely hostile environment of the Internet (or even a wide area network of any scale) without a very deep understanding of the field is very slim indeed. Instead, put the asset management server behind a strong firewall, and use existing technologies such as a VPN (Virtual Private Network) or the secure tunneling and authentication provided by protocols such as SSL (Secure Sockets Layer) to control and protect connections. These systems have been extensively reviewed and tested by experts in the field, and provide the best possible "guarantee" of security, although it is still wise if utilizing such a system to keep a close watch on announcements related to it as no tool can ever offer perfect security.

PROVIDING AN EXTERNAL API

While the GUI tools are the most visible and commonly used interface to any asset management system, arguably more important in many respects is the design of the

API which will provide programmatic access for other tools. This API needs to be designed in such a way that it is robust enough to be reliably embedded into other applications (remember that in most cases, if a plug-in for a content creation package crashes, the host application will crash as well, potentially causing lost work), and straightforward so that programmers not intimately acquainted with the internals of the asset management database can still write tools that interface to it.

In the vast majority of cases, it is strongly advisable to implement the asset management GUI and any other "built in" tools using the API itself, as this ensures that there is no needless duplication of client-side code and that once the GUI is finished and in service, the vast bulk of the API code is complete, tested, and stable. Otherwise, most systems degenerate into a "two tier" structure, where the services available to the main GUI or external programs start to diverge, often with one lagging significantly behind the other.

Single and Multiple Client Models

One of the most critical design decisions to be made when designing the API is if the system will support only a single instance of the client code per machine, or if each API task should have a separate client (and, hence, a separate connection to the main server). The single client approach requires that there is a single task running on the user's machine with which all the programs using the API communicate, this in turn handles the connection to the server. This increases the complexity of the API code (as it must pass all data to and from another process in some fashion), and requires that the client can support either simultaneous execution of requests or some form of queuing system (in general, the latter is preferable, as simultaneously executing requests can result in very complex race conditions if not handled extremely carefully, and as the server communication is a bottleneck there is little potential performance gain). However, there are several major advantages: it is not necessary for every process using the API to perform authentication and negotiation with the server when they start up, and the lower number of connections reduces the load on the server. In addition, client-side caching strategies and state management are much easier to implement since the client application can manage them without worrying about the actions of other local clients invalidating stored data.

The multiple client model does have advantages, though: the client code is simpler, because there is no need to handle multiple tasks simultaneously, and there is no interprocess communication or data passing required. The single point of failure the client represents no longer exists, either, meaning that there is little risk of a crash in one application bringing down every other program that uses the asset management API!

In the single client model, as little of the logic is present in the API stubs themselves, statically linking them to the API libraries is a viable approach. However, with the multiple client system it is preferable to use dynamic linking whenever possible, as otherwise every time a change is made to the client it will be necessary to recompile every application and plug-in that uses the API!

Interface State

The functions provided by the API can either be implemented so as to rely on internal state being stored for each client program (this happens implicitly in a multiple client system), or such that every request contains all the information required to complete it, therefore, no state information needs to be stored.

The primary advantage of using stateless requests is simple: the client code no longer needs to keep track of each program that is using it (beyond the duration of an individual request), and there are far fewer opportunities for problems to arise as a result of the state information becoming invalid or simply being left active if a program crashes. The other major advantage is that a stateless system forces the design of the API to be constructed so that it follows the transaction model. Each request is a logical transaction that can either succeed or fail as a whole, and with the API structured in this way it is most likely (although not certain) that programmers using it will be forced to obey the majority of the transaction rules as well, thereby increasing the robustness of the system as a whole massively. Finally, stateless systems are generally more amenable to being shoehorned into other stateless protocols—for e ample, a stateless system could almost certainly be easily modified to use HTT as a transport if required.

There are some advantages to storing task state, however: it makes it easier for the client program to selectively cache and filter information for the API task, and it generally (although not always) makes the development of programs using the API easier, as the client handles the maintenance of more data.

In most cases, though, the stateless approach leads to a more robust and maintainable system, albeit at the cost of some additional coding. In some cases it may be possible to construct a hybrid system, where state information is stored not in the client task, but in the API itself (that is, in the code that is linked into the target application). In this way, the client still sees the operations as being stateless, but the burden of data maintenance is not shifted onto the application developer. However, this approach should be used with caution as it can easily lead to inefficient code (as the interface the application programmer sees is not a true representation of what the client is executing, leading to incorrect assumptions about the relative overheads of certain tasks), and the additional benefit of forcing application programmers to work with the transactional paradigm is lost.

High-Level APIs

In cases where it is anticipated that there will be many programs using the asset management APIs, it may well be desirable to implement a second API which provides more high-level functionality, usually by hooking system services. For example, on most operating systems it is possible to create an "image filing system" or "virtual filing system," which can make the asset repository appear to be mapped as a drive or folder in the standard filing system. Likewise, as mentioned earlier, integration with the existing shell services (such as Windows Explorer) can be used to very easily extend services to a wide range of applications without having to write specific code for each.

SCRIPTING SUPPORT

While the focus of activity in most asset management systems is in either the main GUI or programs utilizing the plug-in API, the importance of scripting support should not be underestimated. While the primary workflows in games development center around the content creation applications and the asset processing pipeline, there are almost always a number of more minor (but repeated) tasks that must be done using the asset management database, such as compiling lists of assets for project planning or pruning accidentally added and redundant files from the system. These tasks are not significant enough to warrant writing an entire application to perform them, but they are common or complicated enough that automating them to reduce the time taken or remove the possibility of user error is a worthwhile effort.

For these cases, some sort of scripting language is the obvious solution. However, in most cases, implementing a full scripting system simply for manipulating the asset database would be massive overkill; it is much simpler to leverage the services of an existing scripting language.

If an existing scripting system (for example, JavaScript, Perl, or Python are common choices) is already in use, then the obvious choice would be to implement a set of APIs or bindings for that—in many cases, an existing API implemented in C or C++ can be directly exposed to the scripting system with little or no effort. However, the single most widely-used choice in this regard is to simply provide a set of command-line tools that allow interactions with the asset manager to be performed. This is a very low-cost solution, yet enables interactions with a wide range of other scripting systems, as virtually every language allows external programs to be executed. In many cases, the most well-understood and frequently used scripting system is that which is built into the operating system—shell-scripts on Unix systems or simple batch files on Windows. Providing command-line tools is a perfect way to provide a simple interface for these, and it is hard to beat them for sheer simplicity and ubiquity of operation. The only downside of using command-line tools for this is that in some circumstances, the overheads of executing a separate application for each transaction (and, potentially, opening server connections or other interprocess communications resources) may become significant. In general, though, these heavy-load cases are the most likely procedures to be handled by a full-blown application rather than a simple script.

The design of a scripting system will usually be driven by the design of the external API for the asset management system; although in some cases it will be necessary to deviate from this. In particular, although stateless APIs map almost directly onto the command-line tool paradigm, if the API requires stored state information it will be necessary to either translate this into a stateless API for command-line use (as each command executed will start a new process), or provide an intermediate layer to handle the conversion.

Change Notification Handling

One particular aspect of client and API design that is somewhat unusual and deserves special mention, is the handling of change notifications. Unlike virtually every other client operation which consists of a single transaction submitting some data to the server and receiving a response, a change notification requests that the server inform the client when an alteration is made to a particular asset (or selection of assets).

The uses of this are obvious: it allows client applications to selectively refresh their view of the database when a change occurs without having to poll repeatedly to see if anything has changed, adding additional load to both the client and server. It can also be useful in implementing the asset pipeline as it allows the pipeline itself to detect changes as they occur and start processing immediately rather than having to wait until the modifications are detected through some other means. Change notifications can also be vital in making some forms of client-side caching reliable and efficient, as they enable cached data to be invalidated as soon as the server-side copy changes.

There are various solutions to handling change notifications. The obvious approach is to have the server store a list of which assets each client is interested in and send a notification message of some sort when a modification is made to any of them. This can be quite expensive in server CPU time as it requires every submitted change to be checked against a list of files for every client, and potentially a large number of different notifications sent. However, it is by far the most efficient mechanism in terms of network bandwidth, as unwanted notifications are never sent and there is no client-side polling required.

Changelist-Based Notifications

Another fairly efficient way of implementing change notifications is to have the server send each client a simple message when a new change is submitted, listing the files touched by the change. This effectively trades network bandwidth and a small amount of client-side CPU time for server overhead, as it removes the requirement for the server to store and compare lists of which clients are interested in which files. As the same message is sent to every client, it is more viable for the server to perform intelligent processing on it to reduce the overheads further: for example, by recognizing if more than half the assets in a particular section of the repository have changed and simply supplying a global notification of the change to that section instead of enumerating every modified asset individually. (Obviously, in this case the clients will then have to query the server in more detail if they need to know precisely which files have changed, which can negate the overall benefit if large groups of files are being individually monitored, the trade-off here depends on the exact usage patterns the client applications generate.)

An equally valid approach to change notifications is simply to not implement them. This is the route many existing systems take and while there is an additional overhead involved in polling the asset server, it is not necessarily a problem if handled efficiently. In particular, if the system implements changelists or change tagging such that every individual transaction that alters the database state is assigned a unique identifier, this provides a very straightforward mechanism for checking for changes—the client need only store the most recent change identifier at the time of the last modification check, and the server easily determines which files have been modified by listing the files affected by each successive change when it is polled. This can form the basis for a very efficient hybrid system if necessary. The client API can implement change notifications for other tasks using call-backs or some other appropriate OS inter-process communication functionality, but internally the client itself can poll the server for changes regularly using the last seen change ID and then send the notifications based on the response. This way, the server does not have to implement change notifications and the additional polling load is mostly restricted to the client side.

Caching Strategies

A major factor in achieving high performance with a large asset management system is the performance characteristics of the caching systems employed; with relatively simple client-side caching it is possible to cut down the number of server queries required by a large amount, which in turn has a huge impact on the system performance: every query sent to the server incurs network bandwidth and server CPU time overheads, as well as taking several orders of magnitude longer to complete than a local action, even using a fast LAN.

The first thing to recognize is that essentially the local copies of files that users have on their machines are a form of cache. If networks had unlimited bandwidth and zero latency, and the server was sufficiently powerful, there is no reason that users could not simply work directly from the asset server's copy of the data (albeit with some provisions made for local modifications to be sandboxed for each individual user). Many of the same management strategies used for caching other data also apply to the locally stored repository.

Aside from the local copies of actual asset data, however, by far the most important thing to cache is the repository hierarchy itself. In the case of a system which supports different hierarchy views, it may be necessary to cache more than one, but the principle is the same. The vast majority of the operations that take place on the repository start by retrieving a list of assets in some form, either as the result of the user directly requesting a listing of them or as a prelude to performing another operation (in particular, the operation of mapping a specific asset ID onto a local filename or vice versa is almost certain to happen very regularly). The asset hierarchy is also a largely static entity. It changes only when a file is added or removed from the repository, or, in some circumstances when an asset's metadata is modified, depending on the nature of the view in question. Therefore, it is relatively straightforward to either poll the server or use change notifications (if available) to ensure that the cache is always up to date with respect to the server's copy of the hierarchy.

Caching Metadata

Asset metadata is also typically quite small, and hence can also be effectively cached, although the access patterns are a lot less predictable and they change frequently, making caching less attractive. It can still be very useful, particularly for GUI applications, to maintain a partial cache of the most recently accessed metadata as a mechanism for speeding user response times, and possibly even to perform limited predictive caching in situations where the user is likely to examine a known subset of the available metadata (for example, when a search has been performed, or by caching assets linked to the one being viewed). An efficient partial caching strategy for this type of data could simply be a fixed sized pool, from which entries are evicted either when a server-side change is detected, or when the pool becomes full, in which case the least-recently accessed metadata is removed. With a sufficient cache pool size, the set of files the user is currently working with (typically 40 or 50 entries in most systems) should be able to fit in without any being prematurely evicted. In addition, in most of these situations, although change notifications can potentially be used to monitor changes to the metadata and evict outdated entries, it is actually often more useful to simply update the cache as entries are viewed. In a GUI context, the user can be shown the cached data while the update happens in the background, and if a change has been made the display can be updated as the new information arrives. Although the actual response time for the correct data is unchanged, displaying the cached information increases the perceived response speed significantly, particularly in the vast majority of cases where no changes have actually occurred.

This form of lazy cache invalidation can be useful elsewhere in the system as well, particularly when coupled with some features of transactions. The client can operate using cached metadata (and, potentially, hierarchy data) until such time as it submits a transaction that relies on out-of-date information. At this point, the server will detect the error in the transaction and reject it (for example, if the client has attempted to update an asset which no longer exists), which tells the client that it needs to update the cached data it holds about this asset. In some cases, it may be advantageous to include in the data sent to the server the assumptions the client is currently using, more specifically, the last change ID the client has cached. This way, the server can easily determine if the transaction affects any assets that have changed since then, and if so reject it.

Using Virtual File Systems for Caching

One advanced caching system which is possible if the asset manager client uses a virtual filing system or image filing system is that of on-demand retrieval and caching. In this case, the local data stored on the client is literally a cache, the contents do not necessarily physically exist on disc until a program requests them. By avoiding storing assets on the local hard drive, the system not only saves disc space, but significantly reduces the time spent updating assets needlessly every time a change on the server occurs. In the majority of cases, a fair proportion of the assets stored on the hard drive are not read or modified in the time between one change and the next, for example, if the user is working on one specific level and does not play any others for several days. Therefore, by not retrieving the assets until they are actually required, the caching system reduced both the storage requirements and the network bandwidth needed, albeit at the expense of longer initial access times for files that are used.

Obviously, even with this system, it is desirable to keep the local copy of the repository from being "updated" unless the user requests it. This is simply achieved by storing the ID or timestamp for the last change each time the local repository is manually updated, and then requesting that specific revision of each file from the server as it is required.

Depending on the exact architecture in use, the server may be able to perform caching as well. In general, most database systems cache the results of frequently executed queries, as well as ensuring that certain critical tables (such as those containing lists of keys for accessing data in other tables) are kept resident in memory.

As asset management system is no different, in general, with the exception that it is virtually never worth caching the asset data itself in RAM; most assets are too large, and so infrequently accessed, that this is simply not worthwhile.

Finally, in some cases it may be useful for clients to cache copies of files that have been updated since their local data was last synchronized with the server. While it is not desirable to update the local data itself automatically, having the new files ready for the next time a manual synchronization is performed can be useful. This can consume a significant amount of disc space in some circumstances, so it is generally a good idea to cap the amount to be cached. It is also usually a bad idea to retrieve more data than is strictly necessary while the machine is being used for other tasks (or when the network or resource server is busy), so preemptive caching should be restricted to times when both are idle. The challenge with this caching system is generally not in the actual caching itself, but in determining a robust strategy for when to perform cache retrieval operations, and being able to abandon them if necessary should the load on the server, network, or client suddenly increase. If this strategy is in use, then using multicast to send data from the server to multiple clients simultaneously can be a major performance boost if network bandwidth or server overhead is a limiting factor.

ARCHIVING AND PURGING DATA

As the total volume of data created by storing multiple revisions of every file in the asset database will quickly outstrip the available storage, an important part of any asset management system is the ability to archive or simply delete redundant revisions of files to maintain the repository size at a sensible level. This process can either be ongoing and handled automatically by the system, or triggered manually by a user or some external condition (running short of disc space being the obvious candidate).

Choosing Which Asset Revisions to Remove

Whether archiving or deleting the files themselves, the hardest part of this process is determining which files should actually be removed from the repository. It should be noted at this point that in virtually all cases it is only the actual asset data that is removed, the metadata associated with that revision remains, in order to keep the revision history consistent. This is not generally a problem as the metadata is small enough that even over a large number of successive revisions it never accumulates to the point where it consumes a significant amount of storage space. In addition, it may be useful to add a marker to the metadata to indicate when the file was removed, and in the case of archival, where it was archived to.

The primary criteria for choosing revisions to remove is their age, both in terms of time elapsed since they were created, and in terms of the number of successive revisions of the file that exist. Clearly, the latest revision of any file should never be removed (in many cases, the most recent pair of revisions should be retained, to allow for the changes to the latest revision to be viewed, this may not be practical for very large files, however), but the further back in history a file is, the less likely it is to ever be used again. It is best to incorporate some sort of capping system in addition to this metric, so that the latest two revisions of every file are always retained, as are those less than two weeks old (for example), but any revision older than six months or more than 10 revisions "deep" into the history is automatically removed. This prevents revisions from either disappearing prematurely if a lot of activity suddenly occurs on one file, or lingering for an unusual period of time if some other factor prevents their removal under the standard algorithm.

Other information in the repository can also be used to skew the removal policy, however. For example, revisions that are part of a label or the root of a branch should be retained longer as they are likely to be referred to again, as are the most recent revisions which are marked as being "stable" or similar if a status tagging system is in operation. The status of files to be shared between projects should also be carefully considered in terms of both projects they exist in. Obviously, files which have been tagged as "deleted" by the system can be removed earlier than "live" files (and their latest revision can be safely removed if they are sufficiently old).

Deleting Files

Once the files to be removed have been identified, deleting files is unsurprisingly, a fairly straightforward process. One minor problem worth watching out for, however, is that on some filing systems repeatedly deleting and creating files can lead to fragmentation of the disc layout, where the available space is broken up into a large number of small blocks, forcing files to be split up to fit into the unused areas. In these circumstances, it may be worthwhile setting up the asset management system so that it can schedule a defragmentation of the disc after each purge of the database to maintain performance. This can be a tricky operation, however, as it typically involves shutting down all other processes on the machine to perform the defragmentation; so it may be simpler to leave it as a manual operation.

Archiving Files

The preferred action when removing files from the database, rather than deleting them, is to archive them to some form of removable media. This process is most simply implemented in two steps: first, the asset management system moves all of the files to be removed into a separate directory or file (outside the asset repository), and alters the metadata for the files to indicate that they have been archived. Then, these files can be moved manually to the backup media. Direct interfacing to backup devices is possible, but generally more trouble than it is worth unless you are anticipating needing to archive large quantities of data on a regular basis.

The actual archival process is quite straightforward, but the largest problem stems from deciding how to store the data. There may be multiple revisions of the same asset being archived simultaneously, which makes simply writing out the assets in the structure where they appear in the local repository (or one of the structures, in some cases) impractical.

Archive Storage Formats

There are several solutions to this problem, and picking the most suitable generally depends not on the archival procedure, but what the planned system for retrieving archived data involves. If archived data is to be restored entirely manually (without any input from the asset management system), then it is most useful if it is stored in an easily human readable structure. The obvious candidate for this is to use a modified version of one of the repository views (or have a custom view created for this purpose) which maps all the files to a sensible structure. This leaves only the problem of handling multiple revisions of the same file being archived—various possibilities exist here, but the most obvious (and simplest) is to add a version tag to the filename of every file, giving the revision number (so, for example, revision 15 of `mytexture.tga` might become `mytexture.tga.015`). This makes it very straightforward for the desired file to be retrieved manually.

If, however, the asset management system can be used in the restoration process, then a more functionally useful alternative is to store all the assets as they are in the repository itself (for example, referenced by unique identifier). This way, they can simply be re-imported in the same way they were archived, and reappear back in the repository. This approach has the advantage that it maintains the association between the files and their specific revision history and metadata entries, as well as allowing revisions to be easily restored for operations such as synchronizing data against a label or merging branches.

No matter which system is used, however, it is vitally important that the archived data also contains a file or set of files in human readable format containing the metadata for all of the archived revisions, their filenames (as they appear in the archived copy), and any other relevant information (for example, the date and time they were archived). In general, a text file is the best way to do this. This ensures that if it is necessary to restore the assets without a copy of the original database, or in the case where some of the data is unreadable and cannot be recovered and manual recovery is attempted, that the metadata required to separate out which asset is which is still preserved. Without that information, the asset archive is practically useless, as it is simply a huge collection of unsorted files in varying formats and stages of completion. It can also be helpful to include CRCs for the individual assets in this file, both as a means of checking for corruption in the data and so that they can be identified from their contents if for some reason the file structure information is lost completely.

When creating an archive, it can also be useful to compress the contents, both to save space and act as a basic safety measure to detect corruption (virtually all archive formats include CRCs for the stored data). A useful side effect of the compression process, as well, is that it effectively avoids any possibility of filenames, dates, or other information being altered by the archival process, for example, when backing up data onto CD-ROM discs, filenames are often truncated to 8.3 (eight characters of filename, three characters of extension) format.

The downside of compression, however, is that compressed data is much more susceptible to corruption, and in general, if an archive file is corrupted it will be hard or impossible to recover any data stored beyond the point the corruption occurs in the file (although some formats differ in their behavior in this respect). A useful secondary step after compression, therefore, is to create a set of parity files for the compressed data. Parity files are simply additional data files that can be used to correct errors in the original data: in general, the more parity data that is stored, the more errors can be successfully corrected. Parity data can be created with any one of a number of third-party tools, and some archive tools now incorporate the ability to automatically build parity information into the file itself. In ideal circumstances, parity information should be stored on separate physical media to the original data itself, to minimize the possibility of both becoming corrupted; although all good parity systems can cope with corrupt parity data in the same way they cope with the original data becoming corrupted, up to the point where there is simply too much corruption for the data to be successfully reconstructed.

Manually Purging Assets

Every asset management system should include a function that allows the user (after a suitable number of dire warnings) to forcibly delete a single asset revision from the database without any attempt at archival or any more intelligent processing. The reason for this is simple: at some point, no matter what checks are put in place, somehow an asset or file infected with a virus or similarly unpleasant code will get into the system. Hopefully whatever virus scanning software is running will detect this and prevent it from actually being executed (generally speaking, viruses that spread by infecting files pose little threat to the server itself as they usually require manual execution, but they can still easily infect client machines), but it can be very difficult to remove a file that is part of the repository safely under these conditions if the default behavior attempts to perform additional operations on the file besides simply deleting it, especially because many virus scanners will automatically block any access to the file for other purposes! At the very least, it should be possible to shut down the system, delete the file manually, and then restart it without there being any ill-effects besides the removal of that revision.

CONCLUSION

There are several off-the-shelf solutions that can be used to form the basis of an asset management system, which provide varying amounts of the required functionality. Regardless whether you are using an existing system or building a new one, however, understanding the basic concepts behind the underlying database technology and the considerations involved in designing the higher-level components is essential.

As important as the technical requirements, however, is understanding how such a system will be used, and the effect that user interface and workflow design will have on the efficiency of the developers working with it. There are many angles that must be considered carefully before embarking on the construction of such a system.

5 Texture and Image Processing

Assets in the asset pipeline must undergo a number of steps before they can be integrated into the final game. The nature of these steps depends on the type of asset involved, the target platform, and the specifics of the engine in use. In most cases, for efficiency reasons the final file formats produced by the pipeline will be very tightly tied to the game engine code, making the use of general purpose tools for processing much more difficult. That said, it is not uncommon for developers to make use of third-party or cross-engine tools at intermediate stages in the pipeline, and the basic algorithms used for handling asset processing are largely identical across the vast majority of projects.

The next three chapters deal with various often used asset processing tasks. The descriptions given of the various algorithms are intended to provide a good description of the basic techniques in use for common asset types, and the principles needed to understand more esoteric or advanced variants. As mentioned previously, in many of these cases the pre-processing and runtime usage of assets are very tightly linked, so the exact details of the methods used will depend heavily on the specifics of the game engine.

TEXTURES

At their most basic level, textures are generally straightforward 2D arrays of color information. In some systems, more advanced representations can be used at a higher level, but virtually all such systems are still based on some combination of 2D bitmap images. Straightforward 2D images can generally be considered a subset of textures; in many engines both are treated in exactly the same way, and the processing tools which are available can generally be applied to both.

Texture maps are almost universally stored in a simple source format that uses either RGB or RGBA (Red, Green, Blue and Alpha) color channels, generally at 8 bits of resolution (although a few formats that allow higher color depth, such as PNG, are becoming more commonly used). For virtually all pipeline operations, this can be expressed as a simple array of color values: while some applications (such as geographical imaging, for example) require in-memory compression of texture data during processing, even the largest textures used in games generally occupy only a few megabytes of memory in their uncompressed form.

TEXTURE SWIZZLING

While the traditional memory layout for textures is a linear block of memory, this format is not actually the most efficient representation for rendering purposes. This is because of the cache properties of the linear format: while adjacent texels in the horizontal axis are adjacent in memory, vertically adjacent texels will be an entire line's width away. As most texture-mapping operations read adjacent pixels frequently (especially as the GPU must fetch several adjacent texels for every pixel rendered as part of the bilinear filtering process), this causes frequent cache misses during texture mapping operations.

Therefore, in order to improve the cache efficiency of the process, most GPUs support (some exclusively) "swizzled" texture formats. *Swizzling* is the process of rearranging the texels within the texture so that blocks of texels that are adjacent in texture space are also adjacent in memory, thereby making adjacent texel fetches much more likely to find the required data already in the GPU's cache.

To achieve this, swizzling schemes take square blocks of the source texture and map each one to a linear chunk of memory using a mapping commonly known as a "swizzle pattern." Figures 5.1 and 5.2 show how an 8×8 linear and swizzled texture map is stored in memory, the numbers representing the memory locations used for each pixel.

1	2	3	4	5	6	7	8
9	10	11	12	13	14	15	16
17	18	19	20	21	22	23	24
25	26	27	28	29	30	31	32
33	34	35	36	37	38	39	40
41	42	43	44	45	46	47	48
49	50	51	52	53	54	55	56
57	58	59	60	61	62	63	64

FIGURE 5.1   The memory layout of a linear texture.

In Figure 5.2 some of the contiguous blocks of memory formed by the swizzling are shaded to make them easier to see. The basic swizzle pattern is a simple 2×2 block, arranged so that four consecutive memory locations are used. This pattern is then repeated in a recursive manner, so that the four 4×4 blocks that form the entire texture are also laid out in this pattern. Most swizzling algorithms use this recursive mechanism up to a certain block size, after which the blocks are simply laid out in a linear fashion (once the blocks become larger than the cache size, there is no advantage in using the swizzle pattern to arrange them).

1	2	5	6	17	18	21	22
3	4	7	8	19	20	23	24
9	10	13	14	25	26	29	30
11	12	15	16	27	28	31	32
33	34	37	38	49	50	53	54
35	36	39	40	51	52	55	56
41	42	45	46	57	58	61	62
43	44	47	48	59	60	63	64

FIGURE 5.2 The memory layout of a swizzled texture.

Swizzling (or un-swizzling) a texture simply involves moving the pixels in the source texture around to match the swizzle pattern required by the hardware. This can either be done using an appropriate algorithm to look up the corresponding memory location for each pixel, or using code to algorithmically generate the mapping information as a precalculated table. Since the maximum swizzle block size is generally relatively small, either option tends to work well.

While swizzling is a lossless operation, and it is possible (with some care) to perform texture processing on the swizzled version of a texture, it is much simpler to perform the swizzling process as the final step in the processing pipeline, using a standard linear format until then.

It should be noted that although almost all GPU hardware now supports swizzled textures, on some systems (mainly PCs), the swizzled formats are not exposed to applications, but instead the swizzling operation is performed by the driver at runtime. In these cases, the benefits of swizzled textures are obtained without any need for the game to perform any additional processing, albeit at the cost of some CPU usage for the conversion operation.

However, there are some swizzled texture types that can be accessed directly even on PC graphics cards, in the form of the compressed texture formats.

TEXTURE COMPRESSION

Texture compression is used to reduce the amount of storage space and bus bandwidth required by textures at runtime. The exact type of texture compression available depends on the support available in the hardware. However, the vast majority of texture compression schemes in use at the time of this writing are based on the same fundamental principles, so while the implementation details differ, the same processes can be applied in all cases.

As with swizzled textures, compressed textures make use of a swizzle pattern to reorder the texture to improve the cache characteristics. However, they take the process a step further, and each swizzled block is reduced in bit depth, effectively forming the texture from a patchwork of individually palletized chunks.

A typical texture compression scheme works on blocks of approximately 4×4 pixels (as with swizzling, power of two sizes are almost exclusively used), and each of these blocks has a unique palette of four colors. Effectively, this reduces the bit depth of the pixels in the block to only two bits per pixel, allowing the entire set of 16 pixels to be packed into only four bytes. Additional storage is of course required for the palette entries themselves, but these can be easily reduced to 16-bit color values. To reduce this further, some texture compression systems do not store all of the palette entries explicitly, but instead store only some and form the others by interpolating the stored values; for example, by only storing two colors for each block and generating the other two as intermediate values between the stored pair (allowing smooth color gradients within the compressed block).

With this additional modification, the compression ratio can be increased even more; using 16-bit color values and interpolation would reduce the palette in our test case to only four bytes of extra data, making a total of eight bytes for the entire 4×4 block. In a 32 bits per pixel format the same block would occupy 64 bytes, and at 16 bits per pixel it would be 32 bytes, so the compressed version is roughly a quarter of the size of the original for a comparable color depth.

Performing Texture Compression

The actual process of compressing a texture in this way is relatively straightforward, if only due to the simplicity of the compression algorithm. The only significant decision that needs to be made is to decide which palette entries are to be used. While it is possible to use a standard palettization algorithm to do this, the added complexity of interpolated palette entries (if they are in use) and the small block size generally make this pointless.

In fact, while it is theoretically not the most efficient algorithm possible, the very small block size means that brute forcing the decision is a perfectly reasonable solution. This is particularly useful because this technique avoids the necessity to make special provisions for interpolated palette entries.

The brute force method is quite simple: for each block, generate each possible palette from the colors used in the block, and then palletize the pixels with it, matching each pixel to the closest palette entry possible. For each of these, an error metric can be calculated from the sum of the differences between the palette entries and the original pixels, and then the palette that produces the lowest overall error is chosen. For the compression method described previously, there are only 120 possible palettes for any given block (assuming that all 16 colors in the block are unique), therefore, even this approach is fast enough to be usable.

Compressing Alpha Channels

One other point worth mentioning about texture compression is alpha channels. In general, simply including the alpha value in the palette entries does not work very well, as this (if the alpha is interpolated along with the color) results in semitransparent areas of texture "bleeding" into the opaque sections, or vice versa. Using uninterpolated alpha (where pixels are assumed to be opaque unless they use an explicitly set transparent palette entry) works reasonably well, but only generally allows for one bit alpha (fully opaque or fully transparent), as there is no way to control the alpha of pixels using the other palette entries.

As a result, many texture compression schemes compress the alpha channel separately, using the same procedure as for the color channels. This compression can either be done as an entirely independent texture, or by allocating extra bits for each pixel to reference the alpha values of palette entries independently.

TEXTURE QUANTIZATION

Many of the most effective techniques for reducing the size of game assets involve reducing the accuracy of the stored data, thereby removing (hopefully) unnoticeable detail but retaining the more important elements. For textures, there are two ways this can be effectively achieved: by reducing the number of texels (resizing the texture), or by reducing the amount of color information stored for each texel (lowering the "bit depth" or "bits per pixel").

Texture Resizing

There are actually two cases where texture resizing is important as a pre-processing operation: in the reduction of textures to conserve memory (or make them conform to a sizing scheme, which will be discussed later), and when generating mipmaps for textures that will be displayed at a number of different texel densities. Fortunately, exactly the same principles apply to both, so one generic texture resizing algorithm can generally be used in all cases.

The problem of resampling images to a different resolution has been extensively studied, and there are a vast number of different methods that can be employed in the process of doing so. The following are the most commonly used, and "tried and tested" techniques; there are numerous others that can be employed, but most of them have more narrow fields of applicability or are harder to tune, especially for texture maps where the artifacts introduced by the rendering process are significantly different from normal 2D bitmaps.

Point Sampling

The most straightforward method of resizing an image is to use point sampling: for each pixel in the destination, simply pick the pixel closest to it in the source. This results in pixels effectively "becoming larger" (as they are duplicated across an area) if the target is larger than the source, or eliminated entirely if the reverse is true.

Point sampling is very quick and easy to implement, but the quality of the output is very poor since removing pixels results in aliasing artifacts where thin lines can disappear entirely, and likewise expanding pixels to cover larger areas of the image simply looks "blocky."

Box Filters

The next method of resizing images is by far the most common, largely due to the ease of implementation and the fact that the results, while not as good as some other algorithms, are often considered "good enough." In particular, in environments where more advanced processing is too time consuming (such as during loading or as part of a preview process), box filtering is usually the preferred option.

Box filtering works by calculating the rectangular area of the source image that one pixel of the target corresponds to, by taking the four corners of the pixel and rescaling them into the coordinate space of the source. Thus, the resulting rectangle will cover more than one pixel if the image is reduced in size and less than one if the size is increased.

If the rectangle covers more than one pixel, all of the pixels covered by it are averaged to form the output color. Pixels that are partially covered by the rectangle can either be included or excluded from the calculation depending on some criteria (if more than half of the pixel is covered, for example), or have their contribution weighted according to the proportion included.

In the event that the box area is smaller than a pixel, bilinear interpolation can be used to smooth the results by assuming that the color of the pixel represents the color at its center, and there is a smooth color gradient between that point and the centers of the surrounding pixels. To calculate the output color, it is simply necessary to calculate the colors at the four corners of the box, linearly interpolating the adjacent pixel colors. Depending on the position of each of these corner points, the interpolation changes; each quadrant of the source pixel is closer to three neighbors, which provide the other values for the interpolation.

Many 3D graphics APIs, such as OpenGL and the "D3DX" DirectX helper function library include box filtering functionality; in particular, it is frequently used for generating lower level mipmaps for textures when only a single image is supplied by the application.

Weighted Filtering

Weighted filtering works in a similar manner to box filtering, by calculating the output color from a set of input pixels within a rectangular area. However, unlike box filtering, in a weighted filter the contribution of each of these input pixels is biased according to a value taken from a matrix of constants known as the convolution kernel, which is mapped onto the source image. The kernel can either be aligned directly to the pixels in the source (that is, each value is used to weight exactly one source pixel), or the same averaging previously described can be applied to determine the color to be used. It is worth noting that the box filter can be expressed in the weighted filtering algorithm by a kernel where every value in the matrix is identical.

0	0	2	0	0
0	4	8	4	0
2	8	16	8	2
0	4	8	4	0
0	0	2	0	0

FIGURE 5.3 An example convolution kernel.

The kernel shown in Figure 5.3 simply performs a weighted blur on the pixels being sampled for the reduction, the shaded cell indicating the pixel at the center of the area. There are a vast number of different possible kernels that can be employed; while simple blurs tend to work well for down sampling images, there are some more advanced edge detection filters that can be added to improve the sharpness of the resulting image.

Lanczos Convolution Kernel

One of the most popular kernels that can be used to sharpen the image as it is resized is the "Lanczos filter," which can be calculated for any desired kernel size. The filter is calculated based on the distance each cell in the matrix lies from the center point, and the values can be calculated using the following code:

```
float v=(d<r)?0:(sinf(PI*d)/(PI*d)) *
    ((sinf((PI*d)/r)/((PI*d)/r)));
```

Where d is the distance from the center point, r is the radius of the filter, and v is the resulting weight. As can be seen, outside the radius of the filter, all the weights are zero, but inside it two sine waves are used to generate the values. The effect of this filter is to try to preserve high-frequency detail in the area being reduced (hard edges, for example) while still blending the affected pixels to avoid aliasing artifacts.

Handling Edges While Resizing

One problem that frequently arises when resizing images, particularly with the more complex filters, is how to handle the edges of the texture, as there are no values available for the filter to use when calculating the color of pixels near the borders.

There are two approaches to this problem that work well: the first one is to consider the texture to be infinitely wrapping, and take samples from the other side of the texture when near an edge. This approach is almost essential when working with textures that are intended to be tiled, as otherwise the output tends to exhibit filtering artifacts where the edges of the texture do not match correctly. However, for textures that do not tile, there is a strong chance that this approach will cause undesirable colors to be sampled, leading to noticeable bands of color around the texture edges.

The second approach solves that problem, albeit at the cost of some filtering accuracy at the edges of the texture. The technique is to discard any samples that fall outside of the texture area and remove their contribution entirely from the filter (adjusting the sum of the filter weights to match). Therefore, only samples that are valid are included, but the overall behavior of the filter may change (particularly in the corners of the texture) as a significant number of cells may be ignored. How much of an effect this causes will depend on the nature of the convolution kernel in use.

A third method, which is generally not very useful but can work reasonably well in a limited subset of cases (primarily those where the texture in question is an irregular shape placed on a constant color background), is to simply consider any sample which lies outside the area of the texture to be a fixed color—the most common color from all the pixels in the image is a popular choice. The idea is to ensure that a "neutral" color is filtered into the texture as it is reduced. The success rate of this technique is largely dependent on how appropriate the color chosen is. Unfortunately, since this is a very difficult decision to automate in the general case, it is not easy to use this approach for large numbers of textures.

Conforming Textures

The vast majority of graphics hardware imposes restrictions on the sizes of textures, both in terms of the maximum (and sometimes minimum) sizes, and also in the usable intermediate values and the ratio of the sides. The most common restriction is that texture dimensions must be a power of two on every side; at the time of this writing, virtually every GPU either disallows textures that do not meet this criteria entirely, or imposes additional restrictions on them (mipmapping and texture wrapping are frequently disabled, for example). While in some cases it may be desirable to simply reject textures that do not meet the required criteria, it can also be useful to have a mechanism by which they can be forcibly brought into line with the requirements during pre-processing.

After detecting that the size is invalid, the first step when conforming a texture is to determine what size the texture *should* be. There are generally two options: either make the texture larger until each side meets the requirements, or reduce it to fit the next smallest available size. In some cases (for example, if the texture is larger than the largest possible size), there is only one possible choice, but in other cases it is largely a question of "personal preference": increasing the size of textures will retain detail but at the cost of memory, while decreasing the size may reduce the visual quality, but will not adversely impact performance.

When reducing the size of a texture, it is always necessary to resize the actual image, which can be achieved using one of the techniques described previously. However, when increasing the size of a texture, there are two options: either resize the texture to fill the available space, or leave the additional area blank.

Resizing the texture is the simplest option, as it merely requires a bilinear filter or other rescaling mechanism to be applied. However, the artifacts the rescaling process introduces can be very noticeable in some circumstances. They are generally not a problem if the texture is mapped onto a 3D surface, but if it is drawn as a 2D image onto the screen (where a 1:1 texel to pixel ratio would normally be expected), then the filtering artifacts can easily cause the image to appear blurred. In these cases, leaving the image itself alone and simply adding some "white space" around the outside can be the better option.

Unfortunately, adding this extra space to the texture requires that all of the objects using it must also be modified, as their UV coordinates must be rescaled to reference only the area of the texture that actually has the image in it! This in turn presents another problem: with the space around the edge of the texture, it is impossible to wrap it (as the wrap would incorporate the white space as well). On some hardware, both of these problems can be surmounted by setting a "region wrap" flag which causes only a subsection of the texture to be used for the entire texture coordinate space. If this is not available, it may be necessary to use the rescaling method instead.

Color Reduction

The process of color reduction is quantizing the actual color information in each pixel of the image. There are two distinct types of color reduction process, depending on the desired output: simple bit-depth reduction and palettization.

Bit-Depth Reduction

Bit-depth reduction is simply the process of converting one "channel-based" pixel format into one with fewer bits per pixel. Channel-based pixel formats store each pixel directly as a set of values, one for each channel (traditionally red, green, and blue, but as we will examine later there are other color spaces that can also be utilized). No other information is required to reconstruct the color of the pixel for display.

As mentioned previously, most textures or images are initially in an 8 bits per channel format, with either 24 or 32 bits per pixel (for images with an alpha channel). However, to conserve memory it is common to use 16 or even 12 bits per pixel formats, which use 4, 5, or 6 bits per channel. The core bit-depth reduction is simply the process of reducing the number of bits per channel and then repacking the data into the new format required.

At this base level, the reduction process is very simple. All that is required is to take the input data and remove the number of least significant bits required to get the desired output format. The only complication is that simply stripping the bits entirely (while a perfectly acceptable solution in many cases) will always have the effect of rounding the value down. To get a correctly rounded version, it is necessary to first add half of the total value of the removed bits to the number. For n removed bits, this can be calculated as $2^{(n-1)}-1$. For example:

8-bit input value	$= 0010\ 1110$ (decimal 46)
4-bit output value (removed bits in italic)	$= 0010\ 0000$ (decimal 32)
Rounding value ($2^{(4-1)}-1$)	$= 0000\ 0111$ (decimal 7)
8-bit input value with rounding added	$= 0011\ 0101$ (decimal 53)
Rounded 4-bit output value (removed bits in italic)	$= 0011\ 0000$ (decimal 48)

As can be seen from this example, rounding in this way produced a much closer result to the actual input value (an error of 2 rather than 16).

Once the channel values have been successfully quantized in this way, the only remaining task is to pack the resulting color value into the required format. While 8 bits per channel formats can easily be represented using a single byte per channel, smaller formats cannot, and must pack multiple channels into a single byte.

The exact layout of the format will depend largely on the target hardware, but virtually all formats follow a common pattern. This is often expressed as a string giving each channel name and the number of bits it occupies, in the order they appear; for example "R8G8B8A8" represents a typical 32-bit format with Red, Green, Blue, and Alpha channels appearing in that order, from most significant bit to least significant. "X" is often used to signify padding bits that are ignored; for example, "R5G5B5X1" is a 16-bit format with 5 bits used for each of Red, Green, and Blue, and one ignored bit at the end to pad the format to fill 16 bits exactly.

Note that it is not necessarily the case that a packed format will have the same number of bits for each channel; in particular, there are many common formats (such as "R5G5B5A1") which only support a single bit for alpha values (thereby providing a simple opaque/transparent pixel toggle), and some even use different numbers of bits for color channels ("R5G6B5" is a fairly common 16-bit format). It is often the case that the green channel is given more bits of accuracy that others in these cases, as the human eye is slightly better at distinguishing shades of green; however, this trick can sometimes backfire when used on textures containing shades of grey in particular, as it can be hard to avoid a slight green tint appearing as a result of the three color channels not containing exactly the same values on monochrome pixels.

Palettization

The process of palettization is required when producing images that use *indexed-color*; that is, instead of the pixels directly containing the values for the color channels, they contain indexes that reference a palette of colors. The scope of this palette can vary massively according to the details of the engine and hardware in use. Most modern hardware supports one palette for each texture, but less powerful systems may have to use a shared palette for groups of textures, or even for entire levels. As mentioned previously, texture compression schemes often use individual palettes for small groups of pixels, as well.

There are two stages to the palettization process: selecting the colors to include in the palette, and then converting the texture (or textures) to index that palette. The bulk of the difficulty in the process lies in the first step; once the palette is chosen the conversion is largely a mechanical process.

Choosing a Palette

Choosing the palette to be used for the image is a process that must make trade-offs to try to ensure the best quality of output. If there are not enough palette entries available to represent all of the unique colors in the image, then some will have to be removed, resulting in the corresponding areas in the texture being changed to another nearby color. Reducing the error introduced by this as much as possible is the goal of the palettization process.

Before any color reduction process is undertaken, however, there is one step that should always be performed: counting the unique colors in the source image. In fact, it is not necessary to accurately count the colors at this stage, but simply to establish if there are more than the available palette entries. This way, in cases where the texture fits into the palette without any color removal, the task can be completed simply by inserting all of the colors into the palette, avoiding the need for any additional expensive processing. Even if processing time is not a consideration, it is usually worthwhile doing this, as there are some cases in which more advanced palettization algorithms will (unnecessarily) reduce the quality of the image by pre-emptively merging colors.

Assuming, however, that the image does have too many colors to be represented exactly using the available palette entries, then it is necessary to start reducing the number of colors. There are two different algorithms in common use for doing this:

Color Pair Merging

This technique is actually quite a simple iterative process. Starting with a palette containing every color in the image, find the two colors that are nearest to each other and remove one of them, repeating this process until the desired number of colors is reached.

The key to this algorithm is the determination of the "distance" between two colors, which represents the error (per-pixel) which will be introduced by changing one to the other. For most purposes, this can be represented by taking each channel of the image as the axis of a cube (or 4D hyper-cube, in the case of four channel images), as illustrated in Figure 5.4.

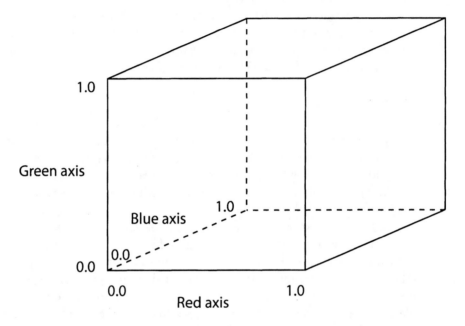

FIGURE 5.4   The structure of a three channel RGB color cube.

The squared distance d^2 between any two points within the cube can be calculated for an RGB image using the distance formula as follows:

$$d^2 = (R1-R2)2+(G1-G2)2+(B1-B2)2$$

or

$$d^2 = (R1-R2)2+(G1-G2)2+(B1-B2)2+(A1-A2)2$$

(in the case of a four channel RGBA image).

In theory, the actual value of d can be calculated and used; however, as this requires an expensive square root calculation, in practice, it is generally easier to skip this and use d^2 instead, because for comparison purposes the squared values are fine. This calculation can also be used for any color space simply by substituting the channels as needed. In fact, as we will discuss later, it may be more appropriate to perform it in a different color-space than the one the image is currently stored in.

With this formula, the pair of colors to be combined can be found simply by calculating the distances between every pair of colors in the palette and picking those with the shortest distance. The act of combining the colors, however, is somewhat more complicated. Essentially, there are three possible ways the colors A and B can be combined: A can be kept as is, B can be kept as is, or the two colors can be averaged to form a third color, half way between the two, which is inserted into the palette instead of both of them.

In practice, however, the third option is rarely used. While in some cases it may reduce the theoretical error, it does so at the expense of introducing colors which *never* appeared in the original image. This can have fairly serious consequences: as well as complicating the palette reduction algorithm slightly (the averaged color may already exist in the palette, for example), the visual appearance of the undesired color may be completely inappropriate (in particular, averaged colors tend to appear "muddy"), particularly if non-trivial quantizations are being performed.

Therefore, the question is: which of the two colors to keep and which to discard? In the absence of any additional information, there is no advantage to either, so the decision must be taken "at random." However, this approach has a significant disadvantage: it can result in a color which is used on a large number of pixels being removed in favor of one which is only used on a handful of pixels.

To avoid this, it is necessary to keep track of not only the colors in the palette, but also how many pixels use each. This information can then be used to determine which color will cause the smallest error if removed.

Knowing the number of pixels which use each palette entry can be useful in the initial stage of selecting which pair of colors to combine. Essentially, rather than simply considering the distance between the colors to be the error introduced, the error becomes the distance multiplied by the smaller of the two pixel counts. This way, large bodies of color are less likely to be merged together than small ones. This works well, although it is usually necessary to have a multiplier on the pixel counts to ensure that the size of the area does not become an overwhelming factor in the decision, especially as this can lead to smooth color transitions (which feature lots of different colors with small numbers of pixels each) being very heavily quantized.

The Median-Cut Algorithm

The median-cut algorithm works on a different principle entirely to the pair merging technique. Instead of starting with a palette containing too many colors and attempting to reduce it, the approach taken is to build up the palette until the maximum number of entries is reached.

The technique works by considering the color space to represent a 3D (n-dimensional for n color channels) cube, in which the colors used in the source image are represented by points. First, the axis aligned bounding box of these points is determined by finding the highest and lowest values on each axis (color channel) of the cube. This bounding box encloses all of the colors that make up the image.

Once the bounding box is found, the longest axis of the box is split, forming two boxes. The point of the split is chosen so that an equal (or as close as possible) number of points are enclosed in each of the resulting subdivided boxes. This can be done quite simply by sorting the points along the chosen axis and then positioning the split at the half-way point through this list. An example of this can be seen in Figure 5.5; the split plane (shown with a thick dashed line) subdivides the bounding box of the image colors so that an equal number fall into each of the two resulting sections (A and B).

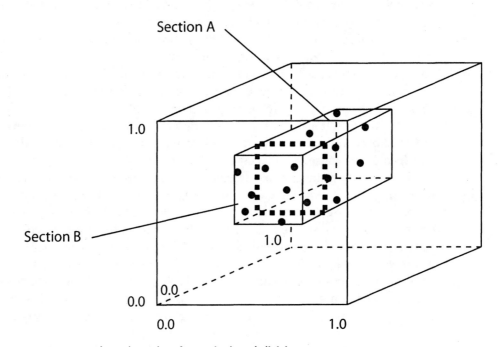

FIGURE 5.5   The color cube after a single subdivision.

The process then repeats, with each of the two subdivided boxes in turn being split until either the box contains only one point, or the number of boxes equals the number of available palette entries. At this point, each box represents one palette color, which is formed from the colors the points inside it represent. As with the pair merging algorithm, they can either be averaged to form the composite color, or the color that appears most in the source image can be chosen instead.

Optimizing the Palette Generation Algorithm

Both of these palette construction algorithms are fairly straightforward, but suffer from one drawback: the processes in each are quite time consuming. Building the initial palette can be quite slow, and in addition, the pair removal algorithm calculating the color distances to determine which pairs to remove is quite time consuming, requiring lots of comparisons between the image colors and palette entries. The median cut algorithm also requires that the colors be sorted on each axis, and both of these tasks require that every palette entry be compared with every other.

There are many optimization techniques that can be applied to speed up these procedures. One of the most commonly used is to build either a three- or four-dimensional tree (the three dimensional case being known as an *octree*) of the palette entries, a data structure that allows colors to be found and compared very quickly.

The principle of an octree is very simple: each node of the tree has eight children, which represent every possible combination of one-bit values in the three channels (000 through 111 in binary). To insert a color into an octree, the process simply starts at the root of the tree and reads the most significant bit of each of the color channels. This gives an index for the child node this color should be inserted into. Moving into this node, the process is then repeated with the next most significant bit in each channel, until there are no bits left. At this point, the node reached is a leaf node which represents the color. In this way, inserting a unique color into an octree palette requires only eight steps, rather than the laborious search of the entire existing palette needed previously.

While this description uses an octree, the procedure for handling a four-dimensional tree is identical, with the exception that each node has 16 children instead. While storing all of the possible nodes in an octree would be prohibitively expensive (16,777,216 nodes in the case of an 8-bit octree), it is only necessary to create nodes as they are traversed during the color addition process. As only a tiny fraction of the possible colors will be used in any one image, and these tend to be clustered together, only a small portion of the tree actually needs to exist in memory.

For the pair merging algorithm, the process of calculating the distances between colors is greatly simplified: as each of the nonleaf nodes represents the most significant n bits of the color (where n is the depth the node is from the root), the subtree beneath each node contains colors that differ only in the remaining bits. So, it is possible to search for colors that are separated only by one node in the tree first, then two, and so on, widening the search until a pair is found.

To enable this optimization to be used with error values that are weighted by the pixel coverage, the error between pairs of nonleaf nodes can be calculated. This enables the algorithm to quickly reject entire subtrees where the error is too high to warrant further consideration.

In the median cut algorithm, the main overhead is the calculation of a sorted list of the colors along one axis; the octree makes this trivial indeed. All that is required is to recurse over the tree, visiting the children of each node in the required order (for any given axis, this simply means visiting the four or eight children that represent a "0" bit on that axis before those that represent a "1" bit). The result is a sorted list. In addition, if desired, the bounding boxes can store pointers to the nodes that represent their extremities, which allows only the subsection of the tree between these to be traversed when building the list.

For very large images (or if a number of textures are being used to construct the palette), the number of leaf nodes in the octree may become unwieldy. In these (relatively rare) cases, it can be useful to only use a certain number of the bits in the color to build the octree, thereby reducing its depth and allowing several colors to reside in one leaf node. Then, a standard linear algorithm can be used on the list of colors in each leaf when searching.

Converting a Texture to Use a Palette

Once the palette is generated, the task of converting the pixels in the image themselves into a set of palette indices is quite straightforward. In general, all that is necessary is to take each pixel's color and find the nearest matching color in the palette. If an octree was used during palette generation, this process can be performed very quickly by traversing the octree in the same manner as was used when the color was added, until a point is reached where either a leaf node is reached, or it is impossible to find the required child node. At that point, the closest color is in one of the leaf nodes beneath the current one, and it can be located with a simple brute force search.

Alternatively, the palette generation process can store information about which colors have been removed, and which colors they were merged with. This can speed up the process somewhat, although care is needed as there may be a "chain" of color removals, where three or more colors were merged. As we will discuss later, it is also possible to use dithering to improve the appearance of palletized images, although the results this technique produces can be highly variable in quality, depending on the nature of the source image.

Generating Palettes for Multiple Images

In some situations, it may be useful to generate a palette to be used for many images, for example, when dealing with engines that do not support one palette per texture, or with mipmaps of a texture. (Filtering can often result in the mipmaps containing colors that did not exist in the original texture!) In these cases, all that is necessary is to add *all* of the colors from the source images into the palette creation algorithm—the result is a palette that includes the best fit colors for all of the input data. The textures can then be palletized individually against this palette as usual.

In some cases, such as when an entire level is using the same palette, it may be more efficient to use only a few "representative" textures when building the palette, and then use this to palletize everything. This can significantly reduce the amount of processing required, at the risk of a texture that was not involved in the palette creation process containing colors that do not appear elsewhere and becoming very quantized.

DITHERING

In traditional 2D graphics, the palettization process is almost always accompanied by some form of dithering pass. Dithering is the process of deliberately interleaving two different colors on adjacent pixels, so as to give the impression of a third, intermediate color when the image is viewed from a distance. In palletized images in particular, dithering can help immensely in breaking up the banding artifacts seen on color gradients when there are insufficient palette entries available to represent the full spectrum of colors used.

There are many established dithering techniques developed for 2D images. Most techniques are based on either ordered dithering or error diffusion—variants of the latter being the more common in actual production use.

Ordered Dithering

Ordered dithering is based on a set of fixed patterns that are used to represent colors that are between one "pure" color (that is, one that appears in the image palette and therefore can be represented directly) and another. Taking a 2×2 grid of pixels, there are three different proportions of two color values that can be represented: entirely one color, a 1:3 ratio between the two colors, or an even split 1:1 ratio. The patterns these three ratios form are shown in Figure 5.6. The dithering process is performed by mapping this fixed 2×2 grid across the image in a repeating pattern, and for each pixel that is not a pure color, finding the two closest palette entries and choosing the appropriate one from this grid.

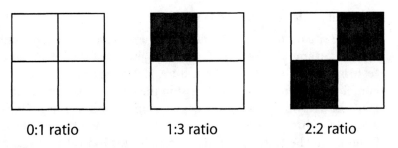

0:1 ratio   1:3 ratio   2:2 ratio

FIGURE 5.6   The three possible 1-bit 2×2 dither patterns.

Ordered dithering is very straightforward to implement, and extremely fast. It is not uncommon to find ordered dithering implemented in hardware on GPUs for the purpose of converting output images from 24 bit to 16 bit color. The downside is that the regular dithering pattern tends to become visible in the output image, even if the size of the patterns used is increased.

Error Diffusion Dithering

Error diffusion dithering works on a slightly different principle to ordered dithering. Instead of having preset dither patterns, the pattern emerges from the use of a filter to distribute the error in nonpure color pixels to neighboring areas. The filter is simply defined as a grid of coefficients, the values of which determine how much of the error is distributed to each neighbor.

The process for performing error diffusion dithering is relatively straightforward. As each pixel of the image is palletized, the difference between the original color and the palette entry chosen is calculated, giving an error metric for each color channel. This error value is added to the cumulative error counts for the surrounding pixels. Then, when those pixels are palletized, the error is first subtracted from the source color, in effect, biasing it to "correct" for the error in its neighbor. This pixel will then in turn generate an error value that is passed on according to the filter coefficients. This process repeats until the entire image has been palletized.

Error diffusion dithering filters are almost always based on the principle that the image is being processed in a linear fashion, top to bottom, left to right. Hence, errors are only propagated "forward" (that is, to pixels below or on the right of the current one), meaning that error values only need to be stored for the pixels on the current and next lines to be processed. This also means that error diffusion dithering can operate in place, there is no need to duplicate the source image data before converting it.

Probably the most famous error diffusion filter is the "Floyd-Steinberg dither" filter, so named because it was devised by R.W. Floyd and L. Steinberg. The filter coefficients are all fractions of 16, which makes optimization of any implementation easier because the costly division can be reduced to a binary shift right of four places instead. Figure 5.7 shows the coefficients for the 3×2 pixel block the filter operates on.

	Current pixel	7/16 of error
3/16 of error	5/16 of error	1/16 of error

FIGURE 5.7 The coefficients of the Floyd-Steinberg dither filter.

As with most error diffusion filters, the performance of the Floyd-Steinberg filter can be improved by alternating the direction in which lines of the image are processed, in other words, by scanning odd-numbered lines from left to right, and even-numbered lines from right to left (or vice versa). When reversing the processing direction, the filter needs to be flipped horizontally as well, so that the error is still passed to the *next* pixel along the line.

Dithering Textures

Dithering works exceptionally well to hide the artifacts generated by lowering the color resolution of 2D images, but it is less useful for texture maps. The problem arises because the sampling of texels in texture maps does not necessarily match the pixels that will be written to the screen. If the texture is on a large object, one texel may cover many pixels (and be filtered with its neighbors), while if the object is small, only one texel in a given area may be drawn. This causes problems when dithering because the illusion that results in the color of an area appearing to be between the two being dithered depends on the pixels being tightly interleaved, so that the eye is fooled into blending them together. Since the orientation and scale the texture will be drawn at is not known in advance, it is very hard to achieve this effect during preprocessing.

Even worse, the noise the dithering process introduces can often cause shimmering or other undesirable artifacts if the interleaved pixels become grouped together on-screen: consider the case of a flat uniformly dithered white and black square (like a chessboard). At a 1:1 pixel to texel ratio, this will appear to be mid grey, but when reduced to half of its original size, each pixel will represent two texels. If mipmapping and bilinear filtering are disabled, then the texture will appear to be either entirely white or entirely black, depending on which pixels are chosen— and as the object moves, it will appear to flash between the two colors! Error diffusion dithering performs much better than ordered dithering in these cases, as the lack of regular patterns tends to prevent the worst case artifacts appearing, but it is still not ideal.

There are some cases in which dithering can be useful for texture maps, however, mainly when the approximate size and orientation can be predicted in advance. A very good example of this is on *sky cubes*, where a series of textures are placed on an infinitely large cube around the viewer to give the illusion of a larger world stretching to the horizon. These textures are often the worst case for palettization algorithms, as they are very noticeable on-screen, and frequently have smooth color gradients that are hard to represent well with a limited palette. Fortunately, because the pixel to texel density does not change much as the player moves around, carefully matching the size of the sky cube textures to the output screen resolution can allow dithering to work well on them.

USING ALTERNATIVE COLOR SPACES

Almost without exception, texture storage, manipulation, and display operations take place in the RGB color space. Since almost all graphics hardware works in the RGB color space, and many common operations are relatively straightforward to perform in it, it is a logical choice for all of these operations. However, there are some cases in which using other color spaces can be beneficial, especially during processing operations such as palettization, which are focused toward getting the best appearance from the output, rather than performing some mathematically correct operation.

The reason that moving to an alternative color space can help greatly with operations such as this is that the RGB color space, while convenient for many other reasons, is not a particularly good match for the way that human eyes perceive color. The RGB color space gives equal precedence to all three color channels, and makes no distinction between the chrominance (color) and luminance (brightness) components of the image. In fact, human perception of color and brightness is significantly different, and in particular, the resolution at which changes in color is detected is significantly lower than that for changes in brightness.

There are several alternatives to the RGB color space, such as HSV ("Hue Saturation Value"), and CMYK ("Cyan Magenta Yellow Black"), but these are primarily designed for other purposes, ease of color selection in the first case, and printing processes in the latter. It can sometimes be useful to provide access to these in tools (particularly HSV, which many artists find more intuitive than RGB), but they have little value in processing tasks.

The YUV Color Space

There is one color space, however, that is designed to mimic in some ways the response of the human eye to colors, by introducing separate channels for luminance and chrominance. This is known as the YUV color space: the Y channel being the luminance of the image, and the U and V channels holding the chrominance, as difference values between the luminance and the blue and red channels respectively. The chrominance channels are also sometimes known as "Cb" and "Cr" (for Chrominance Blue and Chrominance Red), leading to the format itself sometimes being called *YCbCr*.

Converting to and from YUV color values is relatively straightforward. To convert into YUV from RGB, use the following equations:

```
Y=(R*  0.299) + (G*  0.587) + (B*  0.114)
U=(R*-0.169) + (G*-0.331) + (B*  0.500)
V=(R*  0.500) + (G*-0.419) + (B*-0.081)
```

(Note that this will result in signed values for U and V. Most systems working with YUV colors "correct" this by adding half of the maximum value to both the chrominance channels, 127 in the case of 8 bit color channels.)

The conversion back to RGB can be achieved with:

```
R=Y +                (V*  1.403)
G=Y + (U*-0.343) +  (V*-0.714)
B=U + (U*  1.773)
```

This calculation assumes that the values for U and V are signed; again, an adjustment (subtracting half of the maximum value) may be necessary if this is not the case.

One of the main advantages of the YUV color space is that by separating the color and brightness channels, it becomes possible to easily process them individually, for example, to apply gamma correction to textures. In some cases, it is not actually necessary to do a full conversion to and from YUV color space to gain the benefits, for example, when palletizing or dithering images the pixel error calculation alone can be made in the YUV space. This is especially beneficial as the separated luminance and chrominance components can be weighted individually, giving more precedence to errors in the brightness of pixels as these will be more obvious to the eye. It should be noted, however, that if the textures are subject to realtime lighting or other algorithms that alter the final pixel color, this can reduce the usefulness of this technique (and the YUV color space in general), as the alterations to the output pixels can significantly alter the characteristics of the texture.

As well as providing several benefits for processing operations, the ability to convert images into the YUV color space can actually be exploited to provide a form of texture compression.

Using YUV Textures

If engine support is available, it may be possible to convert textures into YUV color space and render from this representation. On its own, this is not a particularly useful technique, but it is possible to exploit the lower resolution at which the eye perceives color detail to achieve a crude (but very effective) form of texture compression, by reducing the resolution (and potentially bit depth as well) of the U and V channels.

This trick is commonly used by video compression systems, which store the color channels at a quarter or less of the resolution of the luminance channel. This gives a significant saving in memory and processing requirements, with relatively little impact on the actual appearance of the image. In particular, YUV textures do not suffer from the artifacts that most other texture compression or palettization schemes introduce on images containing smooth gradients with several colors, such as sky backgrounds.

So, while YUV textures are not a substitute for the more standard palettization or compression techniques (due mainly to the additional complexity involved in rendering them), they can be very useful in giving a quality boost to certain types of images without significantly increasing the storage requirements.

CONCLUSION

There has been a significant amount of research done in the field of image processing, and while some techniques are not applicable to games (most notably because of the different rendering characteristics of texture maps as opposed to flat 2D bitmaps), there are several common algorithms that form the core of virtually every game's asset pipeline for images. Resizing, compressing, and manipulating the color depth of images are the most frequently performed operations, and ensuring that the code used to perform these is efficient and produces good quality output is essential to the performance of the pipeline as a whole.

6 Geometry Processing

In This Chapter

- Mesh Data
- Mesh Geometry Processing
- Stripification
- Triangle Lists
- Sanitizing Input Data
- Regular Mesh Subdivision
- Geometry Compression
- Bone Weight Processing
- Building Bounding Volumes
- Mesh Hierarchy Processing
- Level of Detail Simplification

In the early days of 3D games, there was a vast array of different rendering techniques and engine types in use, usually trading off some flexibility in asset design for higher performance. Many of these systems required special methodologies and custom software for asset creation, which in turn meant that the processing required was almost entirely dependent on the engine and techniques in use.

However, with the proliferation of dedicated 3D hardware, both in recent generations of home consoles and modern PCs, the ability and need to create engines using such a diverse range of techniques has been almost entirely eliminated (at present, the most notable exceptions to this rule are games designed for portable devices such as mobile phones, which are often lacking in both 3D hardware and processor power). Therefore, the 3D graphics in virtually every recently developed game are constructed and rendered in the same way as meshes of triangles, usually texture mapped, with one or more 2D bitmap images.

MESH DATA

In the majority of systems, such a mesh is constructed of a number of vertices, the points in 3D space that define the shape of the model, and triangles or polygons that connect them and form the surface. While in theory arbitrary polygons can be used to construct the surface, for most practical applications, the mesh is restricted to using convex polygons (which can be fairly easily triangulated), or simply triangles. None of the currently available consumer level rendering hardware natively supports drawing n-sided polygons. At some point, either in the game itself or at a driver level, such primitives will be converted into triangles for rendering. Nonetheless, it can sometimes be useful to use the polygon representation of surfaces for processing and some stages of rendering as it is generally more compact, and can be easier to manipulate.

The vertices and polygon information define the shape and surface structure of a mesh, but more information is generally (but not always) needed to render it. The three most commonly used types of additional information are vertex colors, texture coordinates, and normals.

Vertex Colors

As the name suggests, vertex colors are simply a single color value, generally stored for each vertex on the model. In most rendering architectures, these colors are used to shade the surface of the polygons as they are rendered, using a linear interpolation to determine the color of points between the vertices. This form of vertex color interpolation is known as *Gouraud Shading*, and although other shading models have been developed, the universal adoption of this form of shading by consumer hardware has resulted in its becoming the de facto standard.

Vertex colors are useful for many purposes: they can be "painted" onto a model by an artist, giving them some degree of control over the color of areas of the model without modifying the textures used (this is particularly useful for introducing some variation into large areas of tiled texture). They can also be used to encapsulate lighting information (either pre-calculated or generated by the renderer at run-time), or as a component of more complex operations such as blending multiple textures.

While vertex colors are stored on a per vertex basis, in some circumstances it may be desirable to store colors on a per polygon basis instead. This is fairly unusual, however, and in the majority of cases where it is useful (writing polygon IDs into off-screen buffers for shadows or special effects, for example), the face colors are generated by the renderer rather than being supplied as part of the mesh data.

Texture Coordinates

Texture coordinates are used to provide information on how a 2D texture map is applied to the surface of the model. For each vertex on the mesh, a 2D coordinate is stored indicating the point on the texture that should be used. Texture coordinates only indicate where on the texture the polygon is to draw data from, not which texture to use. This information is usually stored on a per polygon basis. The exception to this rule is when multiple textures are being packed onto a single page, in which case a number of textures may appear as one large image, with each using a subset of the available coordinates.

Normals

Most rendering engines use the normals of surfaces as part of their lighting calculations, and in some cases for other special effects (extruding meshes along their normals to make them "balloon" as part of a glow effect, for example). While in theory normals for vertices and faces can be calculated by the engine or a pre-processing step, in many cases it is desirable for the artists to have direct control over them, because adjusting the normals (or normal generation algorithm) by hand can give surfaces smooth, faceted, or uneven appearances as desired.

Normals are generally stored per vertex, because in order to ensure a smooth appearance to surfaces the engine must interpolate either the normals themselves or (more usually) the calculated lighting values. However, polygon, or face, normals can be very useful for certain special effects and other processing, so it is not uncommon for these to be stored as well.

Polygons

In addition to the vertex data, information on the polygons themselves must be stored. In its simplest form, a polygon may simply consist of a list of vertices (three in the case of a triangle), all of the other relevant information can be stored by the vertices themselves. In most cases, however, there will be at least a small amount of information stored for the polygon itself: a reference to the texture map it uses, or a face normal, for example.

In more advanced engines, there may be yet another layer of abstraction, where polygons are sorted into sets according to some criteria (the texture map required is a very common one), and each set possesses a set of properties of its own. This is a very efficient way to deal with meshes that contain a large number of polygons grouped into a relatively small number of sets, avoiding the need to redundantly store a lot of information at the polygon level. This system has advantages and disadvantages: it is closer to the format the renderer itself will probably require, but it can make processing awkward as the sorting must be maintained as changes are made to the polygons themselves.

Indexed Vertices

While the obvious method for storing polygon information is to include a copy of the vertex data with each polygon, this can actually be counterproductive in many ways. Almost all modern 3D hardware supports vertex indexing, which is the separation of vertex data into a flat array of vertices which are then referenced by the polygons using an index into the array (the notable exception to this is the Playstation 2, where if required, indexing must be handled by the engine itself).

Moving the vertex data into a separate array has advantages beyond improving the rendering speed, however. In most cases, it is desirable that mesh manipulations maintain the coherency of the mesh surface, in other words, gaps between polygons are not introduced. If each polygon has a copy of every vertex, then it is necessary to update every polygon that includes it when a change is made to a single vertex. Even worse, as in this case, the only information on the surface topology is in the positions of the vertices, if two vertices are moved on top of another they effectively become one, meaning that there is no way to undo the merge and restore the original structure of the mesh!

Vertex Streams

Most graphics hardware supports the concept of having multiple "streams" of vertex data, each containing one or more of the elements above. These individual streams are then combined to form complete vertices just prior to rendering.

Vertex streams are useful because they give the engine the ability to store and manipulate each type of vertex information separately, and by selecting a different stream, alter the data in one element of the vertices without having to store a second copy of all the unchanged data. This is very useful when performing multi-pass rendering, as well as for vertex animation and some types of level of detail reduction. Some hardware also supports multiple sets of indices, so individual streams can be referenced differently. This allows streams that have a lot of duplicated or redundant data (for example, the vertex normals) to be reduced significantly in size.

Generally speaking, however, it is easiest for pre-processing tasks to work with vertices as complete units, and separate the data into streams as required once all of the other operations are complete.

Model Hierarchy Information

While the term mesh is used for a single set of polygon and vertex data, a model is the term used for a complete 3D object—a character, for example. A model may contain multiple independent meshes, in which case in addition to the mesh information itself, they usually contain a hierarchy of nodes to which the meshes are attached, often along with other invisible nodes such as bones for skinned animation and markers for positioning other objects relative to the mesh. Each node of the hierarchy has an independent set of transforms, but is relative to its parent, meaning that an entire sub-tree can be moved, rotated, or scaled simply by altering the parent node. This mechanism is often used by 3D packages and dedicated animation tools to make animating characters and other jointed structures simpler. In many of these systems, nodes are given constraints on their movement which can in turn be used by systems such as IK solvers to quickly produce realistic movement.

In general, the mesh that each node of the hierarchy possesses must be processed separately, as their movements relative to each other are unpredictable, and at runtime they are drawn with different transformations. However, certain types of processing can be performed on the hierarchy itself, such as animation compression, and in some cases it may also be possible to exploit known game-specific or engine-specific information on the behavior of nodes to enable mesh level optimizations to be performed, such as merging nodes that are always static relative to each other.

MESH GEOMETRY PROCESSING

With this unification of rendering formats, a number of universal techniques for pre-processing triangle mesh geometry have been developed, enabling higher runtime performance, easier control of level of detail, etc. While not all of these are applicable or useful for every individual game, they can often form the basis of a more specific solution tailored for the requirements of a given engine and design.

STRIPIFICATION

As mentioned previously, all current consumer 3D hardware operates on triangles as the most basic primitive. These can be submitted to the hardware for rendering as a simple list, each triangle comprised of three distinct vertices (or vertex indices), but for the majority of meshes this is actually a fairly inefficient way to represent the data. This is because in most meshes, the triangles form a continuous surface, and each triangle shares vertices with its neighbors. Therefore, rather than starting each triangle with a completely new set of vertices, it is possible to construct the next triangle by taking two vertices of the previous one (the edge which connects these triangles), and adding one more vertex to form the new one. This process can be iteratively repeated until a triangle that has only one (unused) connected edge is reached. An example of this is shown in Figure 6.1, the numbered vertices 1 to 5 form three triangles A, B, and C using vertices (1, 2, 3), (2, 3, 4), and (3, 4, 5).

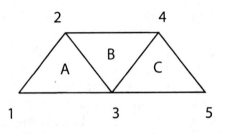

FIGURE 6.1   A triangle strip containing five vertices.

The result is a *triangle strip*, a long list of triangles all joined together. Apart from the first one, each of the successive triangles in the strip only requires one additional vertex, making the overall number of vertices required $n+2$ for a strip of length n, rather than the $3n$ vertices required by a simple list. This not only reduces significantly the storage and transfer overheads of this geometry, but also the processing required as well, each triangle only requires one vertex to be transformed, as the previous two calculated vertex positions can be reused.

Building Triangle Strips

The process of building a triangle strip from an unordered list is a surprisingly complex problem. The primary problem is one of optimization. It is quite straightforward to obtain a solution that works, but very hard to obtain one that is optimal.

The reason for this is because it is generally unlikely that in a real example the geometry will be able to be expressed as a single strip. In most cases, it will require a number of independent strips to cover the whole surface, and this is where the choice of algorithm will make a huge difference, as each additional strip incurs extra overheads in storage and processing (which we will examine in more detail later), in general a more optimal algorithm is one that produces fewer, longer strips, thereby maximizing the benefit that the stripping process gives.

In fact, the stripification of an arbitrary mesh is an NP-complete problem, in other words, there is no (known) completely accurate method to find the optimal solution other than trying every possible combination! However, to obtain significant benefits from the conversion to strips it is fortunately not necessary to find an optimal solution, merely one that is "good enough."

The Greedy Algorithm

The simplest, and most obvious algorithm for generating triangle strips is a greedy approach. This works by selecting a random triangle on the mesh to start from, and then picking one of the adjacent triangles (again at random), and moving on to it. Once the initial "direction" of the strip is established, the next triangle is that which adjoins the edge formed by the last two vertices used. As each triangle is added to the strip, it is removed from the input data, and eventually the process will reach an edge with no adjoining triangle, at which point it stops. The process then repeats (starting a new strip) until there are no triangles left in the input data.

In this basic form, the performance of the greedy algorithm is not particularly good, in particular, it is very prone to leaving "islands" of unconnected triangles stranded in the middle of the mesh, which then require another strip to include in the mesh. However, it is possible to make a few simple modifications that turn this method into a significantly more useful tool.

Picking the Initial Triangle

The first decision that the stripification algorithm must make is the most important, which triangle to actually begin building the strip from. In the basic greedy algorithm, this has a huge impact. If the strip begins in the middle of a surface, it will most likely produce a suboptimal result overall as the mesh will become divided in two. As we will examine shortly, while this can be mitigated to some degree by extending the strip in both directions, a better algorithm for picking the initial triangle is fairly straightforward.

The key to this is to examine the connectivity of each triangle in the mesh. In a well-formed mesh surface, each triangle can be connected to up to three others, one for each of its edges. Ignoring triangles with no connected edges (which clearly can never form part of a strip), those with a single connected edge must lie at the start or end of a strip in any solution. Therefore, if such a triangle exists it is the obvious choice for a starting point, as otherwise the risk is high that another strip will *orphan* it by removing the single triangle it is connected to.

Once no singly connected triangles exist, the next logical step is to pick a triangle with two connected edges. A triangle with two connected edges is effectively already part of a strip. There is one "entry" edge and one "exit" edge, so the only possible solution must be the optimal one.

This leads us to another very simple, but highly effective optimization. After a strip has been built, the algorithm should return to the initial triangle and if another unused connected edge exists, extend the strip *backwards* from it (if more than one connected edge remains, then the same selection algorithm used during strip construction can be employed). This way, even if the strip was started at a point in the middle of the mesh, it will be extended as fully as possible.

If a case is reached where there are only triangles with all three neighbors present in the mesh, then it is largely redundant which one is selected. This is because the only case where this will happen is when the mesh has no edges at all, and the surface wraps around, such as a sphere, for example. Under these circumstances, the choice of a starting point makes very little difference to the overall performance of the algorithm. Also, if it does occur this case will only happen on the very first strip that is built for that surface, because after a strip has been built the removed triangles will break the overall connectivity, introducing surface edges where the triangles have one or two neighbors.

Picking the Initial Direction

Once an initial triangle is selected, the next decision to be made is which *direction* the strip should be extended in, in other words, which of the available adjacent triangles should be used. At this point, there will be between one and three connected edges available that the strip can be extended to. Clearly, for one edge, the decision is simple, as there are no other options available!

In the cases where there are two or three available edges, making a decision at random is a perfectly viable strategy—remember that if the strip is also being extended backwards, then in the case of a triangle with two connected edges, the decision is irrelevant, and in the case where three edges are available it is only one that will be left unused. However, there are techniques that can make this decision more likely to yield useful results.

Recursive Methods

To optimize this further, a commonly used approach is to add recursive processing of strips, or *look-ahead*. Quite simply, this works by taking the case where a decision must be made between three potential directions to extend the strip in, and recursively calling the strip building routine on each one. Whichever results in the longer strip length "wins" and is chosen as the final answer. It should be noted that this test needs to be repeated when extending the strip backwards, rather than simply using the "second place" answer, as this may overlap the solution employed for the first direction chosen!

With these extensions, the greedy algorithm becomes a fairly reasonable solution to the triangle stripification problem. Certainly, the efficiency achieved is more than enough to make the process worthwhile, and the required processing time to build the strips is fairly trivial. For many applications, at this point the cost/benefit ratio involved in extending the algorithm further is not worthwhile, especially as optimizing for other factors (such as vertex cache characteristics) will yield bigger gains.

However, if a more efficient solution is desired, then it is also possible to consider multiple starting points and test each one independently. In this case, again the solution that generates the longer strip is used, with the process then repeating if there are any triangles left to be processed. In some circumstances, it may be possible to select two or more "winners," if the strips produced do not overlap at any point.

Clearly, on a large mesh this has the potential to generate huge amounts of processing as the number of possible combinations grows exponentially with the number of possible starting locations. In addition, care must be taken not to consume large quantities of RAM as each recursive call will need to keep track of which triangles have been visited and removed from the main mesh independently of the others! However, these problems can be tackled by adding further constraints to the recursion, for example, only allowing a certain depth of recursion before making a decision on which direction to take, and early on rejecting strips that generate an unacceptable number of unconnected triangles or are *functionally identical* (i.e., traverse the same triangles in a different order) to previously considered strips.

The SGI Algorithm

The most commonly known derivative of this technique is the so called "SGI algorithm," which as the name suggests was developed at SGI as part of a toolkit of utilities for their Iris GL system, the precursor to OpenGL. The SGI algorithm uses the algorithm as described above, but with one key difference: when considering which triangle to extend the strip to initially, the triangle with the lowest number of connected edges is chosen. If more than one triangle has the same number, then a one step look-ahead is used, examining the number of connected edges each adjacent triangle to the candidates has and again choosing the one with the lowest number of neighbors.

This approach is designed to minimize the number of orphan triangles generated, by ensuring that the triangles with the lowest connectivity (and hence the highest risk of becoming orphaned) are included into strips first. Preferring triangles with fewer neighbors also ensures that strips traverse around the edges of areas first and work their way into the center, minimizing the risk of splitting a large connected surface into two separate sections during stripification.

The SGI algorithm is generally considered to be the benchmark in greedy style algorithms, and it is the one most commonly used in games development, thanks to the combination of relatively high efficiency, low processing overhead, and ease of implementation.

Other Methods

There are some techniques for mesh stripification that are based on entirely different strategies. However, the vast majority of them are only of academic interest to game developers because they either do not perform significantly better than the simpler methods, or because they rely on having higher-order knowledge about the mesh or primitives from which it is constructed, which is generally not available for game models.

That said, one alternative technique that has been successfully employed in games development and does produce more efficient results in many circumstances is the "STRIPE Algorithm," developed by a team at Stony Brook University. STRIPE works by finding "patches" formed of grids of quadrilaterals (each a pair of triangles) in the in mesh, and then building strips that traverse these patches in the most efficient way possible. The group's research [Evans96] has shown this approach to produce strips that are about 15% more efficient (measured in terms of relative strip length and number of strips generated) than those built using the SGI algorithm. The downside of this approach, however, is that it is both more computationally expensive and significantly more complex to implement than any of the greedy algorithm derivates. The original STRIPE source code is available from the STRIPE homepage, and is free for noncommercial use (licenses for commercial use may also be obtained for a nominal fee). More information can be found on the project's homepage at *http://www.cs.sunysb.edu/~stripe.*

Back-Face Culling and Winding Order

One problem which has not yet been mentioned is that of how triangle strips interact with the common practice of back-face culling, considering triangles to be single-sided, and not drawing those that face away from the viewer. While on some systems (most notably the Playstation 2), back-face culling is not often used as it consumes more processing time than simply drawing every polygon, in many cases it provides a straightforward and computationally inexpensive (in fact, usually "free") method of culling about half of the triangles in any given scene.

Back-face culling is usually implemented by assigning a *winding order* to vertices, such that triangles are set up with their vertices in a clockwise (or counter clockwise) direction when they are facing toward the viewer. Since this order is reversed when a triangle is facing in the opposite direction, it is therefore trivial to check which triangles are facing the viewer and need to be drawn.

However, since each triangle in a strip is formed from the last two vertices of the previous one, the winding order reverses each time; every other triangle in the strip is effectively "backwards" as far as the culling is concerned. Therefore, to avoid this resulting in surfaces being drawn with every other triangle missing, when drawing triangle strips the 3D hardware internally flips the expected winding for each successive triangle. Effectively, the odd numbered entries in the strip are culled one way, and the even numbered entries another. This way, the surface is drawn correctly.

This does raise a problem for the triangle stripification algorithm, however. When generating strips, it is necessary to ensure that the vertex winding order is preserved. This can either be done by keeping track of the current expected winding order as the strip is built, or by examining the strip relative to the original triangles once it has been built. In either case, however, the winding order of a strip will be consistent, so the only required change will be to swap the winding order of the entire strip, providing that the source mesh did not include any triangles that were deliberately flipped relative to their neighbors. These cases can either be handled by treating edges between flipped triangles as unconnected during the strip generation itself, or by breaking and re-stitching the strips (a technique we will discuss later) when a flip)ed triangle is identified.

Flipping Winding Order Using Degenerate Triangles

Adding additional vertices to a strip can be very useful, as it allows the winding order to be deliberately manipulated and for strips to be stitched together. This technique relies on the fact that virtually all 3D hardware has a *fast reject* path for degenerate triangles, that is, triangles that have zero area, and hence will never be drawn. In the case of a triangle strip, a degenerate triangle is one in which two or more of the three vertices that comprise the triangle are identical (therefore making the triangle an infinitely thin line or a point).

This allows us to add additional vertices to a triangle strip which are never drawn, but still affect the winding order and the state of the strip itself. For example, if a strip is formed from numbered vertices as follows:

1,2,3,4,5

Then this will draw three triangles, formed of vertices (1, 2, 3), (2, 3, 4), and (3, 4, 5). In addition, assuming the winding order is initially clockwise, (1, 2, 3) and (3,

4, 5) will be drawn with clockwise winding order, while (2, 3, 4) will be drawn with counterclockwise winding order.

Inserting an additional vertex at the head of this list, however, enables us to flip the winding order of the entire strip without otherwise affecting the rendering (and with very minimal processing overhead). The strip:

```
1,1,2,3,4,5
```

produces four triangles: (1, 1, 2), (1, 2, 3), (2, 3, 4), and (3, 4, 5). The first of these is degenerate, as the index 1 appears twice, so it will be rejected by the hardware, leaving only the desired triangles. The presences of the extra triangle, however, causes a winding order flip, meaning that (1, 2, 3) and (3, 4, 5) will be drawn with counterclockwise winding, and (2, 3, 4) with clockwise winding.

This technique can be used to fix cases where the stripification has resulted in the winding order being incorrect for a strip, but it can also be used as a mechanism to stitch two strips together.

Merging Strips

Stitching two strips together is achieved by duplicating the last vertex of the previous strip and the first vertex of the next strip, allowing the transition from one to the other to take place without any valid triangles reaching the hardware. For example, given two strips (1, 2, 3, 4) and (6, 7, 8, 9), which contain the triangles (1, 2, 3), (2, 3, 4), (6, 7, 8), and (7, 8, 9), the following sequence of vertices indices is a single merged strip which will draw the same geometry:

```
1,2,3,4,4,6,6,7,8,9
```

This produces triangles (1, 2, 3), (2, 3, 4), (3, 4, 4), (4, 4, 6), (4, 6, 6), (6, 6, 7), (6, 7, 8), and (7, 8, 9), of which only the original four triangles are not degenerate. However, this may not produce the desired effect if used in conjunction with back-face culling, because unless the first strip contains an odd number of vertices, the second strip will start on an even-numbered entry, effectively reversing the winding order on it. To avoid this, in the case where the first strip length is even, either the last or first vertex must be duplicated a second time, giving:

```
1,2,3,4,4,4,6,6,7,8,9
```

This version now preserves the winding order correctly, rendering both original strips in the single combined strip. Merging strips together in this way can make a huge difference to the drawing efficiency, as sending small batches of vertices to the hardware is generally very inefficient. The overhead of processing the additional degenerate triangles and indices is insignificant compared to that of performing another API call or setting up data transfer to the GPU to process a new primitive.

Making Use of Draw-Cancel Flags

Some hardware (most notably Playstation 2) supports the concept of a draw-cancel flag. This is an additional bit stored for each vertex referenced, which determines if the triangle formed by that vertex and the previous two in the strip should be drawn. By inhibiting the output of undesired triangles in this way, it is possible to stitch strips together without requiring any additional vertices beyond the first two of the new strip (with one more if a winding order flip is also required). It should also be noted that the draw-cancel flag allows triangle strips to represent single triangles equally as efficiently as triangle lists, removing any incentive to support these separately.

In a multi-platform context, it may be desirable to output triangle strip data with either degenerate triangles or draw-cancel flags bridging strips depending on the target platform. Fortunately, it is fairly trivial to convert from one representation to the other.

Converting Draw-Cancel Flags into Degenerate Triangles

The process of converting draw-cancel flags into degenerate triangles is very straightforward. The basic procedure is to walk through the strip, and every time a draw-cancel flag is encountered, duplicate the previous index. In this way, the triangle that needs to be inhibited is converted into two degenerate triangles instead, but the behavior of the rest of the strip is unaffected. If winding order is important, then to preserve it the index must be duplicated twice, but the end result is the same. For example, consider the following strip (with draw-cancel indicated by the underlined index):

1,2,3,$\underline{4}$,5,6

This represents triangles (1, 2, 3), (3, 4, 5), and (4, 5, 6), with the triangle (2, 3, 4) inhibited. With the draw-cancel removed and an extra index inserted to produce a pair of degenerate triangles, the index list becomes:

1,2,3,3,4,5,6

As the triangles (2, 3, 3) and (3, 3, 4) are degenerate, those that are actually drawn are (1, 2, 3), (3, 4, 5), and (4, 5, 6)—the same as the original. To preserve winding order, the index is duplicated twice, giving:

```
1,2,3,3,3,4,5,6
```

which merely introduces an additional degenerate triangle (3, 3, 3). This technique works even if several draw-cancel bits are set in a row.

Converting Degenerate Triangles into Draw-Cancel Flags

The opposite conversion is slightly more complicated, and requires the data to be processed in two passes. In the first pass, degenerate triangles are identified and the draw-cancel flag set for them. This is performed simply by comparing every vertex index against the two previous indices. If any of the three are equal, then the triangle is degenerate. For example, taking the output of the previous conversion, and underlining the final index of the degenerate triangles (2, 3, 3), (3, 3, 3), and (3, 3, 4) gives the following:

```
1,2,3,3,3,4,5,6
```

This achieves the basic goal of setting the draw-cancel flag on the invisible triangles. However, as none of the extra vertices added to stitch the strips together have been removed, the resulting strip still contains the same number of indices, several of which are redundant. To remove these, a second pass through the strip is required, this time examining the draw-cancel flags.

On this pass, vertices with the draw-cancel flag set are removed if they do not form any part of a visible triangle. The obvious criteria for determining this is to look for places where two or more identical vertices occur together. In these cases, all but the first occurrence of the vertex will have their draw-cancel flags set (as the triangles they form are degenerate), and can be safely removed. In the case where strips have been bridged as described previously, this will correctly remove all of the unnecessary vertices from the input stream, leaving:

```
1,2,3,4,5,6
```

which is the original input data. However, there is an additional case in which a vertex may be redundant. If the draw-cancel flag is set on it and both of the subsequent vertices, then it can never form part of a visible triangle, and can be safely removed. If the input data has been processed in the manner described then this situation should never occur, however as it is very straightforward it is usually worth including a check for it just in case.

As with the conversion into degenerate triangle form, special care must be taken when converting back if winding order is to be preserved. Fortunately, the mechanism for ensuring this is again very straightforward: when removing vertices, only concurrent pairs can be safely eliminated. Otherwise, the winding order after that point in the strip will be reversed.

Strips versus Lists

While triangle strips are a highly efficient means to represent the geometry for mesh surfaces which are smooth and have large areas of connected triangles, they become less efficient as the strip length drops. If degenerate triangles are being used to bridge strips, then each bridge adds an additional four or five vertices to the strip, depending on whether a winding order flip is required (two or three extra vertices for the bridge itself, and then the first two vertices of the new strip). This means that a single isolated triangle in a strip will require either five or six vertices, as compared with only three in a simple triangle list. Once there are two connected triangles the strip is as efficient as a list (or slightly more), and beyond that the strip becomes more efficient.

As previously mentioned, on hardware where draw-cancel flags are supported, this is not a problem; no degenerate triangles are required, making strips just as efficient as lists. However, on hardware that does need degenerate triangles, it can sometimes provide a significant performance to move individual orphan triangles into a separate dedicated list, drawn at the same time as the strip by a second draw call. Assuming that the number of orphaned triangles is enough to justify the cost of performing two drawing operations, this enables the most efficient possible representation to be used wherever appropriate.

Triangle Fans

In addition to triangle strips, another primitive that is sometimes used is the triangle fan. A triangle fan is simply a series of triangles formed from a list containing a single vertex for the center of the fan, and then a number of vertices around the edge. In a similar way to triangle strips, each individually rendered triangle of the fan is formed of the current, previous, and the first vertex, an example of this is shown in Figure 6.2.

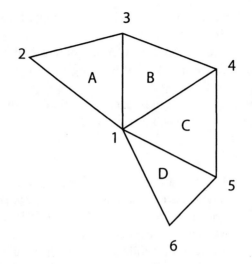

FIGURE 6.2   A triangle fan formed from six vertices (numbered).

Unlike strips, however, as the first vertex is always used as one of the points of the triangle, fans cannot be usefully stitched together into a single draw call, and draw-cancel or degenerate triangle use is generally pointless. Fans do have the useful properties, however, that they are generally the fastest way to render an arbitrary convex polygon with more than four sides (requiring only n vertices for an n-sided polygon), and unlike strips they do not require any winding order reversal.

In fact, from a pre-processing perspective, triangle fans can effectively be regarded as n-sided polygons. The layout of the vertices and the resulting visual effect are identical. It is usually only in cases where inaccuracies in the rendering output cause differences among the individual component triangles that it is necessary to consider the actual triangulated form. In these cases, the polygon can be subdivided as described later to minimize the visual errors.

Vertex Cache Optimization

The primary benefit of both vertex strips and lists is that they provide an explicit form of vertex caching. By reusing two previous vertices for each new triangle, the number of vertex transformations that must be performed for each triangle rendered is reduced from three to one. In addition to this, however, it is common for 3D hardware to also implement an explicit vertex caching scheme, usually in the form of a FIFO or LRU buffer which holds recently processed vertices in their transformed state. Cache entries are referenced by the vertex index (and hence, clearly, such caching systems are only able to operate on primitives that are specified by index streams rather than explicitly supplied vertices).

If the details of the caching structure are known (even roughly), then it is possible to use this knowledge to bias the process of generating triangle strips to make more efficient use of the cache. In virtually all such architectures, vertices that can be retrieved from the cache are effectively "free" in terms of transformation costs, so it may be worthwhile to prematurely break a strip if doing so allows a new strip to be started using mostly cached vertices.

As with the triangle stripping procedure itself, there are many different approaches to integrating this sort of metric into the algorithm. The most common technique, however, is to "emulate" the vertex cache as the strip is built, keeping track of which vertices are in the cache as each new vertex is added to the strip. This way, when considering where to start a new strip, the starting point that offers the most vertex reuse can be chosen. A hybrid solution is to assign a "score" to each possible starting point, calculated from a weighted sum of the number of reused vertices and the original strip criteria (such as triangle connectivity). The starting point with the highest score is then used to begin the next strip.

Determining cases in which it may be advantageous to terminate an existing strip in favor of a new one is somewhat more difficult than merely incorporating cache metrics into the creation of new strips, however, and as a result somewhat less widely used. There are two factors that must be carefully balanced: the potential benefit of reusing cached vertex data, and the costs in terms of additional bandwidth and memory used to transfer the vertices to bridge the strips. Due to the smaller number of bridge vertices required, hardware with support for draw-cancel flags generally requires a much smaller number of cached vertices to make this worthwhile.

The principle generally applied is broadly the same as when starting new strips, however. Before each new triangle is added to the strip, the cost of adding that triangle is compared with the cost of adding bridging vertices and restarting the strip at every candidate triangle with at least one cached vertex (the assumption is made that it will never be worthwhile breaking a strip to move to a starting point that is completely outside the cache). In order to do this, it may be necessary to look-ahead several triangles into both the potential new strips and the existing strip, to allow for the situation where several cached vertices can be reused on subsequent triangles. Once these costs have been calculated, the option with the lowest cost (or highest score, depending on the exact metrics chosen) can be used to continue the strip.

Optimizing in this manner for vertex cache behavior can give a dramatic performance boost, especially in the case of engines making use of programmable vertex shaders or techniques such as matrix skinning which have a high transformation cost per vertex.

Batch Caches

A variant on the standard FIFO or LRU cache which is sometimes encountered is a *batch cache*. This situation is most common on Playstation 2, where the vector unit architecture is designed around vertices being transformed in discrete chunks rather than as a single stream. In the case of a batch cache, vertices are normally sent and processed in an unindexed form, but a special flag can be used to tell the transformation code that instead of transforming a vertex again, it can reuse the transformed result from a previous vertex in the batch. This may be achieved either by keeping a FIFO cache internally and referencing from there, or by simply referencing the required previous vertex directly (by address or index within the batch). In the latter case (and sometimes in the former, depending on the exact architecture), only vertices that have been already processed as part of the current batch can be used as cache entries.

In both of these cases, the effect is the same: the benefits of having a vertex cache are realized without the necessity to actually handle the management of the cache in the vertex processing loop. Instead, the determination of which vertices to store and retrieve from the cache is made offline, allowing the vertex processor to simply retrieve the vertex data from the specified location when prompted.

The pre-processing necessary for a batch cache depends on the specific engine-level implementation, but in general it is fairly straightforward: once a list of indices forming a triangle strip (or other primitive) is generated, the system can walk through the list, dereferencing the indices and inserting the data for each vertex into the batches. By maintaining an emulation of the state of the transform cache, indices that are duplicates of those already transformed and within "cache range" can be inserted into the data stream as references instead.

With this post-processing step in place, the same cache emulation can be used during the triangle strip generation as well to ensure that the ordering of triangles suits the layout of the cache. In a batch cache it may sometimes be difficult to perform a precise emulation of the cache (if, for example, the triangle strip builder does not have guarantees on where the batch boundaries will fall within a strip), but basic heuristics such as "vertices that last occurred more than 60 indices ago will never be in the cache, and the probability of a vertex being cached increases the more recently it was used" can achieve most of the desired effect.

TRIANGLE LISTS

Most of the principles that apply to optimizing triangle strips to make best use of vertex caches also apply to indexed triangle lists. In fact, the process of optimizing triangle lists is made much simpler. In the absence of other factors (such as transparency sorting), the cache optimization process is free to rearrange triangles in any way required within the list to ensure the cache is utilized as much as possible. Doing this is a relatively straightforward process—again, emulating the cache behavior is the key, and as the cost of a given triangle is simply the sum of the vertex costs (which are in turn usually simply dependent on whether the vertex is present in the cache), it is often perfectly reasonable to perform a brute force test of every remaining triangle with at least one vertex in the cache to determine which to insert next.

In advanced cases, look-ahead can be added to improve the optimization this achieves, although this can make the performance of the brute force approach unacceptable even for offline processing. Fortunately, there is a relatively simple optimization that reduces the scope of the problem dramatically, and makes even fairly extensive look-ahead possible: as a precursor to the actual sorting procedure, the connectivity of the mesh can be examined and a table built of which triangles adjoin which others (in fact, an adjacency table is useful in many mesh pre-processing operations, so it may already exist at this point). Since unless the cache size is very large, the cached vertices will almost always be grouped in a relatively small connected area of the mesh, the search space for candidate triangles can be reduced to those that directly adjoin the current one, mimicking the surface walking behavior of the triangle stripification process. With this optimization in place, even very large meshes can be very quickly sorted for cache efficiency.

Depth Sorting

There is one other common reason for sorting triangles in lists, however, which is relatively rarely used for the bulk of the geometry in most games, but can be essential in certain cases. This is depth sorting, the process of arranging (single-sided, or back-face culled) triangles so that they are always drawn from front-to-back or back-to-front.

This trick originates from hardware that did not feature Z-buffers to enable objects to be implicitly depth sorted during rasterization, but is still useful even on most systems that do have pixel level depth comparisons. The reason for this is due to semitransparent, or alpha blended objects. Unlike solid surfaces, as the act of drawing these blends the incoming color with the pixel value stored in the frame buffer, they are order dependent—different drawing orders will alter the final result.

Therefore, in order to ensure that the appearance of alpha blended surfaces does not vary depending on the drawing order or viewing angle, it is necessary for the engine to sort them, usually into back-to-front order, before drawing. While inter-object sorting must be done at runtime (between moving objects, at least), polygon level sorting is usually too expensive to perform on a per frame basis. Fortunately, in the case of static single-sided objects (with no self intersections), the polygons can be sorted in such a way that the drawing order is consistent regardless of the viewing angle.

The mechanism for doing this is a very straightforward iterative process. The algorithm uses two lists of polygons, one for input and one for output, and simply loops over the input list, moving any polygon that cannot obscure any other to the end of the output list. Eventually, no more polygons that can be moved will be found, at which point any remaining entries in the input list are polygons that break the constraints set out earlier (generally by being degenerate or intersecting each other). Since polygons are only placed in the output list once all the polygons that they could have obscured have already been moved, drawing the polygons in the output list order will always result in back-to-front rendering.

The core of the algorithm is the test for determining if a polygon obscures another one. This test is viewing angle independent, and essentially determines if one polygon can ever (that is, for any viewing angle) obscure the other. There are two components to the test: determining the relative facing of the polygons, and then their relative positions.

The first step is necessary to filter out cases where polygons face in opposite directions (directly away or toward each other). If either of these is the case, then they can never obscure each other, as they will never be simultaneously visible (again, assuming that the polygons are single-sided). The test for this is very simple. If the dot product of the normals of the two polygons is greater than zero, then they are facing in the same direction and must be examined further to determine their relative positions. If the dot product is less than or equal to zero, however, then the polygons will never occlude each other and the test is complete.

In the case where the polygons face in the same direction, the next step is to examine their positions to determine which side of one the other lies on. Labeling the two polygons A and B, if polygon A is in front, then it will obscure B, and if it is behind, then it will be obscured by B at some viewing angles.

Testing the polygons to determine the side of A that B lies on is done by examining the angles between the A and the vertices of B. For each vertex in B, constructing a vector from a vertex of A (which one is irrelevant) to it and then taking the dot product of this vector with the normal of A gives an indication of where that vertex falls relative to A. If the dot product result is greater than zero, then it is in front of A, if it is less than zero it is behind. A dot product result of zero indicates that the vertex is coplanar with A.

Once each vertex of B has been tested in this way, the result can be calculated. If the vertices are all either in front or behind A, then B lies entirely on that side of

A and the test is complete. If, however, some vertices are on one side and some are on another, then B crosses the plane A occupies in space, and hence the result is inconclusive. In this case, then the trick is simply to repeat the test, swapping A and B and then inverting the final result. If B crosses the plane of A as well, then the polygons are intersecting and cannot be correctly sorted without being first sub-divided (a process which will be discussed later).

In general, vertices that are coplanar with A can be safely ignored when doing this check, as long as all of the remaining vertices of B are on one side of A, then that is the correct answer. However, in the case where all of the vertices are coplanar, then it is safe to assume that the polygons do not obscure each other, as they lie in the same plane, the only way they could do so is if they physically intersect, in which case the sorting will never be correct, and in many cases other visual errors such as Z-buffer artifacts will be visible as well.

Depth Sorting Double-Sided Polygons

As previously mentioned, this sorting approach cannot handle double-sided poly-gons directly, as their sort order will change depending on the viewing angle. How-ever, there is a very simple shortcut to avoid this problem if back-face culling can be used by the renderer, at the cost of some extra geometry.

The trick is simply to replace every double-sided polygon with two single-sided polygons before performing the sorting. The second single-sided duplicate polygon should have the winding order reversed from the original, and the normal flipped—this way, the polygon is now represented by two single-sided polygons facing in opposite directions. These can then be sorted correctly by the algorithm without requiring any further changes.

SANITIZING INPUT DATA

A fairly large majority of the algorithms for processing geometry data (including many of the algorithms described here), make assumptions about the topology and layout of the input data, such as requiring single-sided nonintersecting polygons or smooth connected surfaces. Sadly, these constraints are not enforced by most 3D modeling packages, and there are many additional oddities that frequently appear in the exported data from artist-generated models and can cause unexpected side effects if not handled correctly.

Fortunately, many of these problems are relatively minor, and the offending data can be removed or corrected without affecting the visual appearance of the model in any way. Cleaning model data at the start of a pipeline is often a very use-ful task as it both increases the robustness of subsequent processing operations and can improve the rendering performance of meshes by removing redundant data. The following are some of the most common problems encountered with model data.

Orphaned Data

In model formats that support indices for referencing vertices or polygons, it is not uncommon for the arrays of these items to include some which are never referenced! While this rarely causes a major problem, it consumes additional memory and processing time, and can occasionally have unexpected knock-on effects. For example, if a bounding box calculation tests every vertex in a mesh by walking through the vertex array, then it may produce a result that is larger than the actual mesh due to outlying vertices which are not used in a polygon and hence never drawn.

Fortunately, the solution to this is obvious enough: simply take every array of such data and build a list of which elements are referenced. Any which aren't can be removed, and the indices of subsequent items adjusted if necessary. This can often be useful when dealing with other mesh data as well, such as materials and skeleton nodes, which are sometimes also left orphaned.

Vertex Welding

In the cases of both indexed and unindexed input data, it is not uncommon for cases to occur where several vertices are almost but not quite, in exactly the same position. This can be caused by a number of factors, although the most common by far is that when the mesh was created the artist closed a gap between polygons by moving the edges of the gap together manually, leaving the vertices that were on either side in slightly different positions. The resulting error in the mesh often isn't visible when it is rendered normally, but can cause problems for further preprocessing steps. For example, vertex compression may move the two vertices apart, widening the gap, and triangle stripification algorithms will not be able to continue a strip across the boundary as it does not appear to be a continuous surface.

The solution to this is very straightforward: examine each vertex in the mesh, and if it is within a small tolerance (a few mm in engine coordinates, for example) of another then the two vertices can be considered to be the same. If this is the case, then the rogue vertex can be deleted and any references changed to point to the original, *welding* the vertices together to form a continuous surface. Determining which is the "rogue" can be done in many ways, such as choosing the vertex with the lowest surface connectivity. However, apart from exceptional cases it is largely irrelevant which algorithm is used for this, as the errors involved are so tiny that even just selecting at random will produce perfectly acceptable results under virtually all circumstances.

As well as vertex positions, the same welding algorithm can be applied to UV coordinates, normals, bone weights, and color information; in fact, virtually any of the data normally stored on a per vertex basis. If these are in separate streams with their own indices then each can be considered independently, but if they are in a combined vertex format then it is necessary to test all of the data, and only perform welding if there is no significant difference in any component of the vertex, otherwise the welding algorithm may destroy this information. In particular, care must be taken when welding vertices on meshes which are skinned or skeletally animated. If the bone indices and weights for each vertex are not compared then vertices that are attached to different bones (and hence may have radically different positions) might be welded together.

Removing Degenerate Triangles

Another common feature of input data that has been heavily hand edited are degenerate triangles, which have zero area as a result of being either a point (all three vertices are identical) or an infinitely thin line (two vertices are identical). Near degenerate triangles can also exist where the vertices are not precisely identical but in almost exactly the same position. Fortunately, if vertex welding is performed before degenerate triangle removal then these cases will become "truly" degenerate as the vertices concerned will be welded into each other.

Finding degenerate triangles of this type is exceptionally trivial, fortunately. All that is required is for each triangle in the input data to be examined, and if two or more of the vertices have identical positions then the triangle is degenerate and can be deleted. Note in general that it does not matter if other data, such as the UV coordinates or colors are different. If two vertices share the same position in space, then the triangle will never be visible (or may be visible as a point or broken line in some engines due to limited arithmetic precision) and it can be safely removed. The one exception to this, however, is if bone weights or data that affects the position in a similar way is different. In these cases, it is impossible to determine if the triangle is degenerate as the positions may be transformed differently by the engine.

One other case in which degenerate triangles may form an important part of the mesh is worth mentioning, because although it is covered by the previous statement, it is becoming increasingly common and the implications are not immediately obvious. One popular technique for forming shadows volumes from meshes (typically for stencil shadow rendering) is to extrude the mesh vertices if they are facing away from the light source, effectively pushing one side of the mesh back to infinity along the silhouette edges. Since the vertices of each triangle use the normal of the triangle (rather than a smoothed vertex normal) in this circumstance, the mesh "tears" along the silhouette edge as one triangle is pushed backwards and the adjacent triangle is not. In order to avoid this situation leaving holes in the resulting volume, additional triangles are inserted along every edge that might lie on the silhouette to close the gap.

In any case where both of the faces they adjoin are facing toward or away from the light, these edge triangles are degenerate and are not drawn, they only become visible when the edge is extruded. Therefore, when removing degenerate triangles from such a mesh, it is important to consider the normals of the vertices as well as their positions, as a difference in normals may cause the two vertices to be transformed differently (as one is extruded and the other is not).

Non-Coplanar Polygons

If the input data contains polygons with more than three sides (i.e., triangles), then it is possible for a polygon to be invalid as a result of the vertices not all lying in the same plane. This can be detected quite simply: taking any three vertices of the polygon will produce two vectors which are the basis vectors for a plane, in which all of the vertices should lie. There should be some tolerance in the calculation to account for precision errors, but if one or more vertices lie a significant distance from the plane, then this represents an error.

The seriousness of this depends on the number of errant vertices, the distance they lie from the plane, and the nature of the processing the mesh is going to undergo before rendering. The reason for this is simple: for rendering purposes (or possibly earlier in the pipeline), the polygon will be triangulated, in the process of which the polygon will be converted into a number of (hopefully) coplanar triangles. The resulting triangles will always be valid (as a triangle only contains three vertices, which therefore always form a single plane), but the exact shape of the resulting mesh will be determined by the manner in which the polygon was triangulated. This is one way to resolve the problem, but it runs the risk of hiding more serious errors as the resultant triangulation may not produce the shape the artist originally intended.

It is also possible to fix non-coplanar vertices without triangulating the polygon. In order to do this, the errant vertices must be moved so that they lie in the plane of the polygon. Of course, in order to do this, it is necessary to determine the "definitive" plane for the polygon, and then modify any vertices that do not lie on it. This definitive plane can be calculated in several ways: the most useful is to calculate the average of the plane equations of every triplet of vertices in the polygon, or simply select the plane in which the most vertices already lie.

Once the definitive plane has been determined, each errant vertex can be brought into line with the plane by taking the normal of the plane and solving the intersection point of the ray from the vertex along this with the plane to give the nearest point which lies on the plane.

Regardless of the approach taken to handling them, any non-trivial errors with non-coplanar polygons should be flagged for later investigation by an artist, as the probability is that the existence of such a surface is a sign of more serious errors in the mesh, and the results of these corrective measures will probably be different from what was originally intended.

REGULAR MESH SUBDIVISION

As well as the triangulation procedures described previously, there are many situations in which it is desirable to subdivide the polygons of an existing mesh in a regular fashion, for example, to provide a higher vertex density in order to improve the accuracy of vertex lighting, or to minimize the errors generated by clipping algorithms. In both of these cases, the goal of the subdivision is to generate a (fairly) even distribution of vertices (and hence polygons) across space, regardless of the relative positions of the original vertices.

Subdivision can be performed on an untriangulated mesh, but in most cases this is relatively undesirable. Triangles are significantly easier to manipulate, and since the overall goal is to ensure an even distribution of vertices in the final mesh, working at a higher level only makes this harder by abstracting the data being manipulated from the final results.

The basic process of mesh subdivision can be split into two steps: identifying the triangles that need subdividing, based on some criteria, and then performing the subdivision itself. This process can then be repeated to subdivide the resulting polygons, meaning that each step need only perform one level of subdivision.

Identifying if a triangle needs subdivision is usually a fairly straightforward process, the most common criteria for this is to subdivide all triangles with more than a certain surface area, or where one of the axes is longer than a certain value. This ensures that a minimum vertex density is maintained across the surface of the mesh.

The process for subdividing a triangle is most easily achieved by splitting it into four smaller triangles, each of equal area, by adding one vertex in the center of each edge of the triangle, and connecting them. If the original triangle is not regular, then the additional vertices along the edge can be shifted to make the distribution of the subdivided triangles more regular. One mechanism for doing this which generates a fairly regular subdivision is to take the shortest edge of the source triangle, and place a vertex half way along it, noting the distance this puts the new vertex along the edge. Then, place the vertices on the other two edges at the same distance along from the shortest edge. This creates three triangles of roughly regular dimensions (the exact ratios will depend on the angles of the sides of the original triangle), and a fourth which encompasses the remaining space in the triangle. This fourth triangle can then be subdivided again if necessary, until sufficient vertex density has been achieved. Figure 6.3 shows examples of both types of subdivision.

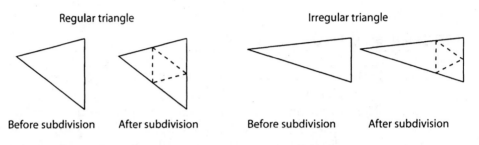

Regular triangle   Irregular triangle

Before subdivision   After subdivision   Before subdivision   After subdivision

FIGURE 6.3 Regular subdivision of regular and irregular triangles.

If an even more rigid vertex layout is required, it is possible to clip triangles to a set of predefined planes, for example, those placed on a regular grid through the mesh, to ensure that vertices always exist at the required positions.

Clipping Triangles

In order to do this, it is necessary to perform a subdivision on the triangles such that a new edge is generated along the desired clipping plane. The procedure for doing this is not too dissimilar from that required to uniformly subdivide a triangle, in many cases, the plane will intersect two of the edges of the polygon. These intersection points form the two additional vertices on this edge for the subdivision.

It is possible to pick a third point on the remaining edge, and then subdivide it in exactly the same way as for a regular subdivision. This will produce a valid triangle, but uses one more triangle in doing so than is needed if the only requirement is to subdivide along the clipping plane. Instead, two triangles can be used to create the quadrilateral formed by the two new points and the remaining edge. In this way, each input triangle becomes three once subdivided; subdividing in this manner can quickly become very expensive in terms of triangle count if a significant number of subdivisions are required. Figure 6.4 shows both of these types of clipping applied to a triangle.

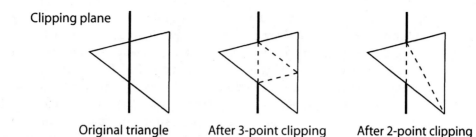

Clipping plane

Original triangle   After 3-point clipping   After 2-point clipping

FIGURE 6.4 Clipping a triangle to a plane.

There is one case that this algorithm does not handle, where the clipping plane passes directly through one of the vertices of the triangle. In this case, it is only necessary to split the triangle into two, by adding one additional vertex at the point where the plane intersects the opposite side. It may also be the case that the clipping plane passes through two of the vertices, in which case, it lies exactly along one of the edges of the triangle and no clipping is required.

Subdividing triangles by clipping in this way can be very useful when performing the depth sorting algorithm described previously. Since it is impossible to correctly sort intersecting polygons, it is necessary to subdivide them so that they do not intersect before performing the sorting procedure. With an algorithm such as this that allows triangles to be clipped to an arbitrary plane, this can be easily achieved by taking each pair of intersecting triangles and clipping each against the plane formed by the vertices of the other. This will result in a number of triangles which form an identical mesh but do not intersect, and hence can be depth sorted correctly.

It is also worth noting that actually clipping geometry to a given plane is as simple as performing this algorithm and removing the triangles formed on one side of the clipping plane. While this is not as common as the need to subdivide triangles, it can be useful for some preprocessing steps, such as eliminating invisible geometry inside meshes or generating shadow volumes.

Clipping Polygons

Although as mentioned previously, it is less useful for subdivision purposes, clipping a convex polygon to an arbitrary plane is a very similar procedure to clipping a triangle. All that is needed is to find the intersection points of the clipping plane with the edges of the polygon, add two vertices at these points, and then form two polygons from the result. There is no need to do any further processing as both polygons formed in this way can be immediately integrated back into the mesh, unlike the quadrilateral formed when clipping a triangle. Unlike when clipping a triangle, there is no special case logic required to handle the situation where the clipping plane passes through a vertex: simply leave the edges as is, and use the vertex already present to subdivide the polygon. Note that unlike in the triangle case, the clipping plane passing through two vertices does not guarantee that it lies along an existing edge. This case must be tested further by checking the two vertices against the polygon's edge list to determine if the clipping plane lies across the polygon or not.

Vertex Interpolation

The core of all of these clipping and subdivision algorithms is the addition of vertices to the mesh along the edges of existing triangles or polygons. In general, this is done by generating a vertex at a given fraction of the length along the edge, both regular subdivision and clipping tend to produce positions in this form, and when this is not the case it is simple to calculate this parametric distance value. If the distance along the edge is known as an absolute value, then simply divide this by the total edge length, and if the vertex position is known, then calculating the line equation of the edge and solving will give the distance.

Once the parametric distance is known, all that is required to generate the new vertex is to interpolate the vertex components using the distance as the interpolation fraction. Note that all of these operations are performed on the edge itself, and hence there are no differences between triangles and polygons. However, the exact procedure for performing this interpolation differs slightly depending on the nature of the different components.

Interpolating Vertex Positions and Normals

Vertex positions can simply be interpolated as individual X, Y, and Z values without any additional processing. In general, the same applies to normals, although they must be re-normalized following the interpolation. It should be noted, however, that virtually all lighting algorithms will cause different results to be generated at the added vertex compared to the original color at that point, regardless of the value of the interpolated normal. If this causes visual artifacts then additional processing may be necessary to remove them, as described later in this chapter.

Interpolating Vertex Colors

Interpolation of color values is simply a case of emulating the interpolation that the graphics hardware would normally perform if the triangle was not subdivided. In virtually all cases, Gouraud shading is being used, and hence simply interpolating the R, G, and B values independently will produce the desired results. For flat shading, obviously enough, no interpolation is necessary. Most advanced shading models (such as Phong shading) actually depend on other parameters than the vertex color, and hence have little impact on this interpolation. However, one common case which does occur is that where the hardware Gouraud shading is not perspective correct—PlayStation 2 being the most frequently encountered example of this.

The reason this causes a problem is because the interpolation is performed in 2D screen space rather than 3D world space (or a variant thereof). When a triangle is parallel to the screen, there is no difference in the results, but as it gets closer to being perpendicular the error resulting from the lack of perspective on the interpolation grows. This can be quite noticeable, especially in cases where large polygons are used to form landscapes or large walls.

Unfortunately, as the effect is view dependent, there is almost nothing that can be done about this during preprocessing. The "best" solution is simply to interpolate the vertex colors as if the Gouraud shading was perspective correct and hope that the visual discrepancies are not obvious! Fortunately, in most cases these artifacts are only noticeable where a subdivided triangle meets a larger (un-subdivided) one, and the interpolation errors create a color difference—this can be handled by subdividing the edges further to ensure a smooth match, as described later. Subdividing polygons or edges will never completely solve the problem, but by introducing additional perspective-correct vertices, the magnitude of the errors can be greatly reduced.

Interpolating Bone Information

While performing an interpolation for bone weights that produces exactly the same output as the renderer would is difficult and generally involves introducing additional bones, it is relatively straightforward to perform an interpolation which, while not necessarily mathematically perfect, is close enough for nearly all purposes. Subdividing a skinned mesh almost always involves performing additional edge match up steps to avoid tearing where vertices have been added, so getting a completely accurate solution is not normally necessary.

The process for doing this is simple: first read the indices for both of the original vertices on the edge. All of these will have an influence on the interpolated vertex, so their indices must all be stored for it. Then, for each of these, the weight can be calculated as a linear interpolation of the weights that bone had on each of the edge vertices, if it was not referenced by one, then assume that weight was zero. If desired, this final list of indices and weights can then be scanned for any bones that have a final weight of zero, and those removed (as they will have no effect on the vertex's position).

If the bone information is stored in a form other than a list of bones and weights (see the later discussion on bone data processing for some examples of these), then it is generally easiest to convert into an index/weight list for the interpolation, and then convert back again afterwards. However, it is much more desirable to perform any processing steps that involve adding vertices to the mesh before compression of any sort is applied, as it both makes the data harder to manipulate and can introduce unwanted quantization or errors.

Interpolating Texture Coordinates

Texture coordinates, like vertex positions, can usually be interpolated linearly without any additional processing. However, there is one case where this is not true: on some graphics hardware (most notably PC graphics cards which support DirectX 8), the GPU can be set up such that polygons always use the shortest section of texture possible when drawn. In other words, in a polygon where one vertex has texture coordinates of (0.9, 0.0) and another has (0.1, 0.0), the area mapped will extend *across the wrap* (a distance of 0.2) rather than stretching backwards across the whole texture (a distance of 0.8).

If this mode is in use, therefore, when interpolating texture coordinates it is necessary to emulate this behavior as well. Fortunately, this is very easy: all that is necessary is for each of the elements of the texture coordinate, calculate the distance (in texture space) between the two original vertices on the edge, and if it is greater than half of the texture size (or 0.5, if normalized texture coordinates are in use), then the lower of the two values should have the texture size added to it before interpolation. Then, if the interpolated values is greater than the texture size (or 1.0), subtract the size (again, or 1.0) to bring it back into range.

In some cases, usually on very old or comparatively underpowered hardware (or software renderers), texture mapping may not have perspective correction applied to it. This results in the same problems that occur with Gouraud shading—as the mapping is view-dependent, it is impossible to fully correct for this except in the renderer itself. However, as in the Gouraud shading case, subdivision of adjacent edges can help reduce the visual artifacts generated to an acceptable level.

Interpolating Other Data

The vast majority of other data usually stored per vertex, such as material properties, bump map tangent vectors, or vertex occlusion values, can be interpolated in one of the ways described above. In most cases, the rule of thumb is to perform interpolation in the same way the renderer does. This will ensure that the pixels on either side of the subdivided edge match as closely as possible. However, there are cases (such as perspective correction problems) where it is impossible to fully ensure that the interpolated vertex on the newly subdivided edge matches the appearance that point would have had before the subdivision occurred.

Edge Match Up

This problem of edge match up occurs primarily when two triangles are adjacent, and one is subdivided in such a way as to insert an additional vertex along the shared edge. This means that when the surface is rendered, the two sides of the edge will appear different if the renderer's interpolation of the pixels is altered by the extra vertex. In cases where this discrepancy cannot be solved by altering the attributes of the vertex, the easiest way to avoid an obvious "seam" along the edge is to subdivide the adjacent polygon edge as well, adding the extra vertex to it and thereby ensuring that the renderer produces consistent results for both sides. In fact, for reasons we will discuss shortly, for many types of mesh this addition subdivision is also crucial because of the effect it has of maintaining the original surface topology.

In the case of a polygon mesh, this procedure is very straightforward: simply identify the polygon(s) that share the subdivided edge, and insert the extra vertex that was added into each. This operation (as with most subdivision) is best performed after vertex welding has been applied to the mesh, as otherwise some adjacent polygons may be overlooked due to slight variations in the vertex positions.

For a triangle mesh, the only difference is that the extra vertex cannot simply be inserted into the adjacent triangles, it is necessary to divide them in two. However, this subdivision need only affect the already subdivided edge, and hence it will not cause any "knock-on" effects forcing the subdivision of more triangles. Effectively, the subdivision can be performed in exactly the same manner as in the case when clipping a triangle to a plane that passes through one of the vertex (that which does not adjoin the subdivided edge).

Another reason for performing this additional edge match up subdivision on adjacent polygons is that it preserves the surface continuity. If an edge is split on one polygon only, then moving the interpolated vertex will cause a tear in the mesh. This is essential if further processing such as level of detail reduction or shadow volume extraction is to be performed on the mesh, and it can vastly improve the performance of algorithms such as triangle stripification by increasing the connectivity of each polygon.

Texture Space Clipping

Although most useful operations on meshes work are achieved by performing clipping based on the actual vertex positions, there is no reason that clipping cannot be performed in the spaces generated by virtually any of the vertex attributes.

Most of the time, these are fairly pointless operations. However, there is one exception, namely clipping in the 2D space formed by the mesh texture coordinates.

The reason this is useful is because it enables constraints on the texture coordinates to be enforced without altering the original appearance of the mesh. For example, some hardware only allows texture coordinates within a certain range, which can place limitations on the number of times a texture can be tiled across a surface or the mappings that artists can generate. By clipping the texture coordinates, the mesh can be subdivided such that they are always kept within range by adding additional geometry to, for example, extend the effective number of times a texture can be wrapped by resetting the coordinates half way across a polygon.

Clipping in texture space (or the space of any other attribute) is virtually identical to the procedure already described, with the only exception being the initial generation of the parametric coordinates. Instead of solving the equation of a clipping plane against the vertex positions to get the edge intersection points, texture space clipping solves the equation of the clipping plane (or, more often, clipping line, as texture coordinates are usually 2D) against the texture coordinates of each vertex. Once the intersection points have been determined, the rest of the process is performed as normal.

All that is then necessary, in the case of clipping in texture space to clamp texture coordinates, is a final step to fix up the texture coordinates of the clipped polygon so that they are brought back into range. It should be noted that in this particular case, it will probably be necessary to duplicate the interpolated vertices, as the polygon on one side will be at one end of the available range, and the polygon on the other will be at the beginning.

Unfortunately, this technique, while useful, is not perfect. If the renderer performs bilinear filtering then there will be a noticeable seam along the clipped vertices where the sampled texels extend beyond the edge of the texture. In some cases this can be avoided by bringing the clipping region in so that it does not extend fully to the hardware coordinate limits, but it can often be quite difficult to avoid at least some artifacts of the process. Also, this process can quickly generate a lot of additional geometry if highly tiled textures are used; it may actually be beneficial to set an upper limit on the subdivision that will be performed so that very large surfaces (water or ground planes, for example) do not get subdivided into huge numbers of polygons! The cost of these additional polygons is also hidden to some degree to the artists creating the original models, so it is wise to ensure that they are aware that using textures in certain ways can cause performance problems.

Edge Creation during Subdivision

One complicating factor to be aware of when doing any operation that creates edges within an existing triangle or polygon, be it subdivision, triangulation, or clipping, is that the linear interpolation used for vertex elements such as vertex coloring can be altered by the newly created edges. The classic example of this is the case of a quadrilateral with two red corners, and two blue corners, opposite each other. If this is subdivided into two triangles, then the orientation of the resulting edge will determine the color of the central point. If the edge is between the two red corners, then it will be red, if it is between the two blue corners, then it will be blue.

Under most circumstances, this problem is not worth worrying about as in real-world meshes it is rare to get such a significant difference in color over the surface of a single primitive, and even in the case where it does occur, there is no way to determine which answer is "right." However, it is worth being aware of as it may cause the occasional visual artifact, particularly if complex surfaces are heavily subdivided, and in those cases it may be necessary to adjust the source artwork to hide the problem, or bias the algorithm so that the orientation of additional edges is more consistent.

GEOMETRY COMPRESSION

Geometry compression is generally used in situations where the meshes have a sufficiently high number of vertices and polygons that they represent a significant amount of memory. However, as with texture compression, the saving achieved is actually twofold: not only is the storage required for the geometry reduced but also the amount of data that is transferred to the GPU to render the model. In many cases, this latter benefit is actually the primary goal of geometry compression.

The primary target of geometry compression is generally the vertices themselves. As the polygon data in most schemes contains little more than a list of vertex indices, there is generally little potential for savings (beyond, in some cases, using 8-bit or 16-bit indices where possible). In general, this vertex compression is achieved by quantizing the source data, trading accuracy for storage space. While this approach does not necessarily yield the highest possible compression ratios, it allows the vertices to still be easily referenced at random and decompression is a very straightforward task.

Compressing Vertex Positions

In most cases, vertex position data can be trivially reduced to a triplet of n-bit X, Y, and Z values. To achieve this, the extents of the model need to be determined, essentially, the minimum and maximum position on each of the three axes. With this information, a new coordinate system can then be defined, which maps the range of the compressed values (−32767 to 32768 in the case of signed 16-bit values, for example) onto the original dimensions of the model. The simplest mechanism for defining this is to calculate the center point of the model (the average of the minimum and maximum values on each axis), and the size (the difference between the minimum and maximum values on each axis). This gives an offset (the center point) and scale factor (half of the size) for each axis to map from the original co-ordinate space into the compressed coordinate space. With this mapping, decom-pression is just the reverse of compression.

For the vast majority of models, using 16-bit vertex coordinates in this way shows no perceptible loss in quality over 32-bit floating point values. In some cases, it may be possible to reduce the data even further—12-bit indices still give accept-able accuracy (4096 discrete vertex positions on each axis) for many smaller objects, and in some cases even 8-bit indices may be acceptable.

The level of quality degradation caused by quantizing the vertices like this depends on the nature of the input data. For small models, it is unlikely that the precision loss will be at all noticeable. Larger models will show the effects more, although in the case of a single mesh it is still relatively unlikely that it will be obvi-ous, unless there are areas of very high detail. Since the quantization applied to each vertex is the same, for a well-formed mesh the process will not generate any seams or cracks, as the surface topology will be preserved. Some care is required, however, when dealing with meshes that may potentially already contain hairline cracks. These need to be removed before compression using one of the techniques de-scribed later, as otherwise the vertex movement can expand them into wider seams.

Adjoining Meshes

However, what is much more of a potential problem is the effect that the precision loss has on meshes which adjoin each other. The problem arises when two meshes are built so that they meet each other in such a way as to form an apparently seam-less boundary. Typical cases for this are walls built in sections and "stuck together" later, or even simply buildings placed onto a landscape mesh.

In this case, what can happen is that the vertices on the meshes are compressed differently, with the effect that the vertices along the join between the two end up in slightly different positions after decompression. This can cause a noticeable crack where the two pieces of geometry no longer meet, or a similar overlapping section. The size of this crack can reach up to just under the average of the distance between the quantized points in the compressed meshes (that is, the size of the bounding box divided by the number of discrete vertex positions offered by the chosen coor-dinate size), so while the problem is relatively minor for small meshes, on larger geometry the effect can be very noticeable, especially on areas like walls where even hairline cracks are generally a problem. There are various solutions to this problem, although to solve it completely for all cases generally requires an increase in the res-olution of the stored vertices, unfortunately.

The simplest solution is to do just this: as the maximum size of the crack (or overlap) is inversely proportional to the resolution of the vertices, increasing it therefore makes the error less noticeable. This can be very simply achieved, although clearly it reduces the benefits of the compression process! Also, it will never completely eliminate the problem unless the vertex resolution is increased back to the pre-compression level, so the geometry edges will never match up perfectly.

The second solution does solve that problem, guaranteeing that there are no cracks or overlaps introduced by the compression. However, it does so at the expense of some resolution within the mesh, and can only be used in situations where the relative positions of the two meshes are known in advance. Essentially, the trick is to ensure that the quantized vertex positions for the two meshes line up with each other, hence guaranteeing that coincident vertices will still have the same position after compression.

This can be done by manipulating the bounding boxes of the meshes prior to the compression process. In order for the vertices to line up, the bounding boxes must both have the same dimensions, so that the size of one "unit" in the compressed coordinate space (that is, the size of that axis of the bounding box divided by the number of discrete vertex positions offered by the chosen resolution) is the same. Therefore the sizes of the two individual bounding boxes are calculated, and a *composite* bounding box formed using the largest size for each axis. Once this is determined, the size of each axis needs to be expanded by two units to account for the fact that the center point of the box will be shifted slightly to align it. (Note that this operation will change the size of the compressed coordinate space, and hence the size of a unit!) This then gives the size of a bounding box which can encompass either mesh, and hence can be used as the bounding box size for both.

With the size of the bounding box determined, all that is left is to locate the center points. In order that the vertex positions line up, the center points for the two meshes must lie a distance which is a whole number of compressed space units apart on each axis. Therefore, starting with the original bounding box centers, the distance between them on each axis is calculated, and one or both points moved to ensure that this value can be divided by the unit size. As the bounding boxes were expanded earlier, this adjustment will not result in any vertices falling outside of them.

This technique can be used for more than two meshes if necessary, simply by taking the largest axis from all of the bounding boxes, and ensuring that the resulting bounding box center points all lie a whole number of units from each other. The loss in precision that results from doing this depends on the relative sizes of the objects, as the precision on smaller objects will effectively be reduced to the level of the largest, minus a small amount for the bounding box expansion.

BONE WEIGHT PROCESSING

Skinned meshes are one of the most commonly used techniques for rendering characters, cloth, and other deformable objects. For the variety of uses and the level of control it offers over the deformation of geometry, the actual implementation is deceptively simple. Essentially, the mesh geometry is attached to a skeleton, a collection of bones, each of which has a position and orientation in space (in general, bones are simply nodes of the object hierarchy that have no associated mesh data). Each vertex in the skin mesh is attached to one or more of these bones, which causes it to move with them. In the case where a vertex is attached to more than one bone, each has an influence, or weight, which is used to blend the contribution that bone makes to the final vertex position. In this way, the mesh can smoothly transition from being rigidly attached to one bone to being rigidly attached to another, introducing seams or tears in the geometry.

In the case of a "classic" skinned mesh renderer, each vertex has an associated set of bone references (usually in the form of indices into a list of bones), and weights for each. This is the format most 3D packages output skinning data in, so it rarely requires any processing to be usable in-game. However, it is usually desirable to perform at least some clean up and optimization on this data, as the output will often contain errors that do not affect the appearance of the mesh, but can dramatically reduce the engine performance.

Removing Redundant Bone Associations

Since each vertex has a weight for each bone it is attached to, it is possible for bones to be attached with a weight of zero, in which case they do not contribute at all to the final position of the vertex. Unfortunately, it is quite common for 3D software to generate bones like this during mesh modification, so filtering the data to remove them is frequently necessary. In addition, under virtually all circumstances (the exception being when one bone has a vastly larger range of motion to the others), any bone with a small weight value (less than 0.05, for example) will make such a negligible difference to the vertex that it can be safely discarded as well. When removing bones with weights other than zero, however, it is necessary to re-normalize the other weights afterwards.

Limiting the Number of Bone Associations

In addition to removing entirely redundant bones from vertices, many engines impose a restriction on the overall number of bones that can be bound to each vertex. Actually removing bones from the vertex is simple (although, as mentioned previously, re-normalization will be required afterwards), so all that remains is to identify which bones to remove, a task most simply achieved by sorting the bones by their weights, and then removing those with the lowest weights until the required number is left.

Normalizing Bone Weights

When rendering, for performance reasons vertex skinning calculations usually require that the bone weights for each vertex are normalized, in other words, that they sum to exactly one. While most 3D formats follow this convention, it is useful to re-normalize bone weights in the processing pipeline, both as a safety measure in case the input data was not normalized, and also to correct any errors introduced by removal of bone associations or weight adjustments in other processing.

The normalization procedure is exactly as would be expected, simply add the weights of all the bones to get the total weight, and then divide every weight by that total.

Using Pre-Multiplied Bones

For performance, some renderers operate by pre-multiplying the bone matrices by a set of weights, rather than repeating the multiplication for the weights on each vertex. This obviously restricts the available weights to those generated during this pre-multiplication process, and as a result the weights used by the bones must be quantized to these values.

In general this is quite straightforward, simply move each weight to the nearest available pre-multiplied value. Ideally, the input values should be normalized at this point, which will cause the result to also be normalized.

A variant on this technique is the use of *bone slots*. This is a technique whereby weights are discarded entirely from the vertex, and a list of a fixed number of bone indices is stored instead. Each of these "slots" is assumed to have an equal weight (so, for example, if there are three slots each has a weight of ⅓), and a bone index may appear in more than one slot. Therefore, with three slots, a vertex can be bound entirely to one bone, with a weight of ⅓ to one and ⅔ to another, or with weights of ⅓ to each of three bones.

To generate the bone data for these slots, an iterative process is needed. For each slot, take the bone with the highest weight in the input data, and insert it into the slot. Then subtract the slot's weight from the bone weight, and repeat the process for the next slot. The resulting approximation will (for low numbers of slots) lose some of the subtlety of the original weights, but for many uses the performance boost is worth the accuracy trade off.

Constructing Composite Bones

In some cases, particularly where skinning is supported in the graphics hardware, the system may only support rigid binding, that is, where each vertex is attached to only one bone. In this situation, it may be necessary to emulate blending by generating additional bones that perform the transform normally carried out by two or more of the original bones when blended together.

Generating the initial input data for such as system is the same as when supporting a renderer which uses pre-multiplied bones or bone slots. However, once this is prepared any vertices that are bound to more than one bone must have a composite bone created for them.

In most engines, the actual matrices for these composite bones are calculated at runtime, as the position of the bones is not known in advance. Hence, the composite bone simply stores the bone indices and weights used to create it, and the vertex bone index is set to point to it. However, in some cases if pre-generated animation data alone is being used for the model, and the skinning is performed in local space, then it may be practical to pre-calculate the composite bone matrices for each frame of the animation.

Since the input data is generated from a set of bones with quantized weights, many of the composite bones required will most likely be identical, and hence one composite can be used for a number of vertices. This dramatically reduces the amount of CPU time and memory required at runtime to generate and store the composite bones.

Subdividing Skinned Meshes

A common constraint on skinned mesh renderers, often imposed by the limited amount of memory available for storing bone matrices, is that only a certain number of bones may be used on the vertices drawn in a single batch. To work around this restriction, it is necessary to subdivide the mesh so that no individual section uses more than the available number of bones.

In addition to simply reducing the bones used to an acceptable level, there are two additional goals when performing this subdivision. First, the number of sections (and hence individual draw operations) should be kept to a minimum. Second, the primitives within each section should be organized as efficiently as possible, to avoid the overhead of unnecessary additional geometry.

Fortunately, in virtually all cases there is a high degree of overlap between these goals, due to the fact that the bones and vertices on the mesh are generally quite tightly coupled spatially, that is, vertices are most likely to be bound to the bone(s) nearest to them. Therefore, exploiting this makes generating an efficient subdivided mesh quite straightforward.

The process starts by creating a new empty mesh, and a blank list of associated bones. Then, all of the primitives of the input mesh are examined, and the bone that is referenced most is copied into the bone list for the new mesh.

An iterative process then starts to build the new mesh. First, any primitives in the original mesh that only reference bones found in the bone list for the new mesh are moved across into the new mesh itself. Then, taking the remaining primitives that reference at least one bone in the new mesh, a frequency table is built of how often each as yet unused bone is referenced. The most frequently referenced bone is then copied into the new bone list and the process repeats until either the maximum number of bones in the new mesh is reached, or there are no primitives left in the source mesh.

Once one new subdivided mesh has been built like this, the entire procedure can then be repeated to create the next, until there are no primitives left in the original mesh. Due to the spatial coupling of vertices and bones, and the fact that each successive bone added to the mesh is sharing the most vertices with an existing bone, the resulting mesh will tend to form a large connected area of the mesh, with a relatively minimal number of orphaned primitives, thereby greatly improving the performance of triangle stripification and similar algorithms.

It should be noted that this procedure operates primarily on primitives, not vertices. This is necessary because a vertex may be shared among several primitives, and so can be duplicated into several of the subdivided meshes if the connected primitives are placed differently.

Rigid-Bound Sections

On renderers where skinning is an expensive operation (for example, if it is performed in software), it may be worthwhile to also subdivide skinned meshes to extract any sections that are actually rigid, that is, where the vertices are bound entirely to one bone. Typically, sections of characters such as heads or hands fall into this category, especially on lower detail meshes. These can be simply rendered using the standard pipeline and the bone's matrix as the transformation for the whole mesh.

In cases where the skinning process is hardware accelerated, the performance impact of drawing an additional mesh to implement this may counteract any benefits gained. For these cases, the best solution is to determine roughly what the overhead per vertex of the skinning system is, and therefore how many vertices need to be transformed before the cost of the additional draw operation is amortized. Then, the preprocessor can split any rigid sections with more than this number of vertices into a separate mesh.

BUILDING BOUNDING VOLUMES

As well as being a prerequisite for many types of object level culling and collision detection solutions, bounding volumes can also be useful during pre-processing, for example, to determine the extents of a mesh for vertex compression. There are many different types of bounding volumes which can be generated, and it is often useful to pre-generate more than one, for use under different circumstances.

In all cases, the goal of a bounding volume is the same: to be as small as possible while still enclosing the entirety of the original mesh. This is easier to achieve in some cases than others, and many of the problems of bounding volume generation can only be "solved" through brute force. However, as long as it encompasses the entire mesh, a bounding volume is still valid, and hence a "good enough" solution is still acceptable, even if it is not optimal.

Axis-Aligned Bounding Boxes

Axis-aligned bounding boxes are the simplest to generate, and also the most generally useful, consisting of a box center point and extents, which are aligned (as the name suggests) to the axes of the current coordinate space. To calculate an axis-aligned bounding box, simply run through all of the vertices of the source data, keeping track of the maximum and minimum values encountered on each axis. The bounding box is then centered at the midpoint of these values, with dimensions of half the difference between the maximum and minimum for each axis. For a given mesh (and orientation) this will always be the smallest possible axis-aligned bounding box, and hence no further optimization is possible.

Bounding Spheres

Bounding spheres are very useful as they can be tested for collisions with other primitives extremely quickly. Bounding spheres consist simply of a center point and a radius, which makes them rotationally independent, thereby simplifying the required intersection calculations significantly. In many engines, it is not uncommon to use the bounding sphere as a quick test for collisions before comparing bounding boxes.

Calculating the bounding sphere that gives the tightest fit over a given mesh is a difficult problem, and there is no solution which is guaranteed to give an optimal result short of using brute force and testing every possibility. Specifically, the problem is that of selecting the center of the sphere. The radius of the bounding sphere for any given center point is simply the longest distance between that point and any vertex. The best fit sphere for the mesh is, logically enough, that which has the smallest radius, such as the one shown in Figure 6.5.

One naïve approach to selecting the center point, which generally produces acceptable (but not particularly optimal) results with minimal effort is to take the center of the axis-aligned bounding box for the mesh. As the center of the bounding box is generally roughly the center of the mesh, this usually gives a relatively

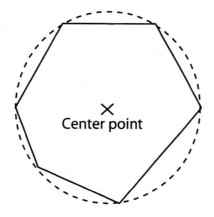

FIGURE 6.5 The smallest bounding sphere for a mesh.

tight fit for meshes which are single, compact shapes. The advantage of this approach is that it requires almost no effort if the axis-aligned bounding box is already known, all that is required is a single pass through the vertices to find the furthest point and calculate the radius.

A more advanced form of this approach, which produces quite tight-fitting spheres for most meshes, works by taking advantage of the fact that after the center point has been placed initially, it can be moved so to minimize the radius, until a local minima for the sphere has been found, effectively, the point where it is impossible to shrink the sphere any further around that point.

To do this, after the initial center point is calculated (again, using the center of the axis-aligned bounding box is a good choice for this), the radius and most distant vertex of the mesh are found. This vertex (or vertices, if several lie the same distance from the center) is the limiting factor on the radius; to reduce it the center point must be moved closer to the vertex.

While there are analytical methods that can be employed to determine how to move the center point, these are largely useful only in the trivial cases (where only one or two vertices are on or near the edge of the sphere), as for larger numbers the problem becomes intractable in the same way as the original bounding sphere problem is. Since a precise solution is not required, therefore, a much simpler but almost as optimal solution can be used.

The approach is simply to randomly select a direction that lies roughly toward the vertices on the sphere edge, and move a fixed distance in it. Then, recalculate the radius and if it has increased, return to the original point and try a different direction, reducing the movement distance slightly. Once the distance to move has dropped below a threshold (1% of the radius, for example), then stop searching as the point found is probably within that threshold of the local minima.

Selecting a direction based on the edge vertices need not be a particularly accurate procedure: simply taking the maximum and minimum values on each axis of the vectors from the center to those vertices and choosing a random value between these limits is one simple approach that works well. In fact, simply choosing a direction entirely at random also works, although this requires more iterations of the process to achieve the same results.

When recalculating the radius for the new center point, there is one optimization that can save a great deal of time with this algorithm. The majority of the time, it is the sphere edge vertices that will determine the new radius, and so by testing these points first (and abandoning the move if one of them produces a radius larger than the previous one), the need to do a costly check of every vertex in the mesh is removed.

Oriented Bounding Boxes

Oriented bounding boxes are very similar to axis-aligned bounding boxes, with one critical difference, namely that in addition to a center point and extents, they also include a set of basis vectors which describe the space the bounding box occupies. Oriented bounding boxes have the advantage over axis-aligned bounding boxes that they can be a much better fit in cases where the mesh is not broadly in line with the axes, and they can be easily rotated with the mesh as it moves, since there is no requirement to keep the bounding box aligned to the coordinate space axes.

The actual procedure for building an oriented bounding box is based on the same principles as that for building an axis-aligned one. However, the key decision that needs to be made is the set of vectors that will form the basis for the bounding box, in other words, the orientation of the box relative to the mesh itself. If the bounding box is oriented such that the axes of the box fall along the natural "sides" of the mesh, then it will be much more efficient than one which is at an angle relative to the mesh. Figure 6.6 shows three possible bounding boxes for a shape: the axis aligned case, a bounding box that is oriented poorly, resulting in a larger than necessary size, and a bounding box that has been orientated to tightly fit the shape, resulting in the most optimal size.

One obvious method for doing this is to use an iterative search, as is used when finding the minimum bounding sphere. This approach can work reasonably quickly and produce good (albeit not optimal) results in most cases. First, a center point for the bounding box is required, the average point along each axis of all the vertex positions is generally a good choice. Then, all that is required is to generate

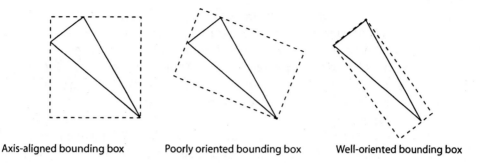

Axis-aligned bounding box   Poorly oriented bounding box   Well-oriented bounding box

FIGURE 6.6 The effect of different bounding box orientations.

set of random orthogonal normalized vectors, which are used as the initial basis vectors for the bounding box.

The next step is that the extents of the resulting bounding box on each axis need to be calculated. This is easily enough done by calculating the minimum and maximum values along each of the axes, the dot product of the vertex position and the axis basis vector will give the distance that the vertex lies along the axis. The maximum distance along each axis between any vertex and the center point gives the extent for that axis.

This process can then be repeated, rotating the basis vectors an amount in a number of (random) directions, and comparing the extents of the result. The new orientation that gives the smallest total extents is chosen, and the process repeats with increasingly small random rotations until a threshold is reached. The final set of basis vectors and extents are then used (together with the initially calculated center point) to form the bounding box.

Aside from the iterative method, the other commonly used technique for doing this is based on statistical analysis. By fitting the layout of the vertices along each axis to an anisotropic Gaussian distribution, a set of basis vectors which represent a likely best fit of the bounding box can be calculated. To do this, a center point for the bounding box is calculated first (again, this is simply the average of all the vertex coordinates).

Next, the *covariance matrix* can be computed. The covariance matrix is a 3×3 matrix representing the average distribution of the vertices on each axis. It can be calculated for a single vertex *(x, y, z)* as follows:

$$x*x \qquad x*y \qquad x*z$$
$$y*x \qquad y*y \qquad y*z$$
$$z*x \qquad z*y \qquad z*z$$

The covariance matrix for the entire set of vertices is simply the average of all the individual matrices, in other words, each element is the sum of the values given above for all of the vertices, divided by the number of vertices. Once the covariance matrix is found, the basis vectors for the bounding box can be found by taking the eigenvectors of the matrix, and then normalizing them. The resulting vectors will be orthogonal to each other, and hence can be used directly as the axes of the bounding box.

With the axes calculated, all that is necessary to complete the bounding box is to determine the bounds themselves. This can be done in exactly the same manner as described for the iterative generation process.

The primary disadvantage that both of these techniques suffer from is that they can be affected by vertices that are internal to the mesh (which will have no impact on the bounding volume), as well as clusters of vertices on the exterior. In the case of the iterative approach, this affects the initial center point calculation, while the statistical method can be easily biased toward a suboptimal orientation as a result of such extraneous vertices.

The problem of interior vertices can be solved by calculating a convex hull for the mesh, and then using this to build the bounding box. Only vertices that are on the hull can affect the box, and this approach improves both the quality and performance of the algorithm, albeit at the not insignificant cost of requiring a convex hull to be constructed first.

The second problem (that of clusters of external vertices) is generally less significant (particularly if a convex hull is used to provide the input data), but can be combated by using the triangles in the source data as input instead of just the vertices, and performing a regular sampling of the surface to build the input points, thereby ensuring that there are no uneven clusters. However, this can considerably increase the amount of processing required, and the resulting gain in bounding box quality is rarely worthwhile.

Convex Hulls

The final type of bounding volume commonly encountered in games is the convex hull—as the name suggests, this is a single, solid convex volume that covers the surface polygons of a mesh, in much the same way that wrapping it in plastic film would. Convex hulls are useful for collision detection and occlusion testing, as they form a very tight fit to the original mesh, but have the useful properties of being convex (and therefore easy to test for collisions), and generally have much lower polygon counts than the original mesh, as interior detail has been removed.

An example of a convex hull can be seen in Figure 6.7. The hull follows the shape of convex sections of the original mesh exactly, but concave areas are "wrapped" in the closest possible convex approximation of the shape.

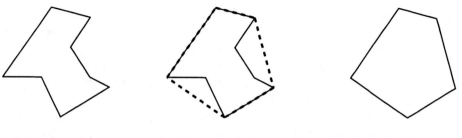

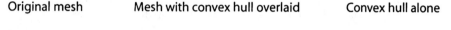

Original mesh   Mesh with convex hull overlaid   Convex hull alone

FIGURE 6.7   The convex hull of a concave mesh.

Unlike the other bounding volumes discussed here, convex hulls are unusual in that rather than being a fixed shape, the volume itself is essentially a mesh of arbitrary complexity. A convex hull is formed from a series of intersecting planes, the volume created on the inside of which is the interior of the hull. The surface of the volume is formed by the planes themselves, each clipped to the surrounding planes. The polygons this creates forms the mesh of the hull.

A convex hull for an object can be constructed from the set of vertices that form the mesh. Given this set of vertices, a simple brute force method for finding the convex hull is to examine every possible triangle that can be formed from these points, and if all of the other vertices lie on one side of that triangle, then the plane it occupies must form part of the hull. By repeating this, the complete set of planes can be found.

One optimization which can be made to this approach (and any other convex hull algorithm) is to reduce the number of vertices in the source data by eliminating those which can never be part of the surface of the volume. This can be achieved by calculating an interior bounding volume (as described later), and then removing all the vertices that lie within that volume (note that vertices on the surface of the interior volume may still contribute to the hull).

There are many different algorithms for performing convex hull generation faster than the brute force approach, each with their own distinct advantages and disadvantages. Further details of several different algorithms and analysis of their execution times can be found in [O'Rourke98]. Two of the most commonly used algorithms, however, are the gift wrapping approach and the incremental algorithm.

The Gift Wrapping Algorithm

The gift wrapping algorithm for computing a convex hull works on a very simple principle. Given a triangle which is known to lie on the hull, it follows that each of the edges of that triangle must be connected to another triangle which also forms part of the hull. Furthermore, those triangles must each be formed by the two vertices on the edge, and one other from the mesh.

Thus, in order to test one of those triangles, it is only necessary to test every other point in the mesh and determine if the triangle it forms in conjunction with the edge is part of the hull. Even using the same test as before (check if every point in the mesh lies on the same side of the triangle), this is still a significant saving in workload over having to examine every *possible* triangle in the brute force approach. However, the technique can be refined even further.

The key to this is that the interior angle formed at the edge between the existing hull triangle and the next point on the hull will be greater than that formed with any other vertex. Hence, all that is required to actually find the next triangle on the hull is to calculate this angle for every vertex in the mesh, and choose the vertex that produces the largest angle to complete the triangle. This dramatically reduces both the complexity and scope of the calculation required.

Since each new triangle found will provide a further set of edges to examine (remember that some edges will adjoin onto hull triangles that have already been found), the gift wrapping algorithm can easily walk across the hull until all of the triangles have been found, hence the name. The only difficulty is in finding the initial hull triangle. However, there is a useful trick which can be used to speed this up considerably as well.

The trick works by first moving the problem into 2D so instead of finding a polygon to start from, we simply find an edge. Ignoring the Z coordinate for now, the first step is to find a vertex that is guaranteed to lie on the hull, in this case, the vertex with the minimum X coordinate (the vertices which appear at the extremes of every axis must form part of the hull surface). Then, the 2D version of the convex hull algorithm can be employed to find an edge that lies on the hull. Taking the angle on the XY plane between every vertex and a vertical line (a theoretical "previous edge" which is guaranteed not to intersect the mesh as it lies at the minimum X extent), the vertex which generates the largest interior angle is found. The edge formed between this and the original vertex is guaranteed to be part of the hull both in the 2D XY plane, and in the 3D mesh.

Then, this edge can be used as the starting point for the 3D gift wrapping procedure. As this edge is part of the 2D convex hull in the XY plane, the interior angle for each candidate vertex can be calculated against the plane formed by this line in the Z axis (imagine that the third point of the "previous triangle" was formed by taking one of the edge points and displacing it in the Z axis). Once the first "real" triangle on the hull has been found, the gift wrapping procedure can then simply walk across the hull surface as described previously.

The gift wrapping algorithm is quite easy to implement, and scales well, particularly in cases where the resulting hull is simple. However, it can be very awkward to debug as the correctness of the output of intermediate steps in the procedure cannot be easily determined, and it can only be performed on complete meshes.

The Incremental Algorithm

The incremental algorithm works by starting with an existing hull (generally a tiny cube, tetrahedron, or even a simple double-faced triangle located at one of the existing vertices), and then expanding it by adding each vertex in the mesh in turn. The expansion procedure is quite straightforward, and mainly relies on calculating the angle between each face of the hull and the vertices.

As mentioned previously, since the hull is convex, no triangles on the hull can ever lie in front of another. Therefore, the first step when adding a vertex is to determine which hull triangles it is in front of, this can be determined with the dot product or a winding order test as before. If the new vertex is behind every triangle in the hull, then it is on the interior and can be discarded. Otherwise, it lies outside the hull and must be added to it.

There are two obvious steps to doing this: creating the new triangles to link this vertex to the hull, and then removing the triangles from the old hull which are on the interior of the newly formed one. In fact, though, it is actually easier to do these operations in the reverse order, removing the internal triangles first.

As stated before, triangles will be internal to the hull if there is another triangle in front of it. It therefore follows that a triangle will be internal if there is any *vertex* in front of it. Therefore, to determine which triangles need to be removed, all that is needed is to find those that have a vertex in front of them, and since only one vertex has been added to the hull (and no triangle could have had a vertex in front of it before), it is only necessary to test against the newly added vertex.

From this, it can be seen that the list of triangles that must be removed are those which the new vertex lies in front of—the same list that was initially calculated to determine if the vertex lay within the volume. Thus, no calculation at all is actually needed, and the triangles in question can simply be deleted.

Once these triangles have been removed, the task of adding the triangles to join the new vertex to the hull is greatly simplified. The removed triangles will have left a hole in the surface of the hull, and it is the edges of this hole that need to be connected to the new vertex. All that is needed is to walk through the list of triangles in the hull, and find any that have one or more unconnected edges. Then, a new triangle can be added comprised of this edge and the new vertex.

Once this is done, the hull will be a fully connected surface again, and the procedure can be repeated for the next vertex. Once all the vertices in the mesh have been processed, the hull is complete.

The incremental algorithm is relatively straightforward to implement, and as the hull should always be valid after each vertex is added, debugging can be significantly easier than with the gift wrapping approach, as each step can be checked to ensure the result is correct. In addition, the incremental algorithm lends itself well to building composite hulls and similar, as additional vertices can be added to an existing hull at any time. Merging two hulls is thus simply a case of adding the vertices in one to the other, as with any mesh.

There is a variation on the incremental hull building algorithm known as the *QuickHull* algorithm. This works in broadly the same way, but uses a data structure that records for each vertex which triangle on the hull it is in front of (if there is more than one, then the closest is used). Then, rather than selecting the next vertex to add at random, a polygon that lies on the current hull exterior is chosen (at random) and the vertex that is farthest in front of it (in terms of perpendicular distance from the polygon) is used to expand the hull.

As triangles are deleted, the vertices assigned to them are either reassigned to whichever of the newly created triangles they lie in front of, or deleted if they now lie inside the volume. This method quite dramatically improves the performance of the algorithm, by deliberately picking vertices that are likely to lie on the extremities of the mesh first, eliminating as many interior points as possible, and using the vertex/triangle association to minimize the number of facing tests required.

Hull Surface Triangles

One interesting problem that can arise when constructing convex hulls using any method is when a number of coplanar triangles form part of the hull surface. The subdivision these can cause does not actually form a useful part of the hull, and the extra vertices introduced are not part of the set of extremities of the mesh. Therefore, it can be a very useful post-processing step on any convex hull to check for any coplanar triangles, and merge those found into a single larger polygon (or simply discard them if only the planes of the hull are being used).

Interior Bounding Volumes

In addition to bounding volumes that are guaranteed to encompass the entire mesh but may contain some space which is not inside the mesh, there is another type of bounding volume that can be useful. Interior bounding volumes are volumes that cover the space which is guaranteed to be inside the mesh, that is, they contain no unused space at all. Interior bounding volumes are useful for many reasons: in collision detection, they provide a quick-accept path; if the interior volumes of two meshes collide then they are certain to be colliding. They can also be used for occlusion culling, to calculate the area of space that the mesh itself occludes, without any possibility of objects inside or behind the volume being visible.

Unlike the procedure for creating normal bounding volumes, where the goal is to optimize the volume so that it is a small as possible, interior volumes are optimized so as to be as large as possible, yet still fit entirely within the original mesh.

The first step in finding an interior bounding volume is to determine a point that is definitely inside the mesh. If the mesh is a continuous, closed surface (which it generally has to be for the interior volume to be valid at all), then this can be done using a ray crossing test. This is done by casting a ray from a point outside the extents of the mesh to a point inside it, and keeping a counter that is altered for each polygon that the ray crosses. If the polygon is facing in the same direction as the ray, the counter is decremented. If the polygon is facing in the opposite direction, however, then the counter is incremented. Assuming the initial count was zero, a positive value indicates that the point being tested is inside the mesh.

Interior Detail Removal

One of the useful properties of interior bounding volumes is that they can be used to identify elements of a mesh that are entirely contained within the model, and therefore can never be seen. While in general these should not exist in the first place, it is not at all uncommon for models to be built and modified in such a way that polygons are left in positions where they are entirely invisible. Removing these can provide a small but potentially important increase in performance for little cost.

Removing entirely interior polygons can be done simply by testing the vertices of each polygon against the interior bounding volume of the object. If all the vertices lie within the volume, then the polygon will never be visible and can be removed. If any vertex lies outside, then the polygon is visible. In the case where some of the vertices lie exactly on the volume surface and others do not, then the polygon will be visible if the remaining vertices are outside the volume, and invisible if they lie inside it.

Polygons whose vertices all lie on the surface of the volume, however, must be treated carefully. There are two possible scenarios that can arise here: either the polygon forms part of the volume surface, or it is stretched between two points on different parts of the volume. In the former case the polygon will be visible, and in the latter it will be invisible. As the volume is convex, any line connecting two points on the surface will be entirely within the volume. To test for this, simply calculate the plane equation of the vertex and compare it to the plane equation for each plane that forms the inner volume. If any match, then the polygon is part of the surface.

In addition, if back-face culling is in operation, and the polygon is facing inwards (toward the center of the volume), then it can be safely removed, as the only angles it could be visible from place it behind the volume.

It is possible to use the polygon clipping techniques described earlier to clip partially obscured polygons so that only the section that falls outside the inner volume is drawn. However, in virtually all cases this is not worthwhile, as the extra polygons generated by the clipping operation cost more to draw than the occluded area. In general, the only time this is useful is when working with a renderer that requires triangles to be non-intersecting, to perform depth sorting, for example, in which case doing the clipping to the inner volume allows the interior sections of the clipped polygon to be easily removed.

Transparency and Bounding Volumes

One area where special care needs to be taken is in the case where meshes can contain textures with alpha channels or other transparency effects. If these are in use, then it may be necessary to discard polygons which have transparent textures when generating the inner volumes. In the case of collision detection routines, this is probably unimportant (as transparent polygons are generally considered to be solid), but for occlusion culling the transparency may allow the viewer to see through part of the inner volume, meaning that it is no longer guaranteed to occlude anything behind it.

Generating Multiple Bounding Volumes

In most circumstances, a single bounding volume is generated for each mesh, especially since the usual goal of these volumes is to provide fast tests for collision and occlusion, generating many volumes often defeats the purpose by adding more complexity and costing CPU time.

However, there are some cases where having several bounding volumes on a single mesh is desirable, for example, if the mesh is very large, or if the volumes are to be used for actual collision checks (rather than just quick-reject or quick-accept optimizations). For these cases, the difficulty is in determining where to position the bounding volumes on the mesh to achieve the most optimal coverage with the minimum number of volumes.

As with many of the bounding volume construction problems, getting a completely optimal solution for doing so is a largely intractable problem, especially since the exact trade-off between the number of volumes used and the efficiency of each depends on the way in which they are being used.

One solution which works very well for generating sets of bounding volumes on most normal meshes is to subdivide the mesh surface into sections, and generate a bounding volume for each section. This can be done by exploiting the surface connectivity of the mesh, and using the efficiency of the volume being created as a metric for deciding how to expand the mesh.

The process is quite simple: an empty mesh is created (the *volume mesh*), which will contain the set of polygons to use to form the volume. Then, a randomly chosen polygon from the original mesh is moved into the volume mesh, and the corresponding bounding volume calculated. After that, each of the polygons adjacent to the polygon now in the volume mesh is examined, and the impact adding it to the volume would have calculated. The polygon with the highest efficiency (that is, the polygon that makes the best use of the volume) is then added to the volume, and the process repeated, with all of the polygons adjacent to any of the polygons in the new volume mesh being considered.

This process will therefore "walk" across the mesh surface, constructing a volume until it runs out of connected polygons. By putting a lower bound on the *efficiency* a candidate polygon must have before it can be added to the volume mesh, the process can be stopped once it is no longer viable to continue adding to the current volume, and a new volume started.

Calculating the efficiency of a polygon is dependent on the type of bounding volume being generated, but in general it is quite straightforward. The simplest metric is to compare the area of the polygon with the increase it causes in the size of the bounding volume. This gives a very rough measure of how much wasted space is introduced by the polygon, if the area is low but the volume size increase high, then it is not very efficient. On the other hand, if the area is high and the volume size increase low, then the polygon is already mostly contained in the volume and therefore adding it is very efficient. Clearly, if the volume size increase is zero, then the polygon already lies entirely within the volume, and adding it carries no cost.

Since this algorithm makes use of the surface connectivity of the mesh, it is highly resistant to building volumes which include polygons from two disparate areas of the mesh, and will tend to form bounding volumes around logical chunks of the input structure. It may also be able to use additional contextual information to bias the split decision if some is available, for example, by breaking the mesh along texture boundaries, thereby potentially saving it from being split twice.

Bounding Volume Hierarchies

It is often the case that in addition to bounding volumes on each individual mesh section in a larger model, it is also useful to have a bounding volume on the whole of the model, to enable it to be quickly rejected from culling or collision queries without having to test all of the sub-meshes. In turn, collections of models (for example, all those in a room, or the individual parts of a larger structure such as a building) may in turn also have an overall bounding volume for the same reason, enabling even more coarse grained tests to be performed.

Essentially, these bounding volumes form a hierarchy, with each parent volume fully enclosing all of its children in the tree. Rejection of any volume in the tree from a test automatically rejects all of the child volumes as well (while it is possible to build hierarchies of inner bounding volumes, they are generally not very useful as the area covered by the parent volumes is so small as to be worthless).

Generating bounding volume hierarchies is very straightforward, as it is possible to use the child volumes as the input data to generate the parent volume (rather than having to re-process the mesh). This serves two purposes: it makes the volume calculation significantly faster, and it guarantees that the parent volume always fully encloses the child volumes. Otherwise, some volume generation methods (such as the bounding sphere center calculation) might result in a tighter fit around mesh areas being achieved by the parent volume than the child volume! While this is not a problem in theory (as both volumes still encompass the entire original mesh), it can lead to some very unusual situations where the parent volume can be quick-rejected but the child volume cannot.

Since the amount of data generated by even a sizable number of bounding volumes is significantly less than that generated by a small mesh, the simplest solution to constructing bounding volumes from other bounding volumes is often the best. With the exception of bounding spheres, all of the volume types discussed can be represented as a polygon mesh, or a collection of vertices forming the points of such. Hence, the parent volume can be formed by converting the child volumes into a mesh, and then using that as the input data instead, applying the same procedure used for the original mesh. Although this is a less efficient method in most cases for constructing the parent volume, as the number of polygons generated is typically very small there is little to be gained from using a more complex approach.

As noted previously, a slightly different tactic is needed for dealing with bounding spheres, as they cannot be easily reduced to a polygon form (a polygonal sphere will never be a completely accurate representation of the true bounding sphere, although it gets closer as the number of polygons increases). Fortunately, it is not necessary to do this, as a relatively simple modification to the original algorithm can be used to allow input data consisting of spheres in their "center and radius" notation.

The required change is to the calculation of the radius of the generated volume, used at each step of the iteration. When using a normal mesh as input, the radius required to encompass any given vertex is simply the distance between it and the center of the bounding sphere. The radius of the bounding sphere for that center point is therefore the largest such distance.

When using spheres as input, however, the center point of each sphere is used instead of the vertices of the mesh. Hence, the size of bounding sphere required to encompass each sphere is the distance to the center point plus the radius. By using this metric to calculate the radius when it is required by the algorithm, the bounding sphere generated will contain all of the spheres given as input.

Bounding Volumes for Animated Meshes

All of the techniques described thus far make the implicit assumption that the mesh in question is static, and hence the bounding volume must also be static. Unfortunately, in most games there will be a fairly large number of animated meshes, such as characters, that do not conform to this. As a result, a strategy for handling animated meshes is also necessary.

The simplest type of mesh animation, hierarchical animation or node-based animation, is by far, the easiest to handle. As each individual node of the hierarchy is a single rigid mesh, a bounding volume can be calculated per node, and then either combined at runtime to generate an overall bounding volume based on the animation pose, or simply left as is and tested against with the node transform applied. In either case, no additional preprocessing effort is required to create the bounding volumes.

Mesh animation, or vertex animation (where the actual vertices of the mesh are animated) is more problematic. In most cases, vertex animation is stored as a number of individual meshes representing the key frames of the animation, which are blended between at runtime. Fortunately, this gives two very useful properties which can be exploited to generate the required bounding volumes. First, the key frames represent the extremes of the animation: no vertex will ever be able to travel to a point outside the extents of a key frame. Second, the key frames represent every state the animation can reach, therefore if a bounding volume is known for each, the overall bounding volume can be calculated.

From this, there are two approaches that can be taken. In many cases, such as a character run animation, the motion does not significantly change the shape of the bounding volume, and hence there is little merit in adjusting the volume at runtime to get a better fit for individual frames of the animation. For these cases, the preprocessor can simply generate the bounding volume for the whole animation, by either calculating the volume for each frame and then constructing a parent volume that encompasses all of these, or by considering every separate key frame mesh as being one large mesh when building the volume. The resulting overall volume will still be a fairly good match for the mesh in all circumstances, and the storage and processing required at runtime is the same as for an unanimated mesh. This approach also has the advantage that the bounding volume does not ever change suddenly, which can cause serious problems for collision systems in some circumstances by generating collisions between objects which are not the direct result of the object moving in the world.

The second approach is more useful in cases where the object does change shape significantly during the animation, for example, if a character "morphs" into an animal. In this case, the bounding volume for each key frame can be·calculated and stored separately, and then recombined at runtime to form a volume for the current animation frame. This is done, quite simply, by combining the volumes from the key frames currently being interpolated (in theory, the volumes could also be interpolated, but the extra computation for this is rarely worthwhile). This combination can either be performed in the same manner as the offline volume generation, in the case of simple volumes such as axis-aligned bounding boxes, or just by testing against both volumes and combining the results.

Aside from vertex animation, there are other cases in which the vertices of a mesh may move after the mesh has been generated. Some of these cases are due to procedural effects (for example, rippling waves on the surface of water) generated at runtime, and hence cannot be accurately predicted by the preprocessor. In these cases, the best solution is generally either not to generate a volume at all and let the engine build one if required, or to pick some arbitrary value for the expected size of the movement and extend the volume by that distance! Generally, these situations are sufficiently rare that "solutions" such as these will not have a particularly adverse affect on performance. However, there is one case in which meshes are deformed by the engine that is common enough to warrant a more complex solution—skinned meshes.

Bounding Volumes for Skinned Meshes

Skinned meshes are an unusual case in that while their vertices are manipulated by the engine, the information it uses to do so is (usually) all available to the mesh preprocessing task. As a result, it is possible to generate bounding volumes for skinned meshes in much the same manner as those for vertex animated meshes, and thus avoid the cost of having to compute volumes at runtime.

The first, and most obvious solution to this problem, is to allow the preprocessor to perform the skinning calculation itself. In this way, it can take each key frame of the animation (which will be represented by a set of bone positions), transform the mesh in the same way as it would be at runtime for that pose, and then calculate a bounding volume for the result. As with vertex animation, these volumes can either be stored separately and references according to the current animation frame, or combined to form one composite volume for the entire animation.

This approach has the advantage that it can be relatively easily implemented, particularly if an existing system for handling vertex animation is available, and it mimics exactly the final output, giving the best possible fit for the bounding volume. However, care must be taken to perform the skinning calculation in the same manner as the engine will (for example, if compressed vertex formats or reduced numbers of bones are in use), otherwise differences between the calculations may cause errors. In cases where the bounding volume accuracy is vital, it may even be necessary to add a small amount to the size of the volume to account for precision or order of operation errors.

The disadvantage of pre-calculating the final vertices for each animation frame when skinning is that this approach only works if the animations are being played back in a "canned" fashion, exactly as they were created. Increasingly, games are using more advanced techniques for character animation, blending several animation sequences into one skeleton, applying physics or procedural animation modifiers, colliding individual bones to avoid characters interpenetrating, etc. Under these circumstances, there is no easy way to predict the final positions bones will assume when the game is actually running.

Bone Bounding Volumes

This leads us one of the most useful techniques for skinned meshes: applying bounding volumes to the bones instead of the mesh itself. This way, the bounding volumes can track the mesh, no matter how the bones themselves move. While this technique does not generate volumes that are absolutely guaranteed to contain the mesh in all circumstances, in general the results are good enough for virtually any practical purpose. With some care, errors can be kept both small in magnitude and very infrequent.

Clearly, the bones themselves have no actual shape, and so cannot be used to generate the bounding volumes. Instead, the mesh information for vertices that are bound to that bone is used to build the volume, taking advantage of the fact that in the vast majority of cases, vertices are attached mostly to a single bone. Vertices which are blended evenly between two or more are comparatively rare in normal meshes.

When building the volume, the first step is to remove any polygon that is not attached in any way to the current bone. After this has been done, the vertices of each polygon need to be examined to determine how they may move during animation. Since this bounding volume calculation is taking place in the space of the current bone (and therefore it is the frame of reference for all the subsequent operations), the weight it has can be used as a measure of how much a vertex can potentially move within that space. A vertex that has a weight of one for the current bone is rigidly bound to it and will never move, while lower weights indicate a higher likelihood (and probable distance) of movement.

Calculating the range of this movement can be done in several ways: a simple solution that works surprisingly well for normal meshes such as characters is to take a sensible value for the *maximum* range of motion (for example, half of the size of the mesh), and then multiply that by one minus the bone weight. This gives a distance within which the vertex could be reasonably expected to stay, unless the model is animated in a very unusual fashion.

This distance can then be used to calculate the bounding volume by considering each vertex as being a bounding sphere, with a radius equal to its potential range of motion. The bounding volume calculation can then be performed either by calculating a series of points on the surface of these spheres as input (these can be quite coarse, as the values being used are only an approximation at best) to one of the standard mesh bounding volume algorithms, or using a more specialized technique such as the parent bounding sphere calculation described earlier.

Another approach is to take the canned animations that the preprocessing tool does have access to and use them calculate the maximum range, this makes the assumption that while the bones may move differently, the overall range of motion exhibited by the animation will remain roughly constant. This can be done simply by calculating the transformed position of the vertex for each frame of the animation, and then either measuring the distance from the position if the vertex is transformed with the current bone alone, or transforming the resulting position back into the space of the bone, which then gives an exact position for the skinned vertex. If this approach is taken, then it may be enough to simply insert all of the possible vertex or polygons generated in this fashion into the mesh before generating the bounding volume.

This technique works very well (and generates significantly smaller bounding volumes than the first approach) in situations where the model is primarily using canned animation data, with only animation blending or some small adjustments (such as matching foot positions to different foot heights) applied. It tends to break down, however, if rag doll physics or other large scale procedural modifications are made to the bones, as these can often generate positions much more extreme that those seen in the source data.

The final approach can be employed if the model only uses jointed animations (that is, bones are connected by joints, and do not move or scale outside the skeleton), and/or some external source of information about bone constraints, such as the input data for a character IK system, is available. In this case, it is possible to pre-calculate every possible configuration of bones that the constraints will allow, and use this data to compute the bounding volume. This can be done in much the same way as when canned animations are used, except that it is only necessary to consider the relative movement of the bones attached to the current vertex or polygon, thereby considerably reducing the scope of the problem.

With only two bones in consideration, it is only necessary to recurse over each degree of freedom of the joint between them (or the composite of the joints linking them) to determine the possible range of motion. If more than two bones are involved then the calculation becomes more time consuming, as each bone will introduce at least one additional degree of freedom. However, only a very coarse level representation of the possible positions is needed, thereby (usually) keeping the calculation within sane bounds.

With some constraint systems, it may also be possible to simply extract the range of motion of the joint, and then apply this to the vertex position, calculating a radius of movement rather than a set of actual positions. With this data, the bounding volume can be calculated in the same way as discussed for the first, most primitive, technique.

As with many of the bounding volume calculation techniques, it may be desirable to add a small margin for error to the calculated volume size. This obviously reduces the efficiency of the volume somewhat, but with the benefit of reducing the potential for errors. The trade-off here will depend on the specifics of the engine being used, and the nature of the input model, more than anything.

Performing Vertex Compression with Animated Bounding Volumes

One point worth discussing is the use of animated bounding volumes alongside vertex compression. In the case of skinned meshes (or meshes subject to other procedural deformations), it is almost always the case that the vertices are decompressed prior to the skinning calculation actually taking place. Therefore, the compression does not need to take any animation of the mesh into account! Therefore, it is usually worthwhile calculating a separate bounding volume based solely on the source mesh (ignoring any skinning information) for compression purposes.

In the case of vertex animated meshes, however, the vertex data being compressed does differ for each animation frame. Therefore, the logical (and most efficient) approach is to calculate a bounding box for each frame of the animation, and use that for the compression. However, this leads to an undesirable side effect: as the size of the bounding box changes, the positions of every compressed vertex (even those not actually moving) shift slightly as the quantization pushes them to slightly different positions. The end result is that as the mesh animates, the entire surface appears to wobble or shimmer.

Fortunately, it is very straightforward to counteract this effect. Instead of using a separate bounding volume for every frame of the animation, simply calculate a single composite volume for the whole animation, and use that for all of the frames. That way, the quantization effect on the vertices is constant, and unmoving vertices stay in their original positions.

MESH HIERARCHY PROCESSING

As mentioned previously, as well as processing on the individual meshes which make up a model, there are some processing operations that can be performed on the hierarchy of nodes that define the structure of the model. These operations are generally more limited, but they can be equally as important as the geometry processing, especially in the cases of optimizations. It is frequently the case that the overheads of calculating the transforms, setting up, and issuing the draw call for a single mesh node far outweigh the actual cost of drawing the polygons!

Unlike the majority of mesh processing operations, however, hierarchy processing generally requires more "domain knowledge"—that is, information about how the model is going to be used in the game. This is because it is frequently the case that hierarchy nodes are manipulated directly by the code at runtime, and hence unwanted modifications to them can cause side effects, particularly in the case of system such as rag doll physics, where the exact structure of the model is important for the calculations.

The feedback mechanism for making this information available to the processing tools varies depending on the structure of the asset pipeline, the desired processing, and how the models are being manipulated, but in general what is required is for each node in a mesh to be marked if the node's transform is going to be manipulated (that is, its position, orientation, or scale change) at runtime, or if the transform is going to be used to position another object (for example, in the case of a marker to indicate where a character should hold an item). With this information and the animation and structure information contained in the mesh itself, it becomes possible to perform some intelligent optimizations on the nodes.

Collapsing Nodes

It is quite common for hierarchies to contain nodes that are entirely redundant, i.e., they contain no geometry of their own, and serve merely to provide transformation data for their children. In particular, character skeletons frequently contain many nodes that are used to provide easy control over the movements of joints, but serve no purpose outside the content creation package.

Determining if a node can be removed is simply a case of examining it to see if it contains any geometry, is flagged as being modifiable or readable at runtime, or is referenced by another part of the model (for example, if it is a bone that is used by a skinned mesh elsewhere). If none of these conditions are true, and the node is not the root node of the hierarchy or a leaf node, then it can be safely removed.

The removal procedure consists of two steps: first the transform of the node being removed is concatenated into the transforms of each of its children. If the nodes are animated, then this step needs to be performed for each frame of the animation. This ensures that the children will be correctly positioned even when the node has been removed (after the concatenation, the node effectively has an identity transform matrix). The second step is to actually remove the node from the hierarchy, making its children become children of its parent. This process can be seen in Figure 6.8.

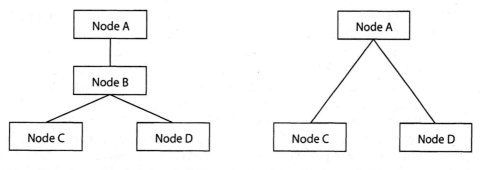

Hierarchy prior to removal of node B   Hierarchy after node B has been removed

FIGURE 6.8   Removing a node from the mesh hierarchy.

The reason that the root and leaf nodes of the hierarchy cannot be collapsed in this manner is obvious: collapsing the root node could potentially result in many new root nodes being formed (if the data format and engine can cope with this, then this may actually be a valid hierarchy, but it is unusual for this to be the case), and collapsing leaf nodes is redundant as they have no children to propagate their transform to.

Removing Leaf Nodes

Therefore, leaf nodes which fulfill the criteria described above (contain no geometry, and are not referenced by either code or other mesh nodes) can simply be removed entirely. In addition, the action of removing a node may in turn cause another node which meets these conditions to become a leaf node, allowing it to be removed as well. Hence, it is important to check the parents of removed nodes, or scan the hierarchy repeatedly until all of the possible leaves have been removed.

Merging Nodes

If two nodes which contain geometry never move relative to one another, then they can be merged together to create a single combined node containing both sets of geometry. This operation can significantly reduce the number of nodes in many meshes, especially if there is little or no animation involved.

The procedure for testing if two nodes can be merged starts by determining if either of the nodes can be safely removed. The criteria for removing a node are almost exactly the same as those for collapsing it: the node must not be read or modified at runtime, or referenced by another part of the mesh. In addition, the node which the removed node is being merged into must not be modifiable at runtime, as in that case the relative position of it to the node being removed cannot be guaranteed. It can still be read at runtime, or referenced from elsewhere in the mesh, however.

The second, and slightly more involved, test to determine if the nodes can be merged is to check if there is any node in the hierarchy that can be modified at runtime in such a way as to affect one of the pair but not the other. The first step in doing this is to find the first common parent of the two nodes, by walking up the tree and building a list of all of the parents of each, and then finding the first node which appears in both lists. This parent is the root of the minimal sub-tree which contains both nodes.

Once the first common parent is found, the nodes on each list below (but not including) that parent must be examined. If any of these are modifiable at runtime, then it is possible that one node may move independently of the other, and hence the merging cannot be performed.

If the second test succeeds, then the final test is to check if the two nodes are static relative to each other. Clearly, if neither node is animated, or has an animated parent (at any point between it and the root node), then they are obviously static, and this test can be skipped. If this is not the case, however, then it is necessary to determine if the animation ever causes the two nodes to move independently.

While in some cases it may be possible to derive this information from the hierarchy itself (specifically, if the path linking the two nodes through their common parent always produces a constant transform when all of the node transformations are concatenated together), it is generally easier to simply calculate the transformations of the two nodes in the local space of the object (or relative to the root node) for each key frame in the animation. Then, the transformation required to map from the space of one node to the other can be calculated by multiplying one node's transform with the inverse of the other. If this matches (to within a small margin of error to account for accuracy problems), then the nodes are relatively static and hence can be merged.

The actual process of merging the node is quite straightforward. The geometry from the node being removed needs to be copied into the other, and the vertices transformed from the coordinate space of the source into that of the destination. This can be achieved simply by taking each vertex and using the transformation previously calculated as part of the node comparison, which maps from one to the other (the transform of the source node concatenated with the inverse transform of the destination node, specifically).

Once the geometry is merged, the source node is left with no geometry. Assuming that the criteria for doing so are met, this can then be removed using the procedure previously described for collapsing nodes which contain only transformation data.

LEVEL OF DETAIL SIMPLIFICATION

A common requirement for modern games is the ability to scale the complexity of models depending on their distance from the viewer, enabling many more objects to be drawn in a scene without compromising the visual quality of objects when inspected close up. In general, the goal is to generate a number of versions of each model (either as a pre-processing step or at runtime), each with fewer independent parts, polygons and/or textures that can be used when the object is sufficiently far away that the loss in detail is not noticeable.

The easiest way to achieve this is to produce and store the reduced detail models in the same way as any other mesh, and have the engine simply select one to display as required. In some cases, the task of building these models is performed by artists, either manually or using one of the various tools built into most 3D packages to reduce the polygon count. However, while this almost always produces better results than automatic detail reduction algorithms, it is time consuming and in many cases the gains achieved in terms of increased graphical quality or performance (due to being able to use lower detail models closer to the camera) are relatively minimal.

To generate a lower detail version of a model, there are three basic types of processing that can be performed: hierarchy merging, polygon reduction, and texture merging.

Hierarchy Merging

Hierarchy merging is simply the process of combining nodes in the hierarchy to reduce the number of individual components on the mesh which need to be drawn. This can be very important, as the cost of the draw call itself becomes increasingly important as the number of polygons decreases. On most hardware, drawing (for example) 100 batches of 10 polygons is approximately the same speed as drawing 100 batches of 100 polygons, as the actual transformation and rasterization time is completely eclipsed by the setup costs for each primitive. By merging as many nodes as possible, the number of polygons per draw call is increased, and the total number of primitives needed decreased.

The actual procedure for merging hierarchy nodes is exactly the same as that described previously for merging nodes that are static relative to each other. The only real difference is in the procedure used for determining which nodes can be removed: instead of only removing nodes that are truly static, nodes that only move a small (unperceivable at the target rendering distance) amount can be merged as well.

Therefore, a tolerance value can be used when considering if nodes are "sufficiently static" relative to each other. An error metric can be calculated by taking the "difference transformation" which maps from the space of one node into the space of another for each frame of the animation, and then calculating the maximum difference between these. This value can then be compared to a threshold based on the desired detail level of the final mesh: some tuning will be necessary to find a balance between the reduction in nodes achieved and the detail loss for a given viewing distance.

If the target nodes are considered to be relatively static, then they can be merged. This can either be done using the transforms from the bind pose, first frame of the animation, or similar set position (which will have the advantage that the resulting merged position should be "neutral"), or by taking the pose from a point in the animation approximately halfway between the extents of the error (thereby reducing the maximum possible error for any frame). The choice of which approach to take is largely dependent on the specifics of the models being processed.

Once the geometry has been merged, the process can be considered "complete," insomuch that the number of draw calls required to render the mesh has been reduced by the merge. However, it is often useful also to remove the (now empty) second node, reducing the computation and storage costs of the mesh as well. Doing this is slightly trickier, as any alteration in the node's transform due to the merge will be propagated to its children, potentially causing a much more serious visual artifact as the error is magnified.

The solution, therefore, is to adjust the child nodes to account for the change in transform the merge will introduce. The simplest way to do this is to take each of the children of the node to be removed, and transform them into the space of either the common parent of the nodes being removed, or simply into the local space of the mesh itself. Then, convert them back into the space of their new (merged) parent by transforming each by the inverse of the parent's transform (relative to whichever space they are currently in). This way, the error is corrected in each of the children, ensuring that no artifacts are introduced in the rest of the hierarchy as a result of the merge.

Removing Redundant Bone Nodes

The same procedure can also be used to remove bones from skinned meshes, although they contain no geometry, they do represent a cost in computation time and storage, and in addition combining bones may enable further optimization to be performed on the skinned mesh itself, such as separation of rigid bound sections, as described previously in the section on skinning processes.

The procedure for merging bones is exactly the same as any other node—the error metric can be calculated in the same way. Obviously there is no geometry to be merged, but again the children can be corrected if necessary as described previously. The major difference when merging bones is that the vertices (or bone palette) of the skinned mesh itself must be updated to reflect the change, and it may be necessary to adjust the binding position of the bone if this is stored separately from the rest of the animation.

Procedurally Modified Nodes

Another optimization that can be performed on reduced detail meshes is that in many circumstances there is little or no need for procedurally modified nodes to be updated when the mesh is in the distance. Equally, in many circumstances the game is highly unlikely to read the positions of nodes in a lower detail mesh. As a result, it may well be possible to discard the constraints these place on the hierarchy optimization process when building reduced detail models, further increasing the number of nodes that can be eliminated.

Polygon Reduction

The most commonly used level of detail reduction process is that of polygon reduction. Sometimes known as "mesh decimation," polygon reduction attempts to combine polygons so that the surface of the mesh is still roughly the same shape, but (generally) less smooth, and using fewer polygons. There are many techniques for doing this, but by far the most popular are variants on the *edge collapse* algorithm.

Polygon Reduction by Removing Edges

The edge collapse algorithm, as its name suggests, operates by removing edges from the mesh. An edge is removed, or "collapsed," by moving the vertices at the ends of the edge together. Doing this will in turn result in the triangles which share that edge becoming degenerate, as they will now have two identical vertices (and hence zero surface area), these can then be removed. In a fully connected mesh, each edge that is collapsed will remove two triangles.

This can be seen in Figure 6.9. The edge between A and B is collapsed, which results in the two shaded triangles becoming degenerate and being removed. This example shows three different choices for the point to collapse the two vertices to: at either end of the edge, and at an intermediate point between A and B. This *collapse point* can lie anywhere along the edge being collapsed.

As with virtually all mesh decimation algorithms, the key to the edge collapse technique is in determining *which* edge to collapse. This can be achieved by calculating an error metric that represents the magnitude of the visual artifact which would be introduced by the collapse, and then collapsing the edges in order, starting with those that will cause the smallest error.

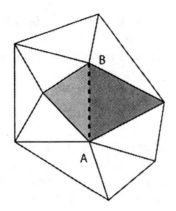

Original mesh

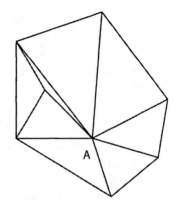

Mesh after collapsing to point A

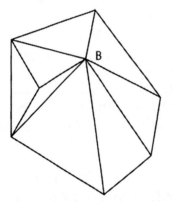

Mesh after collapsing to point B

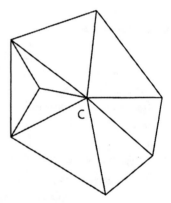

Mesh after collapsing to intermediate point C

FIGURE 6.9 The effect of collapsing an edge to different points.

Detecting Surface Errors

There are many possible error metrics that can be chosen, but most are built from a number of terms, each constraining a different area of the problem in terms of the difference between the original uncollapsed mesh and the version generated after the collapse operation. The most obvious, and important, of these constraints is that on the position of the mesh surface itself. This should match the original mesh as closely as possible.

Calculating an error value for the mesh surface can be done relatively simply through a relatively brute force approach. This is done by taking each triangle in the (post collapse) mesh, and generating a number of points across its surface (the number being based on the size of the triangle to ensure a roughly even distribution). Then, the nearest triangle in the *original* mesh to each of these points is found, and the perpendicular (and hence closest) distance between the point and the triangle found—this gives the error for that point. By averaging the error across all of the points, a value can be calculated for the error introduced into the mesh surface by the collapse.

Obviously, doing this operation for the entire mesh on every potential edge collapse would be quite a time consuming process, but fortunately it is only necessary to examine a very small subsection of the mesh each time. Only triangles that adjoin either of the vertices on the candidate edge may be affected by the collapse operation, and hence only those need to be examined. Every other point in the mesh can be assumed to have an error of zero. This optimization significantly reduces the amount of calculation required to compute the error metric. Note that it is still necessary to know the *number* of other points in the mesh in order to calculate the average error—otherwise a collapse that affects a few very small triangles may have a disproportionately high error value in comparison with the effect it has on the mesh as a whole.

Detecting Other Visual Errors

While the surface position error metric is by far the most important, there are several others that play an important role in ensuring that the detail-reduced process does not introduce visual errors. It is vital to consider all of the elements of each vertex that may be affected by the collapse. In most cases, these will be the vertex texture coordinates, normal and color.

One approach to calculating the error for each of these which is simple to implement and quite efficient is to calculate the error for each of these additional vertex attributes as part of the surface error calculation. They can be calculated for each of the points on the surface (generally by simple linear interpolation), and then compared to a similarly interpolated value for the closest point on the original mesh when it is located. The difference between these can then be used as an error metric. The contribution of these errors to the overall error metric should be weighted according to their visual significance. The importance of, for example, errors in vertex color across the mesh is generally much less important than that of errors in the surface itself or the texture coordinates.

When calculating the error metric, it is necessary to consider that the act of collapsing an edge can be done in a number of ways. By labeling the two vertices on the edge A and B, either A can be moved to the position of B, B moved to the position of A, or A and B both moved to some intermediate point. The varying position of this *collapse point* where A and B are placed can have a massive effect on the error introduced in some circumstances.

While there are some edge collapse algorithms that employ analytical methods to determine the optimum position for the collapse point, by minimizing the error metric function across the edge, for most practical purposes it is simpler and almost as effective to consider only a small number of cases—typically the two extreme ends of the edge (the positions of A and B), and the halfway point along it. By calculating the error metric for the collapse to each of these points, the lowest error (and hence best solution) can be found and used as the error value for that collapse.

If the edge is very long then it may be worth considering subdividing the edge into a large number of points to consider, although since large edges are generally not good candidates for collapsing except in trivial cases, this marginal improvement in performance may not be worth the CPU cost of performing the additional error calculations.

Once the error metrics for all of the edges have been calculated, all that is needed is to walk through the list in order (from least error upwards), actually performing the collapse operations (welding the two vertices and removing any resultant degenerate triangles) until either the desired number of triangles is reached or the error crosses a preset threshold. If the collapse point is at an intermediate position along the edge, the same vertex interpolation described previously for mesh subdivision can be employed to generate the attributes of the new vertex.

Handling Discontinuities

While this algorithm works well on meshes that are entirely smooth and have no texture seams or other discontinuities, for it to be useful on the types of mesh more commonly encountered during game development it is necessary to extend it to take account of these features.

It is relatively straightforward to detect where a discontinuity occurs in the mesh by examining the edges. One type of discontinuity is where the triangles on either side of the edge form an extreme angle (at the edge). In this case, collapsing the edge will have the effect of removing this feature from the mesh, which will probably cause a significant difference in the appearance. An edge also represents a discontinuity if the attributes of the triangles on either side of it are noticeably different, for example, if they have different textures, or if the normals used by each triangle do not vary smoothly across the edge (note that in many mesh representations, this will cause the vertices on the edge to be duplicated). The severity of the discontinuity can be judged by the magnitude of the change across the edge.

The act of collapsing an edge will obviously affect any discontinuity on the edges of the triangles that share that edge (as they will be removed entirely), but it will also affect those that adjoin either of the vertices of the edge. In this case, the discontinuity will still exist but will be moved by the collapse if the corresponding vertex is moved. Therefore, when calculating the error metric for a given collapse operation, it is necessary to consider the effect it will have on any nearby edges which feature discontinuities, and add a value for this to the overall error metric—the magnitude of the discontinuity multiplied by an overall weighting factor for importance is a good choice for this. In some cases (such as texture seams), it may be desirable to simply inhibit the collapse altogether if a discontinuity is affected or will be removed entirely.

Using the Edge Collapse Algorithm on Skinned Meshes

The edge collapse algorithm can also be used to reduce the level of detail in meshes that are skinned—however, some care must be taken to ensure that the effect of the bone weights are taken into account during the collapse process. In general, the weights can be factored into the error metric calculation in the same way as other vertex attributes, by interpolating them and deriving an error vault from the difference between the nearest surface point and each point on the new mesh.

While this does ensure that the resulting collapse point lies roughly on the surface that would have been generated by the skinned mesh, it does not, however, take into account the fact that the movement of bones in a skinned mesh may quite dramatically alter the surface, in many cases introducing creases or discontinuities that are not present when the model is in a neutral pose (consider the elbow or knee joints of a human character, for example). As a result, the algorithm may collapse edges which are in fact vital to the appearance of the mesh in certain poses.

If canned animations are being used, then this problem can be solved through the simple mechanic of calculating the error metric for each vertex across every key frame of the animations, and using the largest value found. However, this is both expensive and generally impractical, as in modern games skinned meshes are rarely used exclusively with pre-built animations.

In the absence of any additional information, the best strategy to use when calculating the vertex error metrics on a skinned mesh is one of caution. Specifically, the error contribution for the bone weights should be weighted quite high, and it may be useful to apply a nonlinear scale to them as well because as the difference in weight on any given bone across the edge increases, so does the likelihood that edge will form a discontinuity or crease when animated.

Progressive Meshes

The edge collapse algorithm is often used as a means of generating static reduced detail meshes, by simply performing the collapses as required and removing the triangles that become degenerate as a result. However, an important feature of the algorithm is that as the majority of the complex calculations are involved in the calculation of the vertex error metrics and hence building the ordered list of edge collapses, the actual collapse and removal process can be performed at runtime if required.

The preprocessing required for this is almost exactly the same as that required for standard edge collapse reduction, except that no actual reduction takes place. Instead, the list of edge collapses that would have been performed is stored, generally in the form of a list of mappings between pairs of vertex indices (most progressive mesh implementations disallow edge collapses which result in the final vertex position being anywhere except the endpoints of the edge, thereby reducing every collapse to a remapping from one vertex to another). At runtime, the engine can then use the first n elements in this list to look up the vertex indices when drawing triangles in the mesh, where n corresponds to the desired number of collapses for the level of detail needed. Some engines may also implement *geomorphing*, where the vertices being collapsed move to their final positions over a number of frames, thereby removing the sometimes obvious "pop" which is seen when an edge suddenly disappears.

Generating Imposter Sprites

For games which need to display very large numbers of objects, or have large playing areas such that objects are often in the far distance, imposters provide a very efficient way of rendering low detail versions of many objects without significant CPU or GPU overhead. The term "imposter" can refer to any object that is used to represent another at distance, but in general it is most commonly used when sprites or arbitrarily constructed geometry are used for this purpose, rather than reduced detail versions of the original model.

Imposter sprites are the simplest form of imposter, and they are extremely simple to generate and use. An imposter sprite is a "snapshot" of an object, from a specific angle, which is then drawn in its place, generally as a *bill-boarded* polygon, i.e., a polygon that always faces the viewer (in the same way as a sprite in a 2D game).

As such, the process for generating an imposter sprite is very simple—all the preprocessing application needs to do is draw the object in the same manner as the game would, and store the result in a texture. The only real difficulty in carrying out this procedure is in setting up the initial rendering parameters so that the imposter is close to the appearance of the model in-game as possible.

Camera Position

The camera position will mostly be dictated by the type of imposter required. Many games make use of a number of imposters from different angles, and then pick the closest to the viewing angle of the model in-game. For objects with rotational symmetry, or at least the illusion of such (for example many types of trees, which tend to look much the same from any angle at a distance), fewer imposters, or even just one, may be necessary.

Projection

For imposter creation, an orthographic or parallel project should generally be used, as distant objects exhibit relatively little perspective effect, and "baking in" the perspective to the model will generally look wrong, unless there is a very close match between the camera distance during imposter creation and the camera distance from the object in-game.

Object Size

The size of the object is important; ideally, it should be set such that the object *just* fills the texture, getting the maximum possible resolution. This can be easily calculated from the bounding volume of the model. Once this is done, either the object can be rescaled or the camera moved to ensure a close fit.

Lighting

In general, imposters will not be able to reflect in-game lighting (this is possible on some hardware through careful use of bumpmaps, but fairly rarely used), and hence they must be lit in as "neutral" a fashion as possible. The specifics of this will depend largely on the game and environment the imposters are to be used in, but in general choosing a pair of light source colors which match roughly the primary lights in the environment (the sun and reflected ground light, for example) and placing these at opposite sides of the model works well. In general, making the lighting subtle works best because people tend to overlook incorrect lighting as long as it is not violently mismatched with the environment.

Animated Imposter Sprites

Animating imposter sprites is relatively rarely done, but can be useful in some cases to get an impression of motion on distant objects by using a few frames of animation. Since each additional frame generated requires more storage space, particularly if multiple angle views are required for the imposter, it is important to keep the number to the minimum needed. Choosing the frames to use is usually a job best left to an artist, and is done either by inserting tags into the model animation itself, or by using some sort of tool to pick the frames needed.

Handling Imposter Edges

When rendering imposter sprites, it is also necessary to generate an alpha channel so that the resulting sprite has the same silhouette as the original model when rendered. This can be achieved simply by rendering the model to a buffer that has a destination alpha channel, or by rendering a second texture with a pure white version of the mesh.

In general, for rendering purposes only 1-bit alpha is desired, as otherwise the edges of the imposter will blend with the background behind it, which can often introduce "fringing" artifacts, particularly if the objects are not depth sorted prior to drawing. Therefore, the alpha channel should be quantized down to a single value after the imposter is created.

Once this has been done, it is often also useful to "smear" the texture, by taking the inverse of the alpha channel, and drawing several copies of the texture back into the original at slightly jittered offsets, using the inverted alpha channel as a mask. This way, the texels outside the visible area of the texture will contain the same colors as their visible neighbors, meaning that if filtering is later applied to the texture, the unwanted background color will not appear in areas between the opaque and transparent texels.

Using Imposter Geometry

As well as imposter schemes which purely use sprites to represent distant objects, it can also be useful in some circumstances to build *imposter geometry,* which is a mesh that is not a reduced detail version of the original, but instead a holder for a specially created texture that mimics the appearance of the model.

There are many different types of imposter geometry, many of which are specific to different types of objects or games. The basic principles are almost always the same: the imposter geometry is constructed, and then one or more rendered "snapshots" of the original model are taken and mapped onto it. The actual construction of the initial geometry can be done in any one of a vast number of ways, although one very general structure that is useful for quite a range of purposes is that of the *axis imposter.*

Axis Imposters

Axis imposters are a very simple example of imposter geometry. The imposter mesh is simply comprised of six quads, each pair aligned with one of the axes of the model, and sized appropriately. An axis imposter is the same size and shape as an axis-aligned bounding box that has been "collapsed" so that the sides meet in the center. The quads in each pair face in opposite directions, so for any given viewing angle only three of them can be seen. Figure 6.10 shows this structure where each of the shaded quads is one of the three currently visible faces of the imposter

FIGURE 6.10 The structure of an axis imposter.

The textures for an axis imposter are simple to generate—they are simply orthographic projections of the model, looking along each axis in both directions. As each pair of quads in the imposter is aligned to one axis, its dimensions will be the bounding box size on the other two, thereby making the sizing of the imposter and textures very straightforward too.

Axis imposters are primarily useful because they are almost as simple as sprite imposters to generate, but they avoid the problem of the transitions among the different viewing angles as the object or camera moves. If the camera is looking directly along one axis, then the resulting imposter is exactly what a normal imposter sprite would generate, but as the camera moves the imposter changes smoothly. While the intermediate appearance of the imposter is not necessarily particularly close to that of the original mesh (depending largely on the layout), the fact the smooth rotation can be clearly seen often makes it much more convincing from a distance.

Axis imposters also have the interesting property that they can be "bolted together" to form larger objects easily. In most cases the imposter occupies roughly the same volume of space as the original mesh from any angle, so axis imposters can represent objects made up of multiple parts without the tendency that imposter sprites have to move apart from each other at certain angles, creating large gaps in composite objects.

7 Audio and Video Processing

In This Chapter

- Audio
- Scripting Languages
- Video

AUDIO

Unlike the somewhat erratic advances seen in 3D graphics technology during the evolution of games as a medium, developments in audio technology have largely followed a steady evolution, with both storage and playback technology having now evolved to the point where game sound can offer a surprisingly close recreation of reality in many circumstances.

Virtually all of the sound processing operations commonly used revolve around *sample data,* which are simply a direct representation of the sound waves themselves, usually encoded at a relatively high resolution and sampling rate (44 KHz samples stored as 16 bit values is a common standard). One waveform is required for each channel of the sound, so stereo audio has two independent sets of sample data. Processing is almost always applied in exactly the same way to all of these sets, as otherwise the balance between the channels is affected.

Somewhat confusingly, the word "sample" is often used to refer to a single set of sample data (rather than, as the strict use of the term would suggest, a single value within that data). For the sake of clarity, in this chapter "sample" is used to refer to a single value, while "sample data" or simply "sound" is used to refer to the whole waveform.

There are various compression schemes for sample data; it is quite common for modern sound hardware to support these natively, so some types of compressed sample can be played directly. As with other compressed data formats, however, it is best to keep sample data in an uncompressed format until the very final stage of processing, as the compression process introduces artifacts.

Resampling

The single most common operation that is required on audio data is to change the sampling rate or the time frequency of the samples in the file. This is most often necessary because of disc space or memory constraints, so reducing the sample rate reduces the amount of data by a corresponding amount. Since the source data is most often sampled at 44 KHz, reducing this to 22 KHz or 11 KHz will halve or quarter the memory requirements respectively. Most sound effects still sound perfectly acceptable at 22 KHz, and even 11 KHz or 8 KHz are reasonable in many cases (background speech, for example).

While in theory it may be necessary to increase the sampling rate of audio data, in practice this is extremely rare in the asset pipeline. In virtually all cases, the input data is at a higher sample rate than the desired output, therefore, it is *decimation*, or sample rate reduction, that is actually required. Essential, though, the solutions to both problems are required, as the processes of increasing and decreasing the sample rate can generally only be performed to integer multiples of the sampling rate.

As a result, the process for decimating the sample data becomes a two-step process. First, the sample rate is increased by an integer multiple to a value which is a common denominator of the source and target rates, and then it is reduced by another integer multiple to the desired final sampling rate.

Both of these processes are fairly straightforward: the sample rate can be increased by an integer multiple simply by padding the sample data and adding the required number of zero values to each sample in the original (this is known as "zero-stuffing"). This produces a sample at the desired rate, but with a certain amount of high-frequency noise added by the addition of the extra zeroed samples.

This noise can be removed using a low-pass filter at the maximum frequency of the original sample (as will be discussed shortly), leaving a complete sample at the new rate. Once this is done, the process of reducing the sample rate to the target is exceptionally simple: all that is required is to throw away samples at regular intervals to achieve the desired final rate.

While in theory these two operations can be performed independently, it is more common to treat the resampling process as a single operation—this way, it is not necessary to calculate and store the entire intermediate high sample rate version of the data, as many of the samples will simply be discarded. Instead, the samples can be generated and filtered as they are required for the output data.

Unfortunately, there is one additional problem that is encountered when decimating samples: the lowered sampling rate will result in some frequency bands in the source violating the *Nyquist criteria*.

The Nyquist Criteria

The Nyquist criteria is a law about discrete digital samples of a continuous analog signal. It simply states that the highest frequency that can be represented in such a form is half of the sampling rate of the signal. On an intuitive level, this can be fairly easily understood: any signal of a frequency higher than this will "fall between" samples and be lost.

The problem, therefore, with reducing the sampling rate is that higher frequencies in the original data will not be able to be represented in the output, and will become aliased. This aliasing will manifest itself as a distortion of the original sample data, and cannot be filtered once it has occurred. The solution, therefore, is to perform a low-pass filtering process on the data before resampling it, removing any sounds above the maximum frequency that can be represented at the target sampling rate.

Low-Pass Filtering

This low-pass filtering process can be performed by using a Fourier transform to convert the sample data into the frequency domain, applying a frequency-based filter (simply a series of coefficients that the frequency data is multiplied by), and then converting the data using an inverse Fourier transform.

While it may seem that the best low-pass filter would be one which simply removes any energy from frequencies above the clipping point, this is not actually the case. While such a filter does work, it also has the effect of smoothing high-frequency artifacts such as the edges of waveforms. The solution is to use a filter that retains a small amount of the frequencies above the clipping point, for example, the *Butterworth filter*, which uses a smooth curve across the clipping point and into the higher frequency bands.

In theory, therefore, what is required to ensure that the data will not violate the Nyquist criteria when the sampling rate is reduced is simply to perform a low-pass filtering operation on it before starting. However, in practice this is not actually necessary, as a low-pass filter is already used on the data to remove the artifacts caused by the intermediate increase in sampling rate. Therefore, this filter can simply be adjusted to use whichever the lower of the two clipping points is, performing both duties simultaneously.

Looping Samples

There are many circumstances in which games require sounds to loop seamlessly. While actually ensuring that there are no audible artifacts across the loop boundary is the job of an audio engineer, it is often necessary for the pipeline to understand about loop points in sample data.

A loop point, quite simply, is the moment in a sound when it returns to a previous point (often the start) of the sample data. On some systems, looping is handled in software, while on others the sound hardware uses data embedded in the samples to perform looping automatically.

On systems with hardware support, therefore, what is needed is simply to insert these markers at the appropriate points in the data. Some care should be taken with the specification of loop points. If they are given as absolute sample numbers, then they need to be shifted appropriately if the sample rate has been altered since the sound was created.

In the case where looping is to be handled manually, however, more effort is usually required. This is because monitoring the audio hardware to determine when a loop point has been reached is a very processor-intensive task, and it is generally not feasible to do so. As a result, looping sounds on these systems are usually handled by detecting the *end* of the sample data (often with an interrupt), and then starting it again.

In the event that it is the whole sound that needs to be looped, no further effort is required to support this. However, if the loop point (and the corresponding point the loop returns to) are in the middle of the sample data, then it is necessary to split it into sections: one for the samples up to the start of the loop, one for the loop itself, and one for the samples after the end of the loop (assuming that there is some means by which the loop can be terminated). These separate sounds can then be played back-to-back by the sound system to provide the illusion of looping at the appropriate points.

Audio Compression

There are many different audio compression schemes in games today, aimed at a variety of different uses. In many cases, there is hardware support for simple compression, which can considerably increase the amount of sample data that can be stored without adding any CPU overhead for decoding.

In many cases, it is not actually necessary to implement a custom encoder for audio data. The manufacturers of the hardware may well provide one, and for popular formats there are usually libraries available (either open source or commercial) which handle the task. Also, on some system (most notably Windows machines), the operating system may provide an API for interfacing to standardized codecs, enabling quick and easy conversion between any format for which a suitable codec is available.

ADPCM

One of the most pervasive compression schemes is ADPCM, which stands for Adaptive Differential Pulse Code Modulation. There are various standardized versions of ADPCM, including many specified by the ITU (most notably G.727 and G.726), which are used in many other types of devices such as mobile phones. Most consoles, however, use a proprietary standard of some description. That said, the differences between ADPCM variants are generally in details of the file format, not the compression algorithm itself. ADPCM is extremely simple both to encode and decode, yet offers surprisingly good sound quality—features which have lead to it being implemented in many hardware audio chipsets.

ADPCM is a fixed-ratio compression format, which represents each sample in coded format as 4 bits. The 4-bit code representing each sample expresses a difference between this sample and the previous one, which is multiplied by a step size that is constantly adjusted according to the previous delta values. The most significant bit stores the sign of the adjustment, and the remaining 3 bits the magnitude.

ADPCM Encoding

To perform ADPCM compression on a single sample, the first step is to take the difference between it and the *decoded* value of the previous sample (that is, the value that the decoder will have generated, not the uncompressed sample value). Then, the 4-bit code for this sample is calculated from the delta.

The first bit is simply set if the delta value is negative, and then the delta is converted into a positive value for the calculation of the remaining three bits. These are determined by taking the delta, multiplying it by 4 (half of the total range the 3 bits can express), and then dividing it by the current *step value*. This stores the magnitude of change the encoder (and hence decoder) is expecting.

The resulting value is then clamped to the range 0 to 7 (3 bits), with 0 representing a delta of 0, 4 representing a delta of exactly the step value, and 7 representing a delta of just under twice the step value. Put together with the sign bit calculated earlier, this gives the 4-bit code for this sample.

The next stage in the process is to calculate the output the decoder will generate, as this will be needed for the next sample. This is simply a case of taking the code and re-calculating the delta value from it by multiplying the lowest 3 bits by the step value, dividing by 4, and negating the result if the sign bit was set. This delta can then be added to the last decoded value to give the new one.

Once this has been done, the final step is to update the step value. This is done using a table of step values, which increase in a nonlinear fashion starting from relatively small values at the low end of the table and reaching the half of the maximum input sample range (generally 32,768 for 16-bit samples) at the high end.

The step value is updated by taking the index within the table of the current value, and moving that index according to the bottom 3 bits (that is, the magnitude) of the last delta code calculated. The specifics of this vary from implementation to implementation, but in general for values of 4 or less, the step value from the *previous* index in the table is used (lowering the expected step size), and for values of 5–7 the step value from an increasing distance ahead in the table is used (increasing the expected step size). This new step value is then used for the next sample compressed.

The effect of this is simple. If the delta value was higher than expected, then the step size is increased to compensate, otherwise it is slowly reduced until the average delta value is approximately half of the step size. This is the "adaptive" quality of the ADPCM algorithm. At the start of compression, the step value is simply initialized to a mid-range value, after a few samples it will quickly converge on an appropriate value.

MP3

MP3 compression, or "MPEG-1 layer 3 audio" to give it its full title, is probably the most famous of all the audio compression technologies. It is part of the ISO MPEG standard, and as such both the compression and the file format are standardized and very well defined. MP3 compression and decompression is a fairly expensive process, which means that until very recently it has not been used much for games. Even now, it is still comparatively rare, although the presence of more hardware decoding support in future audio chipsets may well change that.

MP3 compression uses *psychoacoustic* principles (that is, the science of how human beings perceive sound) as part of the compression process, essentially, the audio data is analyzed in the frequency domain, and bands that are considered inaudible are stripped. The data is then compressed further using more traditional techniques, such as Huffman encoding (see Chapter 10 for a discussion of this) to form the final file.

MP3 can compress audio data very well to surprisingly low bit rates. 128 kbit per second (16 KB/second) is generally considered to be fairly high quality for music, and rates as low as 96 kbit/second (12 Kb/second) or even 64 kbit/second (8 Kb/second) still sound acceptable for some purposes, such as background speech. MP3 can also be used as a variable-rate compression system, where the bit rate of the audio is altered from moment-to-moment depending on the characteristics of the input data. This can considerably improve the sound quality without the need to increase the bit rate of the entire file.

MP3 is almost exclusively used for compressing music and speech, as the CPU overheads of the decoding process make it unsuitable for sound effects or any application where a large number of sounds must be played simultaneously. In addition, most MP3 decoders introduce a degree of latency into the playback process, which can make accurately starting and stopping MP3 streams "at random" problematic, although this is a problem that with some ingenuity, can be solved.

Decoding MP3 audio is a fairly involved task, but encoding it is considerably more so; writing an MP3 encoder that is both efficient and generates high-quality output is not a task to be taken lightly. Fortunately, there are many MP3 encoding programs and libraries that can be used, both open source and commercial. One of the most highly-regarded of these is the open source LAME library, which is used in many MP3 encoding and audio toolkits. LAME can be found at *http://lame.s ourceforge.net.*

Alternatively, on Windows systems there are standard codecs available that perform MP3 encoding and decoding. These can be easily employed through the standard multimedia system APIs as required.

It should be noted, however, that there are number of patents held on various technologies involved in the MP3 encoding process, and some legal research into this area is highly advisable if you intend to use MP3 audio.

Vorbis

In recent years, many other audio codecs based broadly on the same principles as MP3 have been developed, many of which offer claim to better compression, faster decoding, or other such benefits. The various trade-offs these offer is beyond the scope of this book, but one codec that has gained widespread acceptance and offers a clear cut advantage over MP3 is the *Vorbis* format, also known as *Ogg Vorbis* (Ogg being the container file format used to hold the encoded audio data). The homepage for the Vorbis project is at *http://www.vorbis.com.*

Vorbis was designed to offer similar compression to MP3, and it claims to outperform it in terms of quality at similar bit rates. However, it is not the higher quality that makes Vorbis attractive to game developers—but rather the fact that it has been developed as completely open standard, and is claimed to be entirely free of patent encumbrance. While this has not (a the time of this writing) been conclusively proved in a strict legal sense, many people believe that this is the case, and the codec has been used without incident by several high-profile games, including *Unreal Tournament* and *Serious Sam: The Second Encounter.* As with any potentially patented technology, proper legal consultation is advised before deciding to use it, however.

As an open standard, anyone is free to develop a Vorbis encoder or decoder. However, as with MP3, this is not an easy task, so most developers use an external library or tool to perform the task. Xiph.org (the creators of the format) offers a set of libraries for the task under an open source license, and they can also be purchased for commercial use. One of the most interesting Vorbis libraries for games use is *Tremor*, which is a decoder that operates entirely using fixed-point math for processors without fast hardware float-point support.

SCRIPTING LANGUAGES

With the increasing complexity of the "scripted" or predetermined sequences in modern games, more and more developers have started implementing game logic in scripting languages: either those developed in-house, or existing systems such as LUA or Python.

Compiling Script Code

Some scripting languages are designed so that they can be compiled, either into an intermediate bytecode which is interpreted at runtime, or directly into native code for the target platform. This compilation process is sometimes done as part of the asset building process, using whichever tools the language provides for doing so.

The main difficulty encountered with compiling script code in this way is that unlike virtually every other type of asset in the game, script code is usually very tightly bound to the actual game source code. This can cause serious problems if the compiled script and the game code are out of sync. This effect is exacerbated by the fact that scripts tend to change a lot more frequently than most other asset types.

As a result, it is usually advisable to keep script compilation as a separate process from the main asset pipeline, possibly even integrating it into the compilation of the game source code instead. Most of the advantages of the asset pipeline do not particularly apply to script code, and the disadvantages can be quite considerable. That said, there are some circumstances under which limited processing of script code during the asset pipeline can be useful.

Deriving Dependencies from Scripts

The most common use of this is in building information about asset dependencies by parsing script files. For example, in order to package all of the character models required for a particular game level, the asset pipeline needs not only to know which characters have been placed in the level file itself, but also if the scripts for that level might create any *new* characters at runtime. Similarly, it is common for other asset types to be referenced from scripts, such as sound effects being triggered.

How this information is obtained depends quite strongly on the nature of the scripting language being used. In some extreme cases, it may be necessary to actually analyze every possible execution path the script can take and determine what assets it needs (a task that is actually impossible to complete in finite time for some programs in a Turing-complete scripting language—consider the case of a program containing an infinite loop creating randomly named assets). However, this is generally unnecessary, by restricting the manner in which scripts can reference assets, it is easy to extract a list without the need to completely parse the script file.

The key to this is in forbidding scripts from constructing asset names at runtime, as the only way these can be accurately determined is by emulating execution of the script. By forcing scripts to declare all of the assets they need directly in the source code, it is then quite straightforward to examine the file and extract a list— especially if a unique type identifier or similar is used for asset references.

VIDEO

Video, or FMV ("Full Motion Video"), is widely used in modern games as a means of telling the story of the game, and displaying effects that cannot be rendered in realtime. The process of generating and applying effects to video is a complex one, and is almost exclusively the domain of dedicated video editing packages. Therefore, in the vast majority of cases the only processing required in the pipeline for video is compression and management of the associated data.

One of the single most useful applications for manipulating video (on Windows systems, at least), both as part of the asset pipeline and in an interactive capacity, is VirtualDub (*http://www.virtualdub.org*). VirtualDub is an open source "Swiss army knife" for video processing and transcoding, provides a wide range of video filters, and makes use of the Windows codec system so that it can read and write virtually any format with an available suitable codec. It also features a fairly comprehensive scripting interface for interacting with external programs.

Another useful tool for more advanced tasks is AviSynth (*http://www.avisynth. org*). This (also open source) application provides a script-based interface for performing image processing tasks, as well as a very powerful *frameserving* system which allows video to be processed and passed between applications on the fly, without the need to actually process and save the entire file. AviSynth works very well in conjunction with VirtualDub, and the two applications can even share filter plug-ins to a certain extent.

Video Compression

Video compression is also an extremely complex subject, and the massive difficulty in writing an efficient video encoder and decoder, combined with the increasing number of dedicated hardware implementations of common standards such as MPEG, means that virtually all developers use an "off-the-shelf" video compression system.

As with audio, there are various ways to integrate such a system into the pipeline—some tools are provided as standalone applications, while others are available as libraries. The Windows multimedia system provides a standardized interface to video codecs that can be used to control compression and decompression easily—this interface is so pervasive that it has even been ported to other operating systems such as Linux, allowing the same codec binaries to be used by a wide range of different applications.

The field of video compression is littered with a huge number of patents on fundamental elements on the technology, even more so than audio compression. As a result, it is best to assume that the majority of the technologies described here are probably covered by a patent of some sort, unless noted otherwise!

MPEG-1 and MPEG-2

The most widely-known video codecs are probably the MPEG (Motion Picture Experts Group) codecs, specifically MPEG-1 and MPEG-2, the standards used for (among other things) Video CD and DVD discs respectively. The MPEG video formats are widely supported, and many platforms, including Playstation 2, feature hardware support for MPEG decoding.

The MPEG working group (*http://www.chiariglione.org/mpeg*), who designed the MPEG standards, is part of the ISO, and therefore the various MPEG standards are freely available for a small fee, although, as always, many areas of them are covered by patents. There are a vast number of MPEG encoders and decoders available in various forms—one of the best known freely available encoders that supports both MPEG-1 and MPEG-2 is bbMPEG, which can be found at *http://members.cox.net/beyeler/bbmpeg.html.*

For modern hardware, MPEG-1 is generally considered to be out-of-date and too low quality to be usable, although the low CPU requirements of the decoding process can make it attractive for some applications. MPEG-2, however, produces very good output, as data rates of approximately 4–5 Mbit/second generally give a very high quality image with very few or no noticeable compression artifacts.

As with many of the MPEG standards, MPEG-2 is designed to be scalable. In order to achieve this, a number of different *profiles* and *levels* are defined. Each profile sets out which sections of the standard are applicable (as there are often several different options for compressing different types of data defined), and the level sets out the limits the encoder must work within in terms of bit rate, frame size, etc. However, for virtually all purposes in games, the "main profile" (which is used by DVD players and similar) is what is used.

The MPEG standard defines formats for both audio and video streams, and also an overall container format, known as a "program stream," which contains a number of other streams multiplexed together. It is these program stream files that are actually played under most circumstances, as they contain all the required data in an interleaved format which allows the entire set of streams to be played without having to read from many different files.

MPEG-4

Another less widely used MPEG standard, but rapidly gaining popularity, is MPEG-4. MPEG-4 is a more recently developed standard than MPEG-1 and MPEG-2, and achieves better quality results at the same bit rates, albeit at the cost of more CPU time for encoding and decoding.

The MPEG-4 standard defines a very wide range of different profiles and levels for various target applications of the technology, from mobile phone video up to HDTV. In most cases for full-screen video at standard TV resolution, it is the "simple profile" or "advanced simple profile" that is used, however.

While MPEG-4 is the "official" standard, it has actually been largely superseded by a number of variant codecs that are based on the same fundamental technologies, but offer various improvements over MPEG-4 itself. Some of these even offer interoperability (generally in terms of playback) with MPEG-4.

MPEG-4 Variants

By far the most widely known MPEG-4 variant is the DivX codec (not to be confused with the ill-fated DivX DVD rental system). This started life as an unofficial hacked version of an existing (non-standard) MPEG-4 implementation, but then evolved into an entirely independent project, which is now maintained and marketed by DivXNetworks (*http://www.divx.com*), who now license out the technology and software.

In addition to gaining widespread acceptance among consumers, DivX has been used successfully by several games, including *Warcraft 3*. There are also a number of other codecs that can play DivX files, such as the open source FFDShow and XviD codecs, which offer compatibility with both DivX and MPEG-4. FFDShow can be found at *http://sourceforge.net/projects/ffdshow*, and XviD lives at *http://www.xvid.org*.

Bink

Bink is different from the rest of the codecs discussed here, in that it is not an open standard, but instead is a commercial product aimed firmly at the games industry. Bink is developed by RAD Game Tools (*http://www.radgametools.com*), who are also known for their older "Smacker" video system which was very widely adopted on older-generation hardware.

Bink is based on the same fundamental technologies as systems like MPEG-2, but claims to offer significantly better performance both in terms of visual quality for a given bit rate and CPU utilization during playback. However, the big draw of the Bink codec for developers is often not the quality, but the fact that it is supplied as a ready-to-run module for all the major platforms (Windows, Mac, Linux, Xbox, Gamecube and Playstation 2, at the time of writing), and it is very straightforward to integrate into most engines.

Encoding tools are also supplied, which allow most common video formats to be compressed into Bink files very easily. From the asset pipeline, the Bink encoder can be invoked fairly easily as a command-line tool.

Localizing Video

Most games now ship a single SKU to a number of different countries, and as a result it is necessary for the game to support multiple languages. This poses an interesting problem for video sequences: there is rarely enough space on the game disc to store several copies of every video, so instead a mechanism must be used to allow the audio alone to be duplicated.

Fortunately, virtually all video formats allow a number of independent audio streams to be multiplexed into the file, and then the decoder can choose which of these to play and which to discard during playback. However, the process of encoding such a file is usually considerably more complex than simply encoding a simple pair of video and audio streams together.

Since re-encoding the video stream several times in order to create the localized audio would be a significant overhead for the asset pipeline, it is usually necessary to separate the audio streams into a number of audio-only files. Then, these can be compressed separately from the (now audio-less) video file, and the resulting streams multiplexed together as a separate step.

These stages can be combined into a single "tool" from the pipeline's perspective, but although the initial setup effort is greater, it is well worth the time to integrate them as individual steps, defining the dependencies among the input data, compressed streams, and final multiplexed file appropriately. The reason for this is that it is not at all uncommon for the audio or video sections of the file to change independently, and it can be a considerable saving in processing time if the pipeline is able to update only those streams that have changed, rather than re-encoding everything.

Subtitles

Another set of additional data that often needs to be inserted into the video stream is the text for subtitles. These are generally created as a separate file from one of the many subtitle timing applications, and while some video playback software can read them directly from this, others expect the data to be multiplexed into the main video file.

As with separate audio streams, it is often worthwhile separating the subtitle files (usually as one block, as there is no benefit in re-multiplexing only one file) in the pipeline and defining appropriate dependencies for them, as this will enable them to be modified without the need to re-run the time consuming video or audio encoding processes.

Video Standard Conversion

One of the bugbears of game video is the different video standards used in different countries. Most significantly, the fact that PAL and variants (as used in most of Europe) has a vertical refresh rate of 50 Hz, while NTSC (as used in the U.S. and Japan) uses 60 Hz instead. This results in an awkward problem—video encoded for one standard cannot be played back on the other without the need to either generate additional frames (if playing 50 Hz video at 60 Hz) or drop some frames (if playing 60 Hz video at 50 Hz). These processes are known as *pullup* and *pulldown* respectively.

This problem can be solved either during video creation (by rendering at both frame rates, for example, or by performing the conversion during the editing phase), or during playback (which often produces suboptimal results due to the complexity of the problem, but allows either frame rate to be used without requiring data changes), but all too often it falls to the pipeline to perform this conversion.

At the simplest level, it is possible to write a tool that removes or duplicates frames in the video to achieve this effect. However, on many types of video (most notably anything involving smooth horizontal pans), this can cause a very noticeable "juddering" effect because the motion is no longer smooth.

In order to avoid this problem, it is generally necessary to blend frames so that the movement speed is kept constant, essentially, the video needs to be resampled at the new frame rate, in much the same way as resampling of audio data works. However, unfortunately, doing this in a manner that introduces as few visual artifacts during the resampling process is a fairly tricky problem. It is generally not something to be attempted unless you are fairly knowledgeable about video and image processing.

Fortunately there are a number of tools available to perform the task: the previously mentioned VirtualDub and AviSynth are among the better ones. Invoking one of these on the uncompressed video (as otherwise the video will have to be decompressed and recompressed again, introducing additional artifacts) to perform the conversion and then compressing the output is usually the best solution.

CONCLUSION

While there is a much more limited range of processing tasks generally performed on audio data, there are many subtleties that can trap the unwary when implementing custom code to manipulate sound effects and music. Video, on the other hand, is usually a far simpler task *because* it is massively more complex, and as a result the vast majority of developers use off-the-shelf solutions for processing it.

8 Environment Processing

Most games take place in an environment of some description that is handled independently from the rest of the game assets, generally due to its size and importance to the gameplay and graphics. Environments take many forms, but they are generally a large mesh or collection of meshes, which can be processed using the geometry processing techniques described previously. However, there are some additional processing operations that are often performed exclusively on the environment, to generate additional data such as visibility or lighting information.

BSP TREES

BSP, or "Binary Space Partition" trees, are a mechanism for breaking up large worlds into smaller spatially coherent chunks, generally for the purposes of visibility culling, collision detection, etc. BSP trees can be regarded as a general form of more specialized spatial subdivision schemes such as portals and quadtrees, and they are notable in that they provide a fairly efficient way to deal with completely disorganized "polygon soup" data.

The basic principle of a BSP tree is extremely simple: taking a collection of polygons (the world), the tree is built by picking a plane through this space, and splitting the polygons into two groups, depending on which side of the plane they fall on. This process is then recursively repeated with each of the resulting groups, until some criteria is met for the minimum size of a group (either in terms of spatial dimensions or number of polygons) and the recursion stops.

Therefore, the result is a BSP tree structure composed of two types of nodes: the leaf nodes of the tree contain polygons, and the nonleaf nodes represent the split planes. This tree structure effectively represents a series of subdivisions of the space the mesh exists in, with the polygons all categorized into the appropriate "bucket" depending on where they lie.

Figure 8.1 shows this process in more detail. The initial split plane (shown as a dashed line) separates the world into two nodes, node 1 and node 2. Polygons A and B are sorted entirely into those nodes, while polygon C lies across the split plane, and must be either subdivided into two sections, inserted into both nodes, or left at the root. The tree formed by this operation is also shown (the tree assumes that polygon C was duplicated into both nodes 1 and 2).

The recursive process then splits node 2 into two further nodes, 3 and 4, using the split plane shown in the second diagram. This places polygon B in node 3 and polygon C (or the subdivided part thereof) in node 4. It should be noted that this new split plane *only* splits the space of (and hence polygons in) node 2. Polygon A is unaffected as it is in node 1.

This structure is useful for many reasons. For example, collision detection can be massively sped up because the point (or any other shape, for that matter) to be collided can be first sorted into the tree but "walking" from the root node, moving to the appropriate child node based on which side of each split plane the point falls on. In this way, with a minimal amount of effort, the subset of polygons that needs to be checked is reduced to those in the leaf node reached. Another use of BSP trees is in visibility calculation: as the leaf nodes form sections of space bounded by the

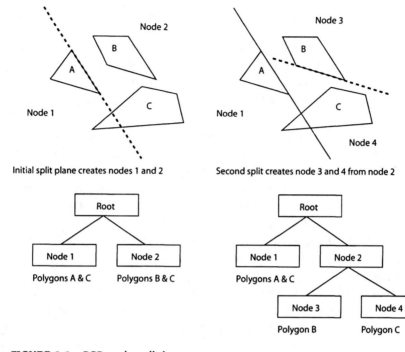

FIGURE 8.1 BSP node splitting.

split planes, they can be used to generate a good set of points for calculating a PVS (Potentially Visible Set), as will be described later.

Building a BSP Tree

The actual process of building a BSP tree is not much more complicated than the brief description given earlier. There are two main steps at each stage in the recursion: choosing a suitable split plane, and then actually splitting the polygons into the two new leaf nodes.

Choosing a Split Plane

The choice of split plane is the most important decision in building the tree. In some ways, the choice of criteria for doing this will depend on the intended use of the tree, but there are some good general guidelines that work in most situations.

First, most BSP tree implementations use the polygons in the mesh to form the split planes, that is, the plane formed by each polygon is used as a candidate split plane, and from the set of these the actual split plane is chosen, based on the further criteria which will be described. In this case, the tree is known as an "auto-partitioning" BSP tree.

Another approach is to use axis-aligned planes to perform the splitting, this method produces a so-called "k-d tree" (k being the dimensionality of the space the tree occupies). Axis-aligned split planes are commonly placed at the midpoint of the bounding box on the axis perpendicular to the plane, or at the vertex half way through a sorted list of vertex positions (again, on the perpendicular axis).

Yet another type of BSP tree is the "general" tree, where an arbitrary split plane is chosen. This gives the best theoretical performance, but it is much harder, and more computationally expensive to narrow down the set of possible split planes for each node.

Once a set of candidate split planes has been found, the relative merits of each can be considered. Generally, there are two metrics that are used to measure this: the relative numbers of polygons on each side of the split, and the number of polygons which actually *cross* the split plane. In most cases, the goal is to balance the tree by ensuring that approximately the same number of polygons lie on either side of the split, and to minimize the number of polygons which span the split (as these will usually need to be subdivided or duplicated).

Taking these metrics, the split plane that best satisfies the criteria can be found. This is stored in the newly-created split node, and then used to split the polygons into two new child leaf nodes.

Splitting the Polygons

The process of splitting the polygons is actually fairly straightforward (the algorithm described previously in the section on mesh subdivision can be used for this purpose). The bulk of the polygons should hopefully lie entirely on one side of the split or the other, and hence can simply be inserted into the corresponding leaf node. Polygons that lie across the split can be handled in one of three ways, depending on the intended use of the tree.

First, they can be subdivided into two sections, one on each side of the split. If this is done then the BSP tree nodes will be entirely contained within their bounding split planes, which can be important for some visibility algorithms, and allows the BSP tree to be used for accurately depth sorting the polygons contained within it. However, the obvious trade-off is that it introduces additional polygons into the tree with every split.

Second, they can be kept in their original form, but duplicated (or, more commonly have pointers inserted) into both leaf nodes. This results in a "loose" BSP tree, as polygons in the leaf nodes may extend beyond the bounding splits of that node, but each node is still guaranteed to include all the polygons *within* those boundaries, an important property for performing collision detection with the tree. When rendering a tree with duplicated polygons, it is usually necessary to keep track of which polygons have already been rendered to avoid rendering duplicated polygons twice if both of the leaf nodes they occupy are visible.

Third, the polygons can be stored at the split node, rather than being placed into one of the leaves. This avoids the need to duplicate or split them, and the rendering process does not need to keep track of them to avoid overdraw. However, doing this does increase the cost of collision checks against the tree (as they must check the polygons which cross *every* split they encounter, even if those polygons do not lie anywhere near the bounding area of the final leaf node).

Once the polygons have all been sorted into the nodes, the building process can be recursively continued on each of the new leaf nodes. The only remaining decision is that of when to stop the recursion.

When to Stop Splitting Nodes

Again, the decision on when to stop the recursion is largely based on the intended usage of the tree. In some cases, it may be desirable to recurse until every leaf contains a single triangle (this is known as a "solid" BSP tree). These are fairly rare, however, and in most cases the aim is to keep splitting the tree until the leaves are sufficiently small so that the polygons within them can be efficiently drawn and tested for collisions.

As such, the most common criteria used is the number of polygons in the node, as this gives the maximum number of polygons that will need to be "brute-force" examined for collisions. The size of the bounding area of the node is also often used to terminate the recursion, as this can be set to avoid the case where a very small dense area of detail gets heavily subdivided because it contains a large number of polygons (this is generally more of an issue when using BSP trees for visibility calculations, where subdivision of such small areas rarely generates any useful occlusion information).

One occasionally useful trait of BSP trees is that even after they have been generated, new polygons can be added simply by walking down the tree and clipping them to each node in turn. This can be very useful in some circumstances where it is necessary to insert objects into the tree at a later stage in the pipeline, although some care should be taken when doing this because since these objects were not considered when choosing the split planes they can end up unbalancing the tree.

POTENTIALLY VISIBLE SETS

As environments are typically very large, it is usually necessary to restrict those areas that are rendered at any given moment. Since environments are usually broken up into sections, for purposes such as collision, using structures such as BSP trees, in addition to the usual rendering techniques such as bounding-box culling, Potentially Visible Set, or PVS-based techniques have become a very common way of occlusion culling environments.

The principle of a PVS is very simple: the environment is partitioned into "sectors" using some other technique, such as a BSP tree, quadtree, or similar. Then, for each of those sectors, the PVS generation pre-processing task calculates which other sections are visible from any point within that sector, and stores a list of these. This provides a very fast way for the renderer to cut down the list of what might be visible from a given viewpoint, as it simply has to determine which sector the camera is in, and then read the list from the PVS.

The goal for a PVS is to provide a *conservative* estimate of what can be seen from a given sector—other methods can be used to cull at runtime the resulting list of sectors and remove those that are determined to be invisible, but even if this does not remove an incorrectly included sector this does not cause a problem as it will simply make the rendering process slightly less efficient. If, on the other hand, the PVS *excludes* a visible sector, then this will cause a visual artifact as it will not be drawn!

Portals

One important concept in many PVS generation algorithms is that of portals. Conceptually, portals are simply holes that allow one sector to be seen from another, for example, a door or window. Portals can be generated in a number of ways: they can be automatically calculated (portals will always lie along the boundary of a sector, and hence can be derived in a somewhat inefficient manner from the BSP split planes), or they can be manually placed during the design of the map—an increasingly common choice, as it ensures relatively sensible portal placement and provides an obvious set of initial split planes for the BSP building process to use.

The process of generating a PVS for a given set of sectors can be done in many different ways. Each has various advantages and disadvantages, and this is an area in which a considerable amount of research is still being done. Most of the existing techniques fall into one of the following categories, however:

Ray Casting

Ray casting can be used to generate the PVS quite simply by casting rays from random points along the edges of one sector, in random directions. All of the sectors that each ray passes through up to the point where it collides with something must be visible from the source sector, and can be added to the list it stores (sector visibility is almost always reciprocal, so it is implicit that if sector A can "see" sector B, sector B can "see" sector A).

This approach works, but the sheer number of rays that must be cast to get even a reasonably correct visibility estimate is staggering. However, it can be optimized in some ways, the main one being through the use of portals. Logically, if there is a portal between two sectors "A" and "B," then they must be able to see each other. Therefore, the next step is to determine if A can see any of the sectors that adjoin B. This can be done by casting a number of rays from the portal between A and B toward each of the portals joining B to other sectors. If any of the rays reach one of these ("C," for example), then that sector must be visible, and the process can be repeated, casting rays from the portal between A and B to the portal between C and each of the sectors it adjoins. This continues until either all the sectors have been marked as visible or there are no portals left in any visible sectors that have not been tested.

This method works quite well, although there can still be problems due to the finite density of the rays cast. If a portal is only visible to another through a very small gap, then there is a chance that no ray will pass through this, and the portal will incorrectly be considered as completely occluded.

Line Stabbing

The principle behind the ray casting approach can be adapted, however, to build a test for inter-portal (and hence sector) visibility which does not suffer from this problem. The key to this is to consider the visibility calculation as a *line stabbing* problem.

Essentially, the problem can be considered as this: given a number of arbitrary oriented polygons, can a line be found that passes through all of them in the same direction? If each portal is considered as one of these polygons, then finding this line is the line of sight between the sectors.

A solution to the line stabbing problem for convex polygons was set out in 1993 in a paper published by Seth Teller and Michael Hohmeyer [Teller93]. Their solution is mathematically complex, involving forming a representation of the polygons in five dimensional space and using that to find the stabbing line (if it exists). This approach, however, is guaranteed to find this line if one exists, and operates in expected $O(n^2)$ time where n is the number of polygon edges. In addition, another of their papers [Teller92] deals directly with the use of line stabbing to calculate portal visibility, and is well worth reading for further details on the implementation of this type of system.

It should be noted that this approach does not consider geometry within each sector as potential occluders, only the sector boundary portals themselves. As a result, it works best when the sector size is small and the area of the connecting portals is as small as possible.

Beam Casting

Another improvement on the basic ray casting approach works by casting beams instead of rays through the portals. Essentially, the beam starts out oriented toward the target portal, and encompassing the entire source portal. It is then clipped against objects (and portals) as they are encountered within the sector. This continues until the beam has been entirely clipped (by which point the beam may have passed through several portals), at which point the list of sectors it passes through is added to the PVS for the source cell. This can be thought of as much the same process as casting light through the portal: the beam represents the light, and every surface it illuminates is visible.

The beam casting approach generates visibility information that takes account of the presence of occluders within sectors, thereby allowing sectors to be larger without significantly decreasing the amount of culling provided by the PVS. However, it can be computational very expensive indeed to clip the beams to objects in the world, and some cases (such as that of a portal that is precisely perpendicular to another) can be hard to handle due to precision problems.

ROUTING INFORMATION

Another common problem in environment generation, which can be quite similar to that of generating visibility data, is the calculation of routing information for pathfinding algorithms. This information generally falls into two categories: accessibility information and connectivity information.

For pathfinding purposes, as with visibility, large environments are usually broken up into a number of sectors linked by portals. This is often the same subdivision that is used for the visibility calculations, although there is no particular requirement that this be the case.

Accessibility Information

Accessibility information gives details of the ability of characters (or any other moving object) to traverse through the space within a sector. The exact nature of this is highly dependent on the game. For example, in a platform game, it may be that the characters can walk on any surface within 45 degrees of a horizontal plane. An RPG might use a specifically created volume for defining where characters can walk, on the other hand, and a game with flying creatures might not be concerned with surfaces at all, but instead the connectivity between areas of open space.

In many cases, the accessibility information for a sector can be trivially derived from the mesh data within it. In the case of the platform game given previously, for example, all that is required is a dot product with each polygon in the mesh, the result being a list of the polygons on which a character can potentially stand.

Surface-Based Accessibility

In general, titles such as platform or adventure games that feature walking characters will almost always be best served by defining accessibility in terms of surfaces, as a character can only stably exist when located on one of these. At any other time, they will be in a state of transition due to gravity, and must eventually come to rest on another surface (or fall out of the world).

The effect of this is that the accessibility of any point in a sector from any other is very simple to define: in the (unusual) case of a game where characters cannot jump or fall, it is possible to reach one point on the surface from another if there is an unbroken connection between the polygons at those points. This can be determined very simply by walking across the mesh, using the connectivity information implicit in the polygons (any two accessible polygons that share an edge must be connected).

Of course, this model does not consider the fact that in most games, the characters are of a fixed size, and therefore cannot pass through any gap smaller than themselves. In cases where the initial surface accessibility is generated by hand, this is not a problem, as it can be taken into account during that process. If this is not the case, however, then a method of deriving this information is required.

Fortunately, this is relatively straightforward to test for, by extruding the surface data to form a volume describing the space the characters can exist in. For example, if the characters are 1 unit high and always stand up vertically, then extruding the surface mesh by 1 unit vertically (and clipping it against any other geometry that intersects this region) will give the volume of space the characters inhabit while standing on that surface. This can then be tested to determine accessibility as described later in the section on volume-based accessibility.

Integrating the ability to jump or fall between two unconnected surface polygons takes slightly more effort. This can be done either by examining the distance between and relative orientation of pairs of polygons and comparing them to the physical characteristics of the characters, thereby automatically generating the connections between accessible polygons, or by marking specific points or routes by hand in the map. Both of these techniques work well, and it is often useful to use them together, applying a conservative estimate of the distances characters can travel when jumping or falling to find "obvious" routes, and then adding manual routing information for more complex or unusual cases.

Volume-Based Accessibility

For games where the characters are not necessarily tied to standing on existing surfaces, or when it is necessary to use extruded surface information to test for character collisions, a method for computing accessibility information in terms of volumes of space is necessary.

The first step in this process is to define a number of initial volumes. This can be done by hand as part of the map editing process, or computed automatically. One method for automatic computation of volumes is done using a "flood-fill" process. Starting with a point in space that is known to be accessible and inside the world (character starting locations or a point just inside a portal are good choices), a ray is cast in a random direction to find a surface that forms part of the volume. From this point, a simple walk across the surfaces using the polygon connectivity will generate the bounds of the volume.

This process can then be repeated for every known accessible point, discarding those that are already inside a section of the volume. The result is a complete set of volumes encompassing the "space" inside the map.

There is one small problem with this approach: it does not take into account the possibility of entirely disconnected groups of polygons existing inside a volume. To locate these, after the volumes have been generated, any polygons that have not formed part of the surface of a volume should be examined. They will either lie entirely outside the accessible area (and therefore can be discarded), or inside a volume, in which case they need to be added to that volume's surface.

These volumes give a measure of the absolute connectivity of the space, any point within one volume is accessible from any point within the same volume, but points in two volumes are not accessible from each other. However, this information only refers to the connectivity between points for an infinitely thin line—in most cases, game characters will have a certain size that must be taken into account.

The easiest way to do this is to take the size of the character, and reduce the volumes by a corresponding amount, effectively extruding all of the exterior polygons inward so that a point collision with the resulting mesh will generate the same result as colliding the character volume with the original mesh. This will have the effect of "collapsing" any section of the volume that cannot be traversed by a character. When this occurs, the volume can be split into two separate volumes, each of which is inaccessible from the other.

Connectivity Information

Essentially, the basis of the information required for high-level pathfinding is connectivity. In order to accurately calculate a route between two points in a large world, the task is generally split into two levels: calculation of a coarse route across the whole map (using sector-level information), and calculation of the exact route within the current sector.

The reason for this distinction is because calculating the entire route in detail as a single operation would be prohibitively expensive, and liable to be rendered invalid due to the movement of dynamic objects or other obstacles. Hence, the precise route is only calculated so as to reach a suitable portal in the current sector; beyond that, all that is needed is to know the list of sectors that must be traversed, so that when the next is reached a new route to the appropriate exit portal can be determined.

The precise route calculation can be carried out using the accessibility information described previously, but for the coarse sector level calculation the sector connectivity information is needed. The form this takes is very simple: for each sector, the sectors it adjoins (and has a portal into) needs to be recorded, along with the details of which of those portals are reachable from each other.

The list of portals and their adjoining sectors is easy to generate, so all that is required is the connectivity information between the portals. For this, the sector-level accessibility data described previously can be used. If two portals can be connected by a route across a traversable surface, or they are in the same volume of accessible space, then they can be considered linked. This test is repeated for each pair of portals in the sector to build the connectivity information.

The other main problem to consider when calculating this information is that of dynamic objects. For example, a door may lie between two points, and whether or not a route can be found between them might depend on its status (open or closed). In general, these problems can be solved by considering the best case (that is, every door is open) situation when building the accessibility and connectivity data, and then flagging any route that passes though such a dynamic object so that it can be modified if necessary. In some cases, it may be possible to deliberately create portals across any object of this nature, making the implementation of this very easy as the problem is reduced to simply marking the portal as unusable while the door is closed.

PRECALCULATED LIGHTING

Due to their size and largely static nature, environments are a very common candidate for pre-calculation of lighting information. This allows higher lighting fidelity than would be possible at runtime, and in many cases removes the workload of applying dynamic lighting to large sections of mesh.

Pre-calculated lighting solutions generally fall into one of three categories: vertex-based lighting, lightmaps, and volumetric solutions.

Vertex Lighting

Vertex lighting is the simplest form of lighting process to implement, and it is very similar to the dynamic lighting performed by most game engines. The fundamental principle is very simple: for each vertex in the mesh, the color of the light at that point in space is calculated and stored. When the mesh is drawn, these colors are interpolated across the polygons, giving the illusion of smooth lighting.

The calculation for vertex lighting is generally very simple; a dot product against the vertex normal is used with each light source to determine the incident light angle (and hence the magnitude of that light's contribution), which is multiplied by the light color, and added together with the results from the other lights and the ambient value.

The results this produces generally look good, but they are no better than what is achieved by realtime dynamic lighting. The big advantage of performing lighting as a preprocess is the ability to perform occlusion checks on light sources, and hence calculate accurate shadows.

The process for adding light occlusion to the vertex lighting calculation is straightforward. All that is needed is to cast a ray between the vertex and each light source, and determine if there is an unobstructed line of sight between them. If there is, then the light's contribution is added as normal, if not then it is discarded as the vertex is in shadow (relative to that light source).

This approach works, although the results do not generally look very good as there is a sudden transition from light to shadow. This is due to the fact that the light source is being considered to be an infinitely small point (and hence casting completely sharp shadows). A more accurate representation of real-world lighting can be achieved by performing "jittered sampling" on the occlusion rays: essentially, picking a number of points within a radius of the light source (either uniformly or at random), and casting rays to all of them. The light contribution is then modulated by the proportion of those rays that were unoccluded, giving a smooth transition between light and shadow with an accurate umbra and penumbra.

The major problem with vertex lighting, unfortunately, is that the accuracy of the lighting is determined by the density of the vertices in the mesh. If sufficient vertices are available, then the results look very good, but if not then it has a tendency to generate very blurred, extended shadow regions (as a result of the bilinear interpolation), and it can be very hard to avoid shadows "smearing" in front of the objects that cast them.

It is possible to deliberately subdivide the mesh to counter these problems, but this often ends up generating a vast number of polygons to preserve the edges of shadows unless the lighting being used is very soft. A preferable solution to this problem, therefore, is to make use of texture maps to encode the lighting information within the polygons without the need to subdivide them.

Lightmaps

This is the basic principle behind *lightmaps*: a lightmap is simply a texture that contains lighting information across a surface, and used as a means to efficiently store and render this information without the need to add additional vertices.

The first step in generating the lightmap for a polygon is to prepare and map a suitable section of texture onto the polygon. There are many ways to perform a procedural mapping of a texture onto groups of polygons, but the simplest is just to take the dimensions in world-space coordinates of the polygon, scale this by the desired lighting density, and allocate a texture of that size (or the nearest suitable size). These individual small textures can then be packed together into a number of larger texture pages at a later stage. It should be noted that it is usually necessary to deliberately oversize the texture somewhat using this technique, adding a number of pixels around the edge (outside the area referenced by the polygon's UV coordinates) to prevent filtering artifacts.

The basic process for generating the actual lightmap data is very similar to that used for generating vertex lighting information. The key process is the evaluation of the lighting color at a point on the surface. The only difference is that instead of only evaluating the lighting at each vertex, a regular grid of points across each polygon that correspond to the mapping of each texel in the texture are evaluated and the results written to the texture.

Obviously, one drawback of this technique over vertex lighting is that many, many more points need to be evaluated. This can cost a significant amount of CPU time, and increasing the number of light sources dramatically increases the amount of processing required.

That said, this approach works very well in situations where there is a single distant primary light source, such as the sun. However, it is less suitable for indoor environments, where the lighting tends to be generated by a larger number of more diffuse light sources; performing the number of samples needed to get acceptable results in this circumstance becomes prohibitively expensive *very* quickly.

For this reason, many games set in such environments (for example *Quake 2)* use *radiosity* calculations instead. Radiosity works by modeling lighting as a transfer of energy between surfaces—essentially, every polygon in the scene not only receives light, but also scatters some of that light back into the scene. The process of lighting a scene using radiosity is an iterative one: first the incident light on every point on each surface is evaluated, by adding the light emitted by every unoccluded point on nearby surfaces. This gives the amount (and color) of the light that is reflected from that point, and this is the color the surface appears to be.

Once this calculation has been performed for every point in the entire scene, it is repeated, using the calculated reflected light at each point as the emitted light values. With each successive iteration, the changes in the reflected light values decrease, causing the radiosity calculation to converge on a solution.

As this description suggests, radiosity calculation is quite an expensive process, although there are various ways in which it can be optimized to make the processing required feasible. The major advantage of radiosity, however, is that unlike the previously described direct ray casting approach to lighting, it can handle unlimited numbers of light sources and arbitrarily shaped lights (with the exception of, ironically, infinitely small point light sources). The reason for this is simple—in a radiosity system, a light source is just a surface with points that already have an emitted light value at the start of the solving process. Therefore, it is even possible with some care to use texture maps to generate shaped lights!

Volumetric Lighting

Volumetric solutions, as the name suggest, work in a radically different manner from either of the lighting systems discussed thus far. Conceptually, they are very simple; the goal is the creation of a mesh that represents the volume of the light, and hence can be used to light the scene by combining it with the physical polygons at runtime (generally through the use of a stencil buffer or other screen space depth technique).

In practice, however, this is a virtually useless approach. In all but the most constrained scenes, the light volume is effectively infinite, or at least very large. Attempting to build and render such a mesh at anything approaching a reasonable speed is generally futile. However, the *inverse* of the light volume is a rather more useful construct.

The inverse of a light volume is, logically enough, a shadow volume: a volume that encompasses the areas of space that are in shadow relative to the light source. This can then be rendered using a stencil buffer or similar technique to darken all of the pixels that are in shadow at runtime. This approach has the major advantage over the techniques described previously that it can be used to shadow arbitrary geometry. World shadow volumes can shadow moving objects such as characters just as efficiently as they shadow the static world geometry (in fact, there is no additional penalty for doing so since the cost of shadow volumes is solely based on the amount of shadow *casting* geometry, not the amount of shadow *receiving* geometry).

The calculation of shadow volumes is based on the geometry that casts the shadows (also known as the light *occluder*). The basic process of building a shadow volume is very simple. First, the facing of each polygon in the occluder mesh is compared with the direction of the light source. If the polygon faces toward the light, it forms part of the leading edge of the shadow volume, and can be inserted directly into it. Otherwise, it is ignored.

Once the leading edge of the volume has been built, it must be extruded along the vector of the light to form an actual volume. This is done by taking every open edge (that is, every edge that is not shared by two polygons), and extruding that edge backwards, moving the two vertices along a vector away from the light source and creating a new polygon. The distance this extrusion needs to cover is the maximum "length" of the shadow; generally, this is the distance between the casting geometry and the furthest potential shadow receiver in the scene.

Finally, the rear of the volume needs to be capped to form a closed volume. This can be done either by taking the vertices that have been extruded and building a number of polygons to form a closed volume, or simply (but less efficiently) by taking the polygons in the leading edge, and creating duplicates with all their vertices pushed back away from the light (and their normals flipped so that they face outwards).

This process builds a valid shadow volume for the geometry in question, although it is not necessarily the most efficient in terms of polygon count and overall size (size is very important for shadow volumes, as the primary cost of rendering them is often the fill rate required to draw the polygons, rather than the vertex transformation time). Many optimizations are possible but one of the most useful is to take the *CSG* (Constructive Solid Geometry, or the mathematics of combining solid volumes of space) union of overlapping volumes, thereby reducing the amount of overdraw significantly.

Another which can be used if the correctness of shading *within* the occluders is not important is to move the leading edge polygons backwards, and remove as much detail as possible while still keeping within the bounds of the original occluder mesh. Convex hulls and interior bounding volumes for shadow occluders can be very useful in reducing the number of polygons needed to form the volumes; in many circumstances shadows can be cast from the silhouette of the convex hull relative to the light source (rather than the object itself) without introducing particularly noticeable artifacts.

This form of volumetric lighting has some very useful properties, such as the ability to shadow dynamic objects at no additional cost. However, it does have some significant drawbacks: the volume only provides a binary indication if pixels are shadowed or not, and therefore it is very difficult to simulate soft-edge shadows (there are techniques that use multiple volumes to do this, but they are generally much too expensive for use on current hardware except in very limited circumstances). For the same reason, it is also usually necessary to encode light contribution magnitudes (based on falloff distance and angle of incidence) into the mesh on a per-vertex basis, as this information is also not encapsulated in the volume.

CONCLUSION

The techniques described in this chapter only scratch the surface of what is possible when processing environment information for gameplay and rendering purposes. This is a very fast moving field, and many of the "established" techniques are actually constantly changing as more advanced hardware capabilities and new design requirements emerge.

It is also the case that the majority of the algorithms described here are unlikely to be best used in the exact way they have been described; virtually every game will have specific conditions which allow different optimizations or variants to be employed.

9 Managing Asset Processing

In This Chapter

- Dependency-Based Processing
- The Make Tool
- Output Data Formats
- Handling File Interdependencies
- Building Robust Tools
- Interfacing to Existing Systems

The actual processing of assets in the pipeline is only half of the story; there is a significant amount of management that must be done to manage the process itself. In recent years, this has become increasingly necessary as the volumes of data and complexity of processing involved have increased massively. As a result, it is no longer a viable strategy to simply reprocess all of the assets for the game, or even all the assets for an individual level when required; more fine-grained control over the process is required.

In most cases, a separate program is required to simply *manage* the execution of the tools that perform the processing. This program is responsible for collecting the input and output data for each step of the pipeline, and determining which tasks need to be run (and in what order) to produce the desired output. Improving the efficiency of this management will in turn greatly increase the efficiency of the pipeline as a whole, since not performing a processing operation at all is the best way to optimize it!

The key to achieving this is to build a system that minimizes the amount of unnecessary work performed when an asset change occurs. This can be done by exploiting the coherence of the input and output data as a whole. Once all the data has been processed once, then only elements of the input that have changed since that time need to be examined, and in turn only the elements of the output that are based on those need updating. It is these *dependencies* between the input and output that must be analyzed to allow this incremental model of processing to function.

DEPENDENCY-BASED PROCESSING

The idea behind this dependency-based strategy is quite simple. A dependency represents a link between a source asset and processed output file, indicating that the latter contains data that is provided (or affected by) the former. So, we say that the output file *depends* on the source asset, and that the asset is a *prerequisite* of the output file. This is a many-to-many relationship; one output file may depend on many source assets (consider, for example, a model file containing a mesh, textures, and animation data), and one source asset may generate many output files.

Dependencies are not limited to being simple links between pairs of files, either; if some files are built using intermediate files, or depend on other output files, then a *dependency chain* emerges, where each of the dependencies of a file may in turn have dependencies of their own. Figure 9.1 shows a simple dependency chain for a character model. If the entire asset pipeline was viewed, elements of this chain (for example, the run animation) might be used in other characters as well, and therefore have additional dependent resources.

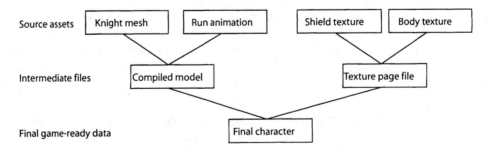

FIGURE 9.1   A simple asset dependency chain.

Walking along the dependency chain for an output file, therefore, provides a list of all of the source (and intermediate) files that affect it, and hence may cause it to be rebuilt if they change. However, while this is a useful view conceptually, in practical terms it is usually more useful to look at dependency chains the other way around: for a given source asset, walking along the chain for its dependents will give a list of output files that must be updated if it is changed.

Dependency chains do not generally exist in isolation, either; chains frequently meet and overlap (for example, if one intermediate file or asset is used by many processes). This is actually another very useful property because in doing so, they provide all the information needed to minimize the amount of effort required to perform a single set of updates.

Consider the case where a number of source assets have all been changed. If each change is processed independently, and the individual dependents of the source asset updated, then some output and intermediate files may be updated several times. This is particularly problematic in the case where there are several "layers" of intermediate files depending on one another; in these cases, it is hard to remove the unnecessary updates because only the *last* update of any given asset is guaranteed to have a complete set of up-to-date intermediate files!

Figure 9.2 shows an example of this type of more complex dependency chain. The knight and paladin models share the same run animation, but have different base meshes. However, they both use the same texture page and therefore, the intermediate texture page file is shared between them.

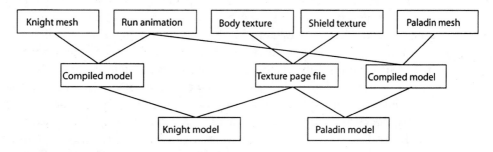

FIGURE 9.2 Dependencies on shared assets.

The dependency chains contain the solution to this, as they store all of the necessary information about the relationships between the files to ensure that every file (both intermediate and output) is updated once only, but in the correct order to ensure that old data is never used. This is done by walking through all of the dependency chains simultaneously, and building a queue of the files that must be processed.

One very straightforward way to do this is to exploit the fact that the dependency chains themselves encode the order that operations must be performed in. To build the queue of operations is a simple iterative process, using a list of potentially modified files as the basis.

The first step of the procedure is to take every source file that has changed, and recursively walk down to all its dependents, adding each to the list (if it is not already present). After this step, the complete set of files that must be updated is stored on the list and the processing order can be determined.

This is done by repeatedly walking through the list and checking each file to see if it is ready to be processed. This is done by examining the files it immediately depends on; that is, those prerequisites that are directly linked to it. If any of those files is still on the list, then it cannot be processed yet, and is skipped. However, if none is present, then the file is moved to the end of the queue. This process is then repeated until there are no files left on the list. With this done, the queue contains an ordered list of the files for processing, so that every file is only updated once, and all of the prerequisite files are updated before each.

While in the majority of cases the files will be processed in a linear manner, and therefore this queue is all that is required for the operation to begin, it is also possible to produce output in a form suitable for processing many assets in parallel, for example, using a distributed network of machines, or a multi-CPU system. To do this, the same procedure is used, but with a marker added to the items on the list. When an item with no prerequisites is found, instead of being moved to the queue immediately it is marked and left in place. Then, when the end of the list is reached, all of the marked files are moved into the queue as a "batch." Each of these batches consist of files that are ready for processing but are also guaranteed to be independent of each other, so they can all be handled simultaneously if needed.

While in many cases analyzing the dependency information once and then processing the resulting queue of output files is enough; in cases where there are large numbers of changes being made to the source assets, it may be desirable to update the processing queue as changes are made. This can be done very simply by taking the current outstanding queue entries and adding the dependents of the newly-modified assets to them, creating a new list of files that need updating. Then, the dependency analysis procedure can be repeated using this input list to generate a new queue for continued processing, thereby ensuring that any changes caused by the new updates are correctly inserted into the processing order.

This technique can be very useful if the asset processing system allows multiple tasks to run concurrently, as it means that a single processing operation does not block the entire system until it completes, though unrelated operations may still be executed in parallel with it.

Determining Asset Dependencies

One of the key problems faced when implementing a system of this nature is how to actually construct the dependency information for the assets in the first place. The mechanisms for doing this will depend to a large degree on the processing tools and files being used, but there are some general areas that most techniques fall into:

Explicitly Stored Dependency Information

In some systems, such as the *make* tool which will be described in more detail later, the dependency information is stored as part of the script that describes all the desired processing operations. In general, this file is human generated, although dependencies can be specified for groups or types of files as well as individual assets, reducing the amount of maintenance required. This approach has the advantage that it is very easy to see and edit the dependency information, especially if it is necessary to add some special case entries for certain assets.

However, there are several fairly significant disadvantages of this system. Dependencies must be consistent across fairly large groups of files, otherwise a lot of manual editing is required. It is also impossible to encode dependency information that is based on the *contents* of the assets. So, for example, making a model file dependent on the textures it uses is impossible unless a human (or another tool) updates the dependency information by hand.

Dependency Information Stored in Assets

Another approach is to store the dependencies of asset files in the file itself. This way, the dependency information can be built by the exporter or tool that creates the file, based on the information it has about the contents. This makes this approach very suitable for handling assets such as models which may be formed from several separate files. It is also generally quite straightforward to implement, although a unified format for storing this information (either as part of the asset file, or in a separate metadata file) is required.

The main disadvantage of this approach is that it is only suitable in circumstances where the dependency chain for an asset can be easily predicted ahead of the processing itself, and is not likely to change often. This is because the information is generally needed to form dependencies for files *other* than the one it is actually stored in. For example, storing a list of textures used in a model file does not actually define prerequisites for the model file itself, as it is a source asset and has none. Instead, this information is used to construct the prerequisites for the processed file(s) created from this model.

Dependency Information Generated by the Processing Code

The final approach is to generate the dependency information "on the fly" by using the processing code (or a subset of it) to read each asset and build the dependency tree. This approach has the major advantage that it can easily handle very complex interdependencies between assets based on their contents, and it is relatively easy to maintain, once the initial framework is in place. Also, by building the dependency information this way, changes in the structure can be easily implemented, without having to edit external files, re-export, or reprocess assets to update their stored data.

However, the process of building the dependency information can be quite slow, and must be repeated whenever an asset changes. It also means that the dependency information is not easily visible for debugging purposes, or editable in the event that a special case change is required.

Of course, there is no requirement that only one of these approaches is taken; it is not uncommon to use a combination, picking the most appropriate technique for different types of assets or processing requirements. Dependency information from a number of different sources can be easily integrated into a single dependency tree for processing, and it is even relatively straightforward to remove all of the dependency information for a given asset or assets and re-insert it if changes to the asset that affect its dependencies occur during processing.

Determining When Assets Have Changed

The procedure for actually determining when an asset has been modified depends largely on the structure of the asset management system in use. If a version control system of some description is employed, then it is simply a case of either comparing the version numbers of each asset in the database with the last processed copy, or just retrieving the list of modifications in every changelist since the last update was performed.

On a flat file system, it is slightly more difficult to detect changes, although there are some methods that work relatively well. The most commonly used system is simply to compare the "last modified" date on each file, and check if it is newer than the last version that was processed (or newer than the processed output file, in some systems). This is not particularly robust, though, as it can be easily confused by actions such as "rolling back" files (by copying a previous version over the top), or if a machine's internal clock is wrong! It does have the major advantage of being very fast, and requiring little or no external information about the files.

Another, more stable method is to take a checksum of the files each time they are processed, and compare that against the stored copy. If a strong checksum or hashing system (the MD5 algorithm is a popular choice for this) is used, then the possibility of a *collision*, where two different files generate the same checksum value, occurring is infinitesimally small. Therefore, the check is a very robust way to determine if a file has changed. However, using this system requires that the entire source asset be read and the checksum calculated every time it needs to be checked, a fairly slow procedure.

If the file formats of the files being used are all under the control of the pipeline developer, or separate metadata storage is available, then one way to avoid this problem is to store the checksum in the file itself, thereby requiring only a handful of bytes to be read and compared to check for updates. However, it is comparatively rare that it is possible to do this for all types of asset files.

Another common compromise is to use both techniques, employing a simple timestamp based test for day-to-day updates, but performing a full checksum comparison on an overnight or weekend basis. This way, any assets that become "stale" as a result of an invalid modification date will be caught and fixed the next time a complete update is performed.

A less widely-employed, but useful in some circumstances, approach is to delegate the task of checking asset versions to the specific tools that perform the processing (sometimes after first checking the timestamp or checksum as an "early out" test). This allows the tool to perform much more fine-grained checking on the file, and determine which sections, if any need updating. For example, in the case of a game where levels are stored as a single large map file, it may be desirable for the map building tool to determine which sections have been modified and only update dependent files related to those, rather than the entire map.

Handling Code Changes

While the dependencies between output files and source assets follow a pattern which can be relatively easily captured in a dependency tree, it is also the case that the processing code itself can (and almost certainly will) change during the development process. The significance of this depends largely on the frequency with which such changes occur. If the engine and pipeline tools are based on stable, mature technology, then changes may be very rare. On the other hand, if the engine is still under development, changes are likely to be much more frequent.

In the case where the processing code only changes rarely, it may well be possible to ignore the possibility altogether in the pipeline, and simply perform a manual "flush" of all of the processed asset data when a change does occur, forcing everything (or the subset affected by the change) to be reprocessed. However, this will quickly become a bottleneck in the procedure, requiring significant time and effort every time a change is required.

On a conceptual level, making the processing pipeline aware of changes to the underlying code is a relatively straightforward procedure, all that is required is to form a set of dependencies between the tool itself and every file that it is involved in processing. This way, a change to the tool will cause all of the files that tool has touched to be updated, and then their dependents, and so on, until everything is up-to-date, in exactly the same way that a change to one of the source assets is handled.

Checking for Code Changes

In many cases, the procedure for determining when a change has been made to the processing code can use exactly the same mechanisms as when detecting changes to source assets. If the processing tool binaries are in a version control system of some description (either the asset database, or a separate source control system), then they can be updated from there as required when a change occurs. Otherwise, the methods described previously for testing asset file timestamps or checksums can be employed. Although, as the number and size of processing tool binaries is generally much smaller than the assets themselves, it is usually worthwhile to *always* perform a checksum test on them to ensure no change is overlooked.

If the individual processing tools that make up the pipeline are in separate binary files, then simply checking for updates to the files may be enough. Likewise, if the pipeline is relatively stable, but the tools are integrated together, then the overhead of reprocessing large numbers of assets when a change occurs may be acceptable. However, if this is not the case, then a more fine-grained approach to tool changes may be necessary.

One method of dealing with this is incredibly simple: by incorporating version numbers for each tool into the binary file (either as a specifically readable block, or simply in a form where invoking the tool outputs all of the included version numbers), changes affecting individual processing operations or asset types can be detected by checking for the increasing version number. This mechanism works very well, although it does rely on the programmer's remembering to update the version number! In fact, this can actually be a blessing as well as a curse, as it allows minor updates or bug-fixes to be made without forcing assets to be rebuilt.

If the asset processing tools have input into the process of deciding which files need to be updated, then another option is to build this versioning logic into the tool, by encoding information in the output files about which versions of the tools were used to build them, and then, based on that, deciding if they need to be updated. This is a good technique to use in cases where the tools are changing rapidly or frequently have new features added, as it allows (with some programmer effort) even more fine-grained control over the process. For example, if a change is made that only affects files containing one particular type of data, the tool could check for that when deciding if files built using the immediately preceding version need to be reprocessed.

THE MAKE TOOL

Probably the single most commonly used dependency-based build tool is *make*, a utility originally developed for Unix systems but later ported to just about every modern operating system. Make is available in every Unix distribution, and there are many Windows ports available, including direct ports of the Unix versions, and variants that are supplied with most compilers. Make's original purpose was to assist with compiling source code, but it is built in a very generic manner, allowing the invocation of virtually any command line tool as part of the process of converting input files into output files.

As such a generic tool, make is not able to use dependency information from the asset files themselves, and instead relies on an external file, known as a *descriptor file* that specifies both the dependencies between inputs and outputs, and the processing steps that should be performed on them. Make uses file timestamps to determine if a file is up-to-date, by comparing the last modifications of the source and destination files for each operation.

Descriptor File Syntax

Make's descriptor files are stored in a text file (typically called "makefile"), which is comprised of a series of *rules*, each of which defines the information needed to build a specific output file. The syntax is very simple: the name of the output file is supplied first, followed by a colon, and then a list of the prerequisites for that file. For example:

```
textures.bin : texture1.tga texture2.tga
```

specifies that the `textures.bin` output file depends on the two .TGA files listed. Therefore, if any of those files have a timestamp newer than that of `textures.bin` (or it simply does not exist), it will be rebuilt. The commands to build the file are specified immediately after the rule, preceded with a tab character to distinguish them.

```
textures.bin : texture1.tga texture2.tga
        packtextures textures.bin texture1.tga texture2.tga
```

In this case, the command is simply executed "as is," and specifies directly the files to be operated on. However, make supports macros that can be used to allow rules to operate more easily on lists of files—for example:

```
TEXTURES = texture1.tga texture2.tga

textures.bin : $(TEXTURES)
    packtextures textures.bin $(TEXTURES)
```

In this example, the list of input textures is defined as a macro, which is then subsequently referenced where it is needed rather than supplying the items explicitly. Macros are defined by supplying a macro name, followed by either "=" or " : =" and then the contents. If a variable is defined with "=", then it is a *recursively expanded* variable. Any reference to other variables will be kept intact in the macro and expanded every time it is used. If, on the other hand, " : =" is used, then it is a *simply expanded* variable. In this case, references to other variables will be expanded at the time the variable is defined, and the results stored instead. For example:

```
CHARACTERTEX = body.tga face.tga
LEVELTEX = grass.tga bluesky.tga
THISLEVELTEX = $(CHARACTERTEX) $(LEVELTEX)
LEVEL1TEX := $(CHARACTERTEX) $(LEVELTEX)

LEVELTEX = earth.tga redsky.tga
```

At this point, LEVEL1TEX will contain "body.tga face.tga grass.tga bluesky.tga," as it was expanded before the definition of LEVELTEX changed. However, if THISLEVELTEX is used instead, then it will be expanded using the *current* values of CHARACTERTEX and LEVELTEX, yielding "body.tga face.tga earth.tga redsky.tga" instead.

As seen in the previous examples, to reference a macro, simply surround the list name in brackets and prefix it with a $ sign (in other words, "$(<macro name>"). There are also some built-in macros (as well as more defined from the host machines' environment, such as the path to installed compiler tools), and a class of macros known as "automatic variables." These are automatically set up every time a command is executed, and contain information such as the target filename and the list of modified dependencies. For a full list of these, see the make documentation.

Make also contains various functions that can be referenced in a similar way to variables, and that similarly insert their results into the rule. These can be used to perform many useful tasks such as string manipulation and wildcard expansion (again, a full list can be found in the make documentation).

The rules in the definition file describe how to actually build the files referenced, but they will not actually cause anything to happen unless make has a reason to build the file. This will only occur if it is either explicitly asked to (by the user typing "`make texture.bin`," for example), or the file appears as a prerequisite in another rule that it needs to build (which, in turn, must have either been explicitly specified or invoked from a third rule).

In order to provide a convenient way to specify "top-level" rules that build a number of files, make supports *phony targets*. A phony target is a file that does not actually exist (and will never be created), but is always considered to be out-of-date. This can be used to write a rule solely for the purpose of triggering other rules, for example:

```
.PHONY : alltextures
alltextures : textures.bin textures2.bin
```

The ".`PHONY`" declaration defines that the target `alltextures` should be considered phony; in fact, even without this the rule would still operate normally. However, if for some reason a file called `alltextures` happened to exist on the disc, and it was newer than the source files (`textures.bin` and `texture2.bin`), then the rule would be considered to be up-to-date and skipped. Marking it as phony simply ensure that this can never happen.

In this case, the phony rule tells make that when it is asked to build `alltextures`, it should build the `textures.bin` and `textures2.bin` targets (because they are specified as dependencies). This rule can then be invoked by issuing the command "`make alltextures`" from the command line, or as a dependency of another rule, for example, a rule that makes all of the resources for the game. In addition, asking make to build the special target "`all`" causes it to build all of the top-level targets in the file (that is, all targets that are not prerequisites of another target).

Pattern Rules

As make was originally designed for processing and compiling source code, the early versions of the tool required every input file to be explicitly specified somewhere in the input rules. This is generally fine for programs, as the number of source files is usually relatively small, and additions are infrequent. However, this is not generally the case with game assets, and therefore maintaining a file that must contain the name of every single asset in the game soon becomes very unwieldy.

Fortunately, later version of make introduced a feature known as *pattern rules*. Pattern rules are a form of *implicit rule* (that is, a rule that operates on an entire class of targets, rather than an explicitly specified list) that allow a rule to be defined that is executed on every target whose name matches a specified string pattern. This way, rules that operate on specific types of assets can be easily built. Pattern rules follow exactly the same syntax as normal rules, except that the % character is used to indicate "one or more arbitrary characters" in the names specified. For example:

```
%.tex : %.tga
        converttexture $@ $<
```

This rule enables any target with a .tex extension to be built from a corresponding .tga file. The $@ and $< entries are automatic variables that correspond to the name of the target file and the source file for the rule, respectively. For example, if the target file grass.tex exists, then this command would expand to "converttexture grass.tga grass.tex."

It should be noted that, like all other make rules, this does not actually perform any actions unless another rule references a file matching it.

Wildcards

Therefore, what is needed as the logical companion to pattern rules is some mechanism for specifying groups of files as the prerequisites of a target without actually listing them. This can be very easily achieved through the use of wildcards, for example:

```
alltextures : *.tex
```

This rule causes all of the files with a .tex extension in the current directory to be built (using whatever rules are available to do so, such as the pattern rule given above) when the alltextures target is referenced. However, this rule will only *update* existing files so that if a corresponding .tex file for the asset does not exist, it will not be built. Note also that while wildcards will be automatically expanded if they appear in a target or dependency list, in a variable declaration they must be explicitly expanded by wrapping them in the built-in wildcard function, "$(wildcard $.tex)," for example.

This is where the string manipulation features of make come in handy. Since what is actually required is not a list of the output files that exist, but a list of the output files that *should* exist, we can build that list by taking the list of input files and changing the extensions; we know that in this case, every .tga file should generate a corresponding .tex file. This can be done with the following rule:

```
TEXTURELIST := $(patsubst %.tga,%.tex,$(wildcard $.tga))
alltextures : $(TEXTURELIST)
```

This rule uses the patsubst function, which performs a pattern substitution. The first argument is the pattern to match (with, as before, % indicating any sequence of one or more characters), the second is the replacement pattern, and the third argument is the input data, in this case, taken from the list of .tga files generated by the wildcard function.

This pattern substitution has the effect of creating a list of the target files, by stripping the .tga extension and replacing it with .tex. The creation of this list is placed in a variable definition to improve performance. Since the variable is defined as being simply expanded, the wildcard and pattern substitution operators are only evaluated once, and then the resulting list is stored for re-use.

Overriding Rules

With this, it is possible to build make files that take source assets of different types from various locations, and build them as required without having to provide explicit rules for every single asset. However, there are often cases where it is desirable to be able to do just that, for example, when there is one texture that looks poor under the default compression settings, or if a special-case is needed to handle the player's character model differently from other NPCs.

Fortunately, make provides a very convenient mechanism for doing this. When searching for a rule to build a specific target, make will always use a rule that explicitly names that target if one is available, only examining implicit and pattern rules if none is found. Thus, even though a rule exists that specifies how to build .tga files into .tex files, if another rule is written with a target of player.tex, it will be used to build that file rather than the more general rule. If the same target is explicitly specified by two rules, make will generate an error.

Advantages and Limitations of Make

Make is a very powerful tool, and the description given here only covers a relatively small fraction of the available functionality. Make is very widely used, and has been tested on many large scale projects. There is even (albeit somewhat primitive) functionality included for running multiple tasks in parallel to improve performance on multi-CPU machines. The descriptor file syntax is somewhat arcane at first sight, but is quite readable and can be easily read and edited by both humans and other applications. In particular, it can be very useful to use external tools to generate portions of these, as a mechanism for encoding dependency information from asset files.

Make works very well on Unix systems, where just about any conceivable task can be achieved through shell scripts or other command line tools. However, on Windows systems, less basic functionality is available to command line programs. In practice, though, this is a relatively minor hurdle. Most of the important tools for asset processing can be command line driven (or must be written in-house), and the other "glue" utilities can be fairly simply replaced or rewritten.

The main disadvantages of using make are that it only checks for file modification through the file timestamps, and adding support for more complex dependencies (such as those based on asset contents) can be complex, and require many custom tools to build additional dependency information in a format make can understand. Also, make has no native support for integrating with asset management systems, it works strictly from a local filing system. Therefore, for most purposes some form of external program will be needed to handle the task of getting asset updates from the database and invoking make when required to perform the processing tasks.

OUTPUT DATA FORMATS

If you are using a middleware engine solution, or have an existing engine to work with, then in all probability the format of the files the asset pipeline must produce is already fixed and there is little room for modifications. However, if there is scope for modifying or creating new formats, then there are several areas worthy of consideration:

Standardizing Wrapper Formats

First, as mentioned previously with regard to intermediate file formats, having a standard "wrapper" format for data can be exceptionally useful. The wrapper format does not have to actually specify a format for the fine-grained data that makes up the bulk of the file, but merely provide a framework that it and other data can be easily slotted into. Many common file formats such as AIFF, ELF, and JPEG files use such structures. The layout of the file allows tools to easily read certain information and ignore anything they do not need or understand.

This is usually achieved by splitting the file into blocks, each of which has a fixed header giving the type of the block and its size. This way, only a trivial amount of code is required to enumerate the blocks present in a file, and extract those of interest. In some cases, the format may also allow for blocks to be nested inside each other, which enables a hierarchical structure to be employed, further encapsulating certain types of information.

It is also useful to include a master header block on the whole file, giving such information as the version of the wrapper format (while this is highly unlikely to change, it is possible), the byte-ordering of the file, a dirty flag (which indicates if the file was correctly closed the last time it was written to), and possibly a checksum of the contents for integrity-verification and version control purposes. If possible, this header should also include an easily recognizable fixed byte sequence at a known offset; this is known as the "magic" value (the first 4 bytes of the file are the traditional location for these). This enables tools to very quickly identify the type of the file simply by reading these bytes, even if the filename or extension is corrupt, and provides a small degree of protection from loading completely corrupted data.

Including Metadata

Another feature of most wrapper formats is that it is easily possible to mark different blocks within the file as being intended for different uses, and treat them differently during the loading process. For example, the ELF executable format uses this so that debugging information can be stored in the file, but the sections containing this are not loaded into memory when the program is run normally, as this would waste memory. The debugger, however, looks for these sections and loads them to get the information it needs.

This can be a very useful trick, as it enables additional metadata for processing, debugging, or other purposes to be included directly into the compiled asset file, thereby avoiding the need to have several different files containing this information, and ensuring that they are always available when needed. Yet since these blocks are not actually loaded by the game, they do not cost any memory or processing time, beyond the drive seek needed to skip them.

For pipeline tools, one of the most useful types of metadata that can be included is a processing history of the file. This is simply a description of how the file was built: which tool (and version) performed each step in the processing, which source assets (and again, versions) were used, and what options each took. This, along with the details of when the processing took place, can be vital, both for debugging problems, and in allowing tools to make intelligent decisions about when files should be updated. For example, if the pipeline can determine which version of a tool built a given file, then it can easily determine if there is a newer version it should be rebuilt with.

These blocks do not necessarily need to be used strictly for debugging or tools information, either. For example, versions of assets for several platforms could be packed into the same file and read as required, or optional data (higher resolution textures) to be used on machines with more memory included.

When being read from a hard drive (as is typically the case during development, or on the PC platform), the time required to skip the unwanted sections of the file is generally negligible. However, on CD or DVD-based consoles it can prove to be more of a problem. Fortunately, it is very simple to counteract this: a simple tool can be written that strips out all of the unnecessary blocks from a file before it is burned onto the game disc, thereby removing the overhead. Alternatively, the blocks can all be moved to the end of the file and a marker inserted to tell the target system to stop reading at that point, thereby keeping the data intact but preventing it from slowing the loading process.

Memory Ready and Parsed Formats

Within the individual blocks, there are many possible layouts the data can take, again mostly depending on the nature of the engine and target platform. However, these can virtually all be categorized into one of two types (with a few hybrid schemes): memory ready data formats, or parsed data formats.

Memory Ready Formats

As the name suggests, memory ready data is stored in the same layout and form as it will be needed in the game's memory. This enables the data to be simply read directly into the block it is to be used from. In general, the only additional work required to make it ready for use is that it perform "pointer fix-up," correcting the values of any pointers within the data by relocating them according to the address it was loaded at (or finding the object they reference and inserting the address).

This means that the speed at which the data is loaded is as close to the theoretical maximum as possible (as there is little redundant data, and no need to move it after loading), and there is very little CPU overhead from doing so. In addition, it can also save memory by removing the need for additional buffers during loading. These properties make memory ready formats almost essential for streaming data, as any CPU load caused by the loading process will directly impact the game. In many ways, they are the most desirable type of formats to use, as they shift the maximum amount of overhead possible onto the preprocessing tasks, and store no more data than is absolutely necessary on the disc.

However, memory ready formats have one huge drawback: they tie the output from the asset pipeline very heavily to the code in the game. If the layout of a structure in the game code changes, then it is necessary not only to change the tool that outputs that data, but also to reprocess all of the existing output files to make them use the new format. Attempting to engineer backwards or forwards compatibility into memory ready formats is difficult, and most frequently simply reduces the loading speed by requiring more of the loaded data to be processed.

This can cause serious headaches, not only from the perspective of pipeline management, but also because it results in a scenario where during development, if any change is made to the low-level formats, code or data from before the change will be incompatible with that from after it. This problem can quickly become a very serious issue if the process of building or obtaining either is at all lengthy or convoluted, as people will spend a significant proportion of their time simply trying to get an up-to-date version of both that work together only to, inevitably, discover that another change has been made since they started.

Even worse, if sufficient checks are not implemented to ensure that the code and data are both using the same structures, very unusual bugs can result from the mismatch, wasting even more time as people try to debug problems that are symptoms of old data, or disregard real issues as such. Subtle bugs can also creep in as a result of structure alignment or packing issues, which can even vary as compiler settings are changed. When working with C++ there are many potential problems with loading classes that make use of inheritance (in particular, virtual function table pointers that are inserted into the middle of the class memory need to be *very* carefully avoided, lest they become corrupted and cause difficult to debug crashes).

These are not easy problems to solve, although there are workarounds that can alleviate the effects somewhat. One of the most important of these is to make the process of packing the data into memory-ready structures the absolute last step in the processing pipeline, and completely separate from all of the other operations. This way, if the format does change, only this relatively fast step needs to be performed again, rather than any more costly pre-processing.

Another helpful mechanism is to store the structure information that a data file was built using in the file itself (typically in a metadata section). This way, debug builds of the game can check that their own structures match these before loading each file, and likewise the tools pipeline can check if a file needs to be reprocessed. It may also be possible, where this is the case, to write a tool that simply rearranges the data in the file to fit the new layout, providing a "quick and dirty" way of updating files to match code changes without having to reprocess them completely.

Parsed Formats

At the opposite end of the spectrum from memory ready formats are parsed formats. These are based on the principle that each element in the file is read individually, and then inserted into the structure as required by the game. Parsed files can take many forms, but the most common are arranged as simple groups of values in a fairly arbitrary order (defined by the order they are read or written in), often broken up into blocks in the same way as the wrapper format is.

The big advantage of parsed files is that they give the game the opportunity to store the data differently from the way it is laid out on disc, and the parser can easily make intelligent decisions about what to do in the case where the data does not match what is expected, for example, by inserting default values. By decoupling the memory and disc representations of data, a degree of independence is given so that code and data structure changes can occur without necessarily rendering old files (or code) useless, and parsed file formats are easier to share between different platforms or tools.

Parsed formats are also less prone to introducing bugs, both because any discrepancies between the stored and memory structures will either be handled or (usually) cause an error during loading, and because there is less scope for errors to be introduced by "unpredictable" compiler behavior such as structure packing or virtual function table pointer positions.

The big disadvantage of parsed formats, logically enough, is the overhead they add to the loading process. The additional storage (and hence data loading) requirements added by the format varies depending on how it is laid out, but as the code has to individually move each element of the data into place in memory, there is a considerable CPU overhead for reading and parsing a file.

Parsed formats are also somewhat harder to maintain than memory ready ones, as they generally require specific code to handle loading and saving of each type of structure. This code can also easily become quite bloated if backwards compatibility is maintained, as it tends to quickly become a mess of conditionals for different file versions.

For practical applications, most formats are a mix of the two systems: it makes sense to use memory ready formats for certain key structures (such as texture and meshes) which are loaded frequently or streamed, but most other data is relatively small and not loaded often, and therefore the overheads of parsing it during loading are far outweighed by the convenience of being able to alter the format without serious repercussions.

Probably the single most important thing when designing any format of this nature, however, is to make sure that it is clear in the code itself which system is in use for any given structure or area, and what the criteria are for deciding how new structures should be handled. While hybrid systems are very powerful, consistency is the most important thing in keeping the format maintainable and unlikely to introduce obscure bugs.

Byte Order Considerations

One problem that manifests itself in virtually any file format is that of handling systems with different byte orders. *Little-endian* systems such as the PC store multi byte values with the least significant byte in the lowest address, while *big-endian* systems such as the Apple Macintosh and Nintendo Gamecube store the least significant byte in the highest address. This, needless to say, can cause significant problems when building files on one platform for use on another.

The byte order problem can be tackled at load time, by swapping the order of values as they are read or stored in the structures. This works best with a parsed file format, although it can be done with memory ready formats, albeit at the cost of completely defeating the purpose of them by manually touching every value!

What is generally more useful is to perform the byte order conversion as a final processing step when the files are created. Some care must be taken, however, as in order to swap the ordering the tool doing the creation of the files must know what the type of every value is, a well-structured intermediate file format that stores type information is very useful in this situation.

In general, if the problem is foreseen early enough, then handling byte order conversion is not a particularly difficult task. However, it can be hard to retrofit to an existing system, and the performance penalty of having to convert all but the most trivial structures during loading can be quite severe, especially when streaming data.

HANDLING FILE INTERDEPENDENCIES

One of the problems that occurs with many types of assets, and can be particularly tricky to handle when using memory ready file formats, is that of interdependencies between different assets. This occurs when one asset needs to reference another which is not part of the same structure or file, for example, when the materials in a model file need to refer to the textures they use.

During processing, this relationship can be easily represented using a filename or unique identifier for the asset in question, but at runtime a more efficient mechanism is generally needed. In most cases, the actual in-game structure will simply store a pointer to the object it wishes to reference, but because in virtually all cases the actual memory location will not be known in advance, it is not possible to calculate and store the pointer in the file itself.

Furthermore, unlike pointers to other objects within the file, which can be stored as offsets relative to the start of the structure and the relocated at runtime, an external object may well be stored in a completely different location entirely, or simply not be loaded at all when the reference is found. Hence, some mechanism for looking up the address of another asset during loading is required.

One simple mechanism for doing this is to make use of an external references table. This is a separate block of data from the actual structure, which is read after it (into a temporary area of memory), and parsed. Each entry in the table gives an identifier for an external resource, typically a name or unique ID, along with an offset within the original structure pointing to the location of the pointer that should reference that resource. The loading code can then search for that asset (even load it if necessary), and then insert the pointer in the appropriate location.

This process can be made even more efficient if the layout of the structure is known: in the copy of the structure stored on disc, instead of pointers being stored as pointers, a unique identifier is stored instead. As most current architectures use 32-bit pointers, either a full UID or a hybrid type identifier and UID can be easily stored without overrunning the pointer field. Then, after loading, the same process as described previously takes place, with the value stored in each pointer location used to look up the resource, and then the real pointer written back over the top of the UID. This avoids the need to load and parse a separate structure containing the pointer information.

One handy trick if this technique is used is to ensure that the UID scheme actually only uses 31 bits (or one less than whatever the size of a pointer is), and that the least-significant bit of the UID is always set to 1. This way, the value stored in the pointer will always be an odd number, which on virtually every architecture is an invalid address to read or write anything other than a byte to, and a highly implausible place for a structure to be positioned. This means that it is very easy to see in the debugger if a UID has not been replaced with a pointer correctly, and in most cases any attempt to read from or write to the structure being referenced will cause an immediate crash due to the unaligned memory address, rather than accessing a random location in memory.

BUILDING ROBUST TOOLS

One of the key requirements of any asset processing system is that it must be robust under as many conditions as possible. Various mechanisms for dealing with broken source assets were discussed previously, but little mention was made of the steps the tools themselves can take to make sure that they fail as infrequently as possible, and that failures are handled sensibly.

Be Lenient in What You Accept, but Strict in What You Output

When writing any system that must interoperate with others outside your control, this is a good mantra to adopt. While your internal file formats will only be seen by a small number of programs, quite likely all written by one person or based on the same source code and libraries, when handling files created by or for the use of external applications, it is necessary to allow for a wide variation in the interpretations of the format specifications.

Most common file formats have been reasonably well documented, but even the best documentation still leaves vague areas or places where the precise behavior is deliberately left undefined for some reason. In some cases there are several sets of (often conflicting) documentation, or even worse, none at all. In these cases, a useful addendum to the above is "expect the unexpected." If it's at all possible within the basic structure of the format, chances are someone will have done it.

In recent years, many specification documents have adopted an "RFC-like" ("Request For Comments" documents are a set of publicly available technical notes, mostly defining protocols and standards for Internet use) style when describing the behavior expected from applications. Many RFC notes use a common set of strict definitions of the words "must," "should," and "may" to avoid any possibility of misunderstandings. These definitions are as follows:

MUST: indicates something that is an absolute requirement. For example, "the index field MUST be an unsigned 32-bit integer."

SHOULD: indicates that there may be valid reasons that this requirement can be ignored, but applications should not do this without first considering the consequences of doing so. For example "the header SHOULD include the name of the source file."

MAY: indicates that this requirement is optional, and it is up to the application to decide if it should implement it or not. For example "this block MAY be followed by one containing additional metadata."

From the perspective of an application reading a file that has been specified in such a manner, it is "safe" to assume that any compliant application will have implemented any "MUST" requirement, but the possibility that "SHOULD" or "MAY" requirements have not been met must be taken into account. However, as the description states, when writing to a file, unless there is a very good reason to do otherwise, "SHOULD" requirements should be met. This ensures the maximum possibility that another application (which potentially may have ignored these rules) can read the file correctly.

Regardless of these specifications, it is good practice to perform sanity checks on values read in from any file if there is the potential for them to cause significant harm (for example, indices that are used to reference arrays or the sizes of structures. In particular, one point worthy of special mention is that many formats do not explicitly state if values are signed or unsigned (and even when they do, this is often ignored). This can lead to serious problems if a negative value is inserted, as it will appear to be a very large positive number when read in an unsigned fashion (and, indeed, vice versa). Performing bounds checking on input values can help catch these problems quickly.

Handling Tool Failure

In addition to performing input validation, some mechanism for reporting failure in tools is also required, to handle situations where the data is sufficiently broken that recovery is impossible. Ideally, this should allow the system to take a suitable response to the broken data, as described previously in Chapter 3, for example, by rolling back to a previous version of the source asset file and retrying the processing step.

When reporting an error, it is generally best for the tool to supply as much descriptive information as possible about the problem. This can then be logged by the system, and used to diagnose the fault. If an e-mail server is available, then e-mailing this information to the pipeline or tool's maintainer is often a good idea. This way, they can often immediately see what the cause of the problem is, without having to actually track down the offending file's log entry.

The error report should also include, in machine-readable form, the names of the input files that caused the problem, and the state of any output files that were altered by the processing. This will enable the pipeline to perform the necessary recovery actions, removing or replacing the (potentially) corrupted output, and finding an alternative set of input files if they exist. It is particularly important that this is done whenever possible on more complex processing operations, as they may involve a large number of files, and in the absence of this information the pipeline may have to assume that all of the input or output files are potentially invalid.

When actually logging the error, this information can be added to by the pipeline; the most useful additional information is that which allows the problem to be recreated. In general, this will include the names and versions of all of the input files for the tool (and the tool itself), the command line it was executed with, and any other relevant system information such as environment variable values, available memory, and so on. With this, when a problem occurs there is a good chance that the fault can easily be recreated in a controlled environment (such as under a debugger).

In circumstances where tools are frequently being called with ephemeral intermediate input files, it can even be useful to store a copy of all the input data for the task that caused the error along with the report. This way, it is not necessary to perform all of the preceding processing steps to recreate the problem, and if the failure was due to a fault in an intermediate tool the broken data will be available to examine.

Redirecting Output

Another technique that can make debugging asset problems much simpler is if *all* the output from the tools is archived in a consistent location, for example, in a database or directory structure that mirrors the layout of the files in the pipeline. This way, for any given intermediate or output file (even if the pipeline detected no errors), the debug output can be quickly located. This can be very useful when trying to diagnose problems the pipeline has missed, such as "why is this model ten times smaller than it should be?" With some care, it can also be used to gather detailed statistics about various parts of the pipeline, such as the average performance of the triangle stripification or the distribution of mesh compression schemes.

This output redirection can be done on an individual tool level, but it is generally more useful to implement it as part of the overall pipeline functionality. This can be easily done by redirecting the standard I/O streams, and, if necessary, hooking the debug output functions (OutputDebugString() on Windows systems). Handling the redirection in this high-level manner both reduces the amount of code required in each tool, and provides redirection for third-party utilities or other similar "black box" components.

Fatal Errors

Regardless of the amount of protection in place, however, there will always be cases where either as the result of an invalid file or simply due to a bug, one of the processing tools crashes completely. These situations can be very difficult to deal with, because in the absence of detailed debugging information, the only solution is to run the offending tool under a debugger to find out where the crash occurred. This is quite time consuming, and in mature toolsets often leads not to an actual bug, but rather to an unexpected set of conditions in the input data. Having as much debugging information as possible can help considerably here.

Infinite Loops

One particularly nasty class of fatal error is that where a tool enters an infinite loop. This is quite hard to detect, as no actual *error* occurs, but instead the processing never completes.

The basic mechanism for detecting infinite loops is to implement a timeout, whereby the tool is forcibly terminated if the processing takes more than a specified amount of time. However, this time can vary wildly among different tools. For example, if a texture resizing operation takes more than a few minutes it has almost certainly crashed, but calculating lighting information for a large level may easily take a few *hours* to normally complete. Therefore, some amount of manual tweaking of timeouts will usually be necessary to avoid terminating tools prematurely.

Another mechanism that can be used to assist in detecting infinite loops is to allow the tool to expose a "progress meter" to the pipeline. Essentially, this is just a value between 0 and 100 (or any other arbitrary value) that indicates how far through the processing the tool has got. The pipeline can then implement a timeout that triggers if no *progress* has been made for a certain period of time, or if the progress meter goes backwards (a fairly sure sign of a bug!). This approach is more efficient, both because less manual tweaking of timeouts is required, and it is capable of detecting crashes that occur early in long processing operations without having to wait until the full time limit expires.

A progress meter can also be a useful tool for other purposes, such as judging how long a process is likely to take, and as a means of preventing human induced crashes when someone decides that a process has taken "too long" and kills it manually!

Debugging the Pipeline

If detailed logs are kept of tool execution, then many problems can be diagnosed simply by examining these, especially if the failure was caused by an assert() statement or some other situation that the code was able to catch and respond to. However, there will always be cases where a crash in a tool must be debugged "directly," by examining the code executed up to the point of the failure.

Regardless of the circumstances, whenever a crash in a tool is detected, if at all possible, either the tool itself or the pipeline should attempt to write out a stack track, register list, and possibly a memory dump; on most operating systems there are relatively straightforward functions provided for doing these. This can be absolutely invaluable in debugging hard to recreate problems, because all the information that can be obtained from viewing the crash in a normal debugger can be gleaned (with a greater or lesser degree of effort) from the dump information. Some debuggers even allow crash dumps to be loaded and viewed directly as though the crash had occurred locally, making the process even more efficient.

If a crash dump is not available, or the problem cannot be diagnosed from it, then it will be necessary to recreate the circumstances that led to the failure. This is where the detailed execution environment information the pipeline should report in the log file comes in useful. By retrieving the versions of the input files specified, and re-running the tool with the same command line and options, it should be possible to cause the crash to happen again. This is essential both for diagnosing the problem and then verifying that it has indeed been fixed.

Un-Reproducible Bugs

As with any complex system, any asset pipeline will always exhibit a few bugs that cannot be reproduced in a controlled environment, or may even disappear when the pipeline runs exactly the same processing operation a second time! These are often due to the precise timing between events (this is particularly an issue if multiple processing tasks are being executed simultaneously), the layout of memory at the time of the failure, or simply hardware or OS faults.

As recreating them is nearly impossible, debugging such problems is almost always possible only with detailed logs and crash dump information. Even worse, it can be very hard to prove that such a bug has been fixed: sometimes changing another unrelated section of the code can cause it to disappear, simply because the sequence of events that revealed the problem now occurs more rarely.

There is little that can be done to mitigate these problems, except for ensuring that all of the tool code is as robust as possible, and that the maximum amount of available information is gathered when a crash does happen. In the worst case scenario, it may be necessary to run the entire pipeline in debug mode or under a debugger to find the problem. Although, it is worth noting that in some rare cases this additional instrumentation can prevent the fault from occurring!

Maintaining Data Integrity

Aside from producing as much information as possible to help locate the problem, the other main task of the pipeline when a crash occurs is to recover as safely as possible, and continue in as normal a manner as possible. A critical part of this process is ensuring that any data files that were modified by the tool that crashed are safely removed or reverted to known good versions. Otherwise a single error can cause a cascade of failures as each successive step in the pipeline tries to use the corrupt data output by the first tool!

This "clean up" process mainly involves removing any temporary files that were created and deleting or invalidating output data that may be truncated or corrupt. Having a dirty flag in the file headers can be a big help here, as it allows partially written files to be easily detected. If checksums of files are being stored for the purposes of detecting changes, then these, too, can be used to detect modifications.

Modified intermediate files can either be deleted entirely and then recreated by re-running the tool with the previous set of input data, or by replacing them with the last versions directly (assuming that these are stored somewhere). Either approach works well, although the latter is generally preferable where possible as it reduces the amount of time needed for the recovery operation.

Another possible approach to take to ensure the integrity of data in the pipeline is to "sandbox" each tool's execution. In this case, the files the tool may modify are copied prior to its execution, and the tool operates on those copies. Only once the task has been successfully completed do the original files get overwritten with the updated versions.

This approach makes sure that an errant tool cannot corrupt files when it fails (clearly, no such guarantee can be made if the tool claims to have executed successfully), and for further safety all of the tool's input and output files can be moved to another directory before processing, thereby ensuring that no files other than those specified as outputs can be accidentally modified. In this case, the truly paranoid can even take the step of making the rest of the pipeline data unwritable to the tools if desired. Sandboxing the execution in this manner is a very effective safeguard, but it does introduce additional overheads in the execution of each processing step.

INTERFACING TO EXISTING SYSTEMS

While the majority of the tools that the asset pipeline will need to use will probably be custom applications developed in-house, there is frequently still the need to invoke third-party programs to perform some tasks. The complexity of performing this operation will depend largely on the manner in which these tools have been written, and how the other tools the pipeline utilized have been set up.

In general, the more of the common logic, such as file location, error handling, and sandboxing which has been built into the framework of the pipeline (rather than the individual tools), the easier it will be to integrate an external program, as all of this functionality will still be usable.

The process of invoking an external application generally breaks into three stages. First, the data required by the application must be acquired and formatted so that it can understand it (this is particularly important if the data is stored in a database, or a nonstandard wrapper file format). Then, the executable can be invoked and the processing done. Finally, the output must be reformatted into a form suitable for the rest of the pipeline.

One very common way of encapsulating these processes is to write a wrapper tool, which appears to the rest of the pipeline as every other stage, but internally reformats the data and executes the external application as necessary. This provides a layer of abstraction so that tool specific logic (such as the reformatting code) is separated from the rest of the pipeline, and no other task needs to know details required to invoke the third-party tool.

One disadvantage of this encapsulation, however, is that some of the details it hides are necessary to ensure the pipeline functions correctly. For example, it is no longer obvious that the executable for the external tool is used to process some files, and that there is a dependency between it and them (and hence, if it changes, those files must be reprocessed). This information must be supplied by the wrapper itself, or a decision made to ignore the problem and accept that changes to the tool will have to be managed by hand.

Another effect of the wrapper is that error handling becomes more obfuscated—in particular, the procedures for handling crashes in tools will probably fail to gather the required information about the external task if an error occurs. Likewise, progress monitoring may well be more difficult or impossible depending on the nature of the tool being used.

An additional set of problems are posed if the external tool is GUI-based: executing a GUI application in an automated fashion is generally possible by "faking" the sequence of messages that the windowing system would send during operation, but this is not a task for the faint of heart! Even if the tool can be *controlled* entirely from the command line, there are some interesting additional problems that can arise simply from the creation of GUI elements. For example, on Windows, many 3D accelerated applications will fail to initialize if the workstation is locked (as is often the case on servers), because they cannot acquire the graphics card resources necessary.

CONCLUSION

Dependency analysis plays a vital role in improving the efficiency of asset process-ing operations, by ensuring that only the files directly affected by each change to the source assets are updated. As this is a common problem, particular in source code compilation, there are many existing tools available that perform this task well— the make utility being the most popular.

Another important prerequisite for building an effective asset pipeline is a strong framework for tools, and well-defined file formats for interchange of infor-mation. The effort expended on getting these aspects of the system right is well worth it, as they will have an effect on virtually every stage of the process. Wherever possible, common functionality should be integrated into this framework, speeding the development and improving the robustness of every tool based on it. Isolating tools from each other as much as possible is also a useful technique for ensuring that failures in one section of the pipeline do not affect others.

10 Final Data

In This Chapter

- File Packing
- Data Layout
- Integrity Checking
- Digital Signatures
- Encryption
- Compression
- Distribution Media
- After Shipping

The final step in the asset pipeline is the generation of the actual data that will appear on the game disc or cartridge. At this point, all of the processing that needs to be done on the asset data itself has been completed, and the disc building process is largely concerned with packing and rearranging this data to optimize the loading process.

This step is generally only performed when building an actual physical disc, and sometimes even then only when it is strictly required, as it can be quite time-consuming. During development, under most circumstances the game will read directly from the individual asset files (often on the hard drive of a PC connected to the development system, in the case of console development), and the increased efficiency of this arrangement over the final distribution media usually outweighs any performance cost for doing so. In addition, it is often necessary for developers to change assets frequently, particularly for previewing purposes, and having to repackage the data each time would quickly become a major bottleneck.

This data packing process is intended to be largely a one-way step; clearly, the game itself will read from the packed data, but there should never be any need for any other tool to do so. Therefore, any extraneous information such as debugging logs, dependency information, or metadata should be stripped as part of this process, both to increase efficiency when loading and to reduce the size of the data on disc. Likewise, the files will never be written to, so there is no need to consider the possibility of files being deleted, their sizes changing, etc.

FILE PACKING

The first step generally required when building any form of disc or cartridge version is to pack all of the files on the disc into one or more (but generally less than a handful) large combined files (often referred to as "pack files" or "package files"), with a table providing information on where each file has been placed—effectively a miniature filing system. There are several reasons for this, but most of them are related to one core factor: *control.*

On cartridge-based systems, it is common for there simply to be no filing system at all; if the game wishes to "load" assets using their name or other identifier, they must be stored in a packed file or other custom filing system structure. Most disc-based games consoles (and, obviously, PCs) do provide some form of native filing system for their media, usually based on one of the standards for that type of storage (for example, the ISO 9660 standard for CD-ROM filing systems).

However, these frequently impose limitations on the layout of the files on the disc. It is not uncommon to be restricted to single case filenames of very limited length (often only eight characters), with similarly tight limits on the number of files and subdirectories. Unless a great deal of care has been taken during development, it is highly likely that the file structure the game uses will not fit into these constraints, particularly if has been developed for several platforms, in which case it must fit into the limitations of *all* of them!

This in itself is often enough of a reason for using packed files, but an additional factor is that the implementations of these filing systems are often very slow, and can have unpredictable performance effects; for example, several common console systems will re-read the TOC (Table Of Contents) on the disc every time a new file is opened, reducing performance to a crawl if this is done frequently. Other common quirks are the lack of some filing system functions (such as enumerating the contents of a directory) and strict limits on the number of files that can be opened simultaneously.

Packed File Formats

The format of a packed file does not have to be particularly complex. In general there are two parts to the file: the file table and the data in the files themselves.

The File Table

The file table is used when the game needs to access a specific file in the package, generally by filename. As such, all that is needed is to store the filename itself (generally as a fully-qualified path from the root of the game data directory, since this way, files in subdirectories can be located without any extra effort), the offset within the package at which this file occurs, and its length. Even for games with large numbers of files, this information is generally compact enough that it can simply be loaded and kept in memory for speedy access.

It is possible to construct a more complex hierarchical file table, where files are stored as single entries and subdirectories are pointers to a separate table for that directory (more like a traditional computer filing system). These can be useful under some circumstances, as they allow faster lookups of file information and easier enumeration of directory contents, but in general the extra complexity is not worth the performance boost unless the game relies very heavily on these operations.

The file table can be stored anywhere within the package, as long as the game knows how to find it. The most common choices, however, are to place it either at the start or the end of the file, along with a marker indicating how big it is—this allows it to be located easily, and keeps it separate from the data itself.

The File Data

The data in the packed file is generally formed simply by copying the contents of the included files, one after another, into the package. The only unusual requirement is that it is often useful to align the start points of files to the sector boundaries of the target media (2 K in the case of DVDs) because this improves the speed at which files can be read, and can make dealing with very large package files easier. Since the start of the package file on the disc is always (by definition) aligned to a sector boundary, as long as the offsets within the file are also multiples of the sector size, it is guaranteed that each file will start on a new sector.

Handling Very Large Package Files

Large package files can pose a problem because of the limits on the size of the data that can be addressed by a 32-bit integer: only 2 GB is available with signed values, and 4 GB with unsigned values. Since the capacity of a single-layer DVD disc is approximately 4.5 GB, it is easily possible to hit this limit if all of the files are in a single package.

One way to avoid this problem is to use 64-bit integers to store the offsets of files; however, this can introduce a lot of additional complexity into the code. Fortunately, another option that works just as well is to make use of the alignment of the files. If every file starts on a 2 K sector boundary, then it is only necessary to store the *sector number* instead of the absolute address of the file, the value of which is 1/2048 the size, effectively increasing the addressable space to 8192 GB! Obviously, the sector number needs to be translated into a 64-bit value for the absolute disc address when performing the physical seek operation to the file, but it is much easier to deal with this within the seek function than at every location in the code that uses file offsets.

It is also worth noting that even if the offsets are stored as sector numbers, the file sizes must still be stored in bytes. This is not generally a problem, however, as in most circumstances it is highly unlikely than a single file will exceed 4 GB.

Using Multiple Package Files

It can be very useful for the game and pipeline to support using multiple package files to store the game assets, searching through each in turn until the required file is found. This allows infrequently modified data such as FMV or speech to be packed separately from other game data, thereby removing the necessity to repackage it every time a change occurs. It may also be useful to have language-dependent data separated, for example, so that only the required files are included on different versions of the game disc.

Another reason for doing this is that on some platforms there is a limit on the maximum size of any single file on the game disc, generally because of other data that must be placed at specific locations by the system. In order to avoid running into this limitation, it may be necessary to split the game over several separate packages, each of a suitable size.

Obfuscating Data

Package files also have the useful trait of hiding the data within them, thereby providing a (very small) degree of protection from the prying eyes of cheats, crackers, or simply overly-curious gamers. This can be quite important if the game uses easily disassembled or common file formats, or there is data that is not used by the game present (although this is generally not a good idea in the first place). If protecting the game data from viewing or modification is important, however, then it is worth considering actually encrypting and signing the data; the protection a package file offers is paper thin at best.

Package files also give the developer the ability to lay out the data in a precise format, rather than being subject to the whims of their disc building tool, which can be critical in helping to speed up the process of loading many files in sequence. In particular, streaming systems can benefit massively from optimizing the positioning of files to minimize the seek distance needed.

DATA LAYOUT

While cartridge-based media has the luxury of equal speed access to all locations (in most cases), disc-based systems must deal with the limitations of the drive technology they are based on. Most modern consoles are capable of sustaining quite high data rates when loading data sequentially from media, but the major bottleneck in the optical drive is simply that the act of physically moving the laser transport to a new location on the disc takes a considerable amount of time.

It is not unusual for average seek times to be in excess of 100 ms, meaning that on a drive with a data rate of 5 Mb/sec, seeking to the start of a new file can easily take the same amount of time as reading half a megabyte of data! Even worse, actual hardware often performs considerably slower as the drive mechanisms become worn over time and both the sustained read speed and seek time are affected.

The read speed of the drive is largely a fixed value (although there is some variance with the position of files on the disc, as will be discussed later); therefore, the single most important factor in improving load times and streaming performance is the number (and distance) of seeks the drive must perform.

Optimizing Linear Loading Procedures

The easiest case to optimize data layout for is a traditional linear load; that is, one where the game loads (for example) an entire level in one operation, reading in each piece of data required in turn. Typically, each file will be loaded in its entirety, and there will be no (or very few) other disc operations such as streaming music taking place at the same time, so the sequence of reads performed will be very deterministic.

If the files are ordered on the disc in the same sequence they are read in, then after each file is loaded the laser head will already be positioned ready to read the next, and so no seek operation is necessary. Note that if the files are padded to sector boundaries, in some cases it will be necessary to "read" the entirety of the final, padded sector of each file to position the seek address precisely on the start of the next. This is nearly always a zero-cost operation, however, since the drive hardware itself generally operates in whole sector blocks anyway.

The hard part of optimizing this process, therefore, is determining the order in which files are read. There are many ways to do this; in simple cases, even just examining the loading code and manually deciding on an order will work. Another approach is to add instrumentation to a special version of the game, which dumps a list of file accesses when it is run. This way, the precise order of accesses for each section of the game can be determined easily. Yet another is to parse the level files and build a list of all the resources that will be loaded, effectively "emulating" the loading process the game uses to do so.

These lists do not need to be 100% accurate and can be safely reused even if changes occur to the loading order, because deviating from them will simply cause additional seek delays, rather than actually breaking anything. Clearly, however, it is desirable to keep them as accurate as possible for the maximum performance gains.

In most cases, there will be files that are used by more than one section of the game (such as the main character model), and therefore cannot be easily sorted into the load order. One option is to group such files in a random order, thereby reducing the cost of seeks between them, but keeping them separate from the optimized ordered sets of files. Another, which can be useful if there is spare space on the disc, is to duplicate them several times, inserting the duplicates into the set of ordered files for each individual section of the game.

In this case, the game can then pick the copy of the file that is nearest to the current laser head position (which will generally be exactly on the current location, if the last file read was ordered correctly), thereby minimizing or removing entirely the seek delay.

Optimizing Streaming

Optimizing files for streaming processes is somewhat more difficult than optimizing for linear loads, because the vast majority of streaming systems read files in a "random" order, and at "random" times! Therefore, reordering the files to remove seek delays is generally not possible, as the precise sequence in which they will be loaded is not known in advance. However, it is possible to group files that are commonly accessed together into the same location, thereby minimizing the seek time when switching between them.

The general principle is therefore fairly similar to that used when optimizing section loads, but without the requirement to collect precise data on the sequence in which the files are loaded. All that is necessary is to know which groups of files tend to be loaded at roughly the same time; for example, all of the textures used in one room. This information can be obtained in much the same manner as described previously.

As with linear loading, with streaming data there will be files that are loaded frequently from many different places. It can be highly advantageous to duplicate these into several different locations across the disc. In some cases, even simply including a handful of the most commonly accessed resources three or four times can have a massive impact, as the worst case seek time to access them will be reduced to ? or ? of the maximum value, and this saving is often effectively doubled as the time needed to seek to the next file is similarly reduced.

One other technique that can be used to speed up streaming is the very simple mechanic of ensuring that the block size that the streaming system reads is a multiple of the media sector size. This ensures that no unnecessary data is read from the disc each time the streaming code loads a new block. While in the case of single streams of data this generally does not require any preprocessing to achieve, in the case of interleaved streams (described later), it can require some additional effort when preparing the data.

Audio Streams

A very common use of streaming in games is in providing background music and speech, the process of which involves constantly reading small quantities of data from a larger file to keep the playback buffers full. As such, it is not uncommon for the drive to have to seek to the currently playing audio stream every few seconds (sometimes even less than that), and the time it takes to do so can have a major impact on the speed of other streaming operations.

If there are several streams being played (for example, for providing ambient sounds as well as music), then this problem is made much worse. In extreme cases, the drive can easily spend the majority of its time seeking between the audio streams in order to ensure that the buffers are kept full and the sound does not "skip," leaving very little time for loading any other data.

As such, audio streams are a very good candidate for being duplicated several times across the disc, as they will be accessed extremely frequently with the head at "random" other positions on the disc. In addition, in cases where several streams of audio or other data need to be accessed simultaneously, it may be worthwhile interleaving them to cut down the number of drive seeks required even further.

Interleaved Streams

Interleaved streams, as the name suggests, consist of data from several files interleaved together, typically using chunks of a few KB for each file. This is useful when working with files such as music or speech tracks that are not read in their entirety in a single operation, but rather streamed over time as they are playing.

Interleaving the files in this way allows the blocks to be read sequentially, delivering data for all the streams (albeit at a reduced rate) simultaneously from a single read. The benefits of this are quite noticeable; as the seek time (rather than the data transfer rate) is generally the limiting factor in determining how many simultaneous streams can be accessed without running out of buffered data, interleaving streams effectively allows the additional streams to be handled for a very minimal cost. In some circumstances it can even be a viable option to interleave additional streams that may *potentially* be used and simply discard the data from them if they are not currently needed; for example, a number of different ambient sound tracks interleaved together with the main music stream.

The main disadvantage of interleaving streams like this is that the relative timing of the streams is fixed once the interleaving has been done; it is impossible to have two interleaved audio streams that are playing from different positions, without having to read the stream twice (completely defeating the purpose of the interleaving). Likewise, if the streams loop, they must loop at the same point. This makes interleaved streams unsuitable for sound effects or speech that can be triggered at arbitrary moments, unfortunately.

The block sizes of the interleaved data are important, as they determine the rate at which each stream receives data. If the block size is too large, then one stream may *starve* (run out of buffered data) while waiting for the next block to arrive. However, if it is too small, then the overheads of parsing the different blocks of data become prohibitively expensive. This trade-off largely depends on the exact nature of the interleaved data, but one point of universal importance is that the block size should ideally be a multiple of the media sector size. This ensures that each new stream read operation will begin (and end) on a sector boundary, and no unnecessary data will be loaded.

The vast majority of games use interleaved streams exclusively for audio, as they are very well suited to this task. However, there is no reason that other types of data cannot be interleaved, such as a compressed video and audio stream for a cutscene (which would actually be interleaved in the first place!) interleaved with the data required for the next game level, enabling a seamless transition at the end of the cutscene.

INTEGRITY CHECKING

The need for runtime verification of data integrity varies from platform to platform. On some systems, the libraries automatically perform CRC checks on data as it is loaded (using CRCs embedded in the sectors on the disc). Some do not, and others even make it a requirement that data errors are detected by the game and "handled" (insomuch that it does not simply crash!). For these reasons, it is often necessary to implement an integrity verification system for data as it is loaded.

The actual mechanics of such a system are quite straightforward and in general, speed of execution is the primary requirement. As such, a standard 32-bit block CRC is generally a good choice, as more sophisticated algorithms such as MD5 are computationally more expensive, and the additional security such cryptographically secure systems offer is unnecessary (and, in fact, useless, as the checksum value must also be stored in the data file).

The main difficulty when integrating an integrity verification system is in deciding where the boundaries of checksum blocks should go, and where the checksums themselves should be stored. The obvious choice is to calculate one checksum for each file in the package, and store the value in the file table.

This approach works well if files are generally read in their entirety, and are small enough that the whole file can be buffered before processing begins on it. In this case, the loader or the processing code can calculate the checksum before any operations are performed on the loaded file, and determine if it is corrupt. This is a very efficient system, as only one checksum is required for each file, and the check can be performed at a high level.

However, it suffers from the major drawback that it is impossible to test the integrity of part of a file. If only a small portion is to be read, then the entire file must still be loaded in order to calculate the checksum. This is a problem in particular if files are too large to be read in a single block, or a streaming system is in use. While in the former case the checksum can be calculated on an ongoing basis as each section of the file is loaded, this introduces the problem that the data's integrity is not known until after the majority of the file has been processed!

An extension of this, which partially solves this problem, is to calculate a number of checksums, each for one fixed size block of every file. This way, rather than having to read the whole file, only the block(s) that contain the data required need to be loaded and checked. This solution works, but it introduces an unpleasant trade-off: the block size needs to be small to avoid potentially having to load significant quantities of unwanted data, but at the same time this creates more checksum values for each file, increasing the size of the file table.

For optimal performance, the checksum block size should be the same as the media sector size (2 K on DVD discs), as this is usually the minimum block size that the drive itself will be able to read. However, on full 4.5 GB DVD, this produces 9 MB of checksum values (assuming they are 32 bits each)! While this overhead is perfectly reasonable on the disc itself, adding 9 MB to the memory file table is not a viable option.

The solution to this is to insert the checksum values into the data stream, so that they are read along with the data itself. This way, no memory is required to store them, and the block size can be brought down to the optimal level. This can be done conveniently by emulating the system that the disc itself uses to store checksums for drive level error detection: allocating 4 bytes out of every sector to the checksum.

This reduces the size of a sector slightly, but the overhead is minimal (as previously mentioned, 9 MB on a full single-layer DVD). Inserting the checksums at a sector level has another major advantage: the error detection code can be made completely transparent to the rest of the game.

The first step needed is for the package file builder to calculate and insert the checksum values at every sector. Effectively, this means that the package file is now laid out so that the first 4 bytes out of every 2048 contain the checksum, and the remaining 2044 contain the data (assuming DVD sector sizes). The file padding remains the same, so every file still starts on a 2048 byte boundary.

Then, when the package file reading code in the game is called upon to read data from a file inside the package, it simply calculates the range of sectors the read operation spans (by dividing the start and end offsets by the amount of *data* in the sectors, 2044 bytes), and then requests that chunk of the package file. As the data arrives, it can compare the first 4 bytes of each 2048 byte block with the checksum calculated for the rest, and then throw away that data, copying the remaining 2044 bytes into the target block for the load. In fact, it is possible to do the checksum calculation at the same time as the copy, to avoid having to read the memory twice, which makes the calculation effectively "free" on most processors.

Using this technique, the overhead for verifying the integrity of the data is almost negligible: a 4/2048 reduction in data transfer rate, and a handful of extra cycles to verify the loaded data. It also works perfectly with streamed data, assuming that the stream is read in multiples of the sector size, which is generally a requirement for obtaining good streaming performance anyway.

While using simple CRC checks in this way works very well for detecting accidental data corruption and disc errors, it is in no way secure against deliberate modification; the checksum for each block is easily computable, so it is easy to fix the checksum on a modified block so that it appears to be correct.

DIGITAL SIGNATURES

There are some cases where it is desirable to protect against this deliberate (and sometimes malicious) modification of data. These cases include preventing pirates from modifying game data files to defeat the protection, or from creating cheats altering data to give themselves an advantage in multiplayer games.

In order to do this, a cryptographically secure system of verifying the integrity of the data is required. As both the data and the checksum values are stored on the disc (and therefore both can be modified), it is necessary to use a system that allows the checksum to be easily *verified* by the game code, but makes it unfeasible to *generate* a new checksum given the data available to the game (and hence, the "attacker").

Trapdoor Functions

This is the core principle of "Public Key Cryptography." Essentially, public key cryptography is based around mathematical "trapdoor functions." These are functions where a number of input values can be combined to form an output value that is unique to that set of inputs, but is mathematically intractable to reverse the function and generate the inputs from the outputs if none of the original input values are known.

The classic example of such a function is taking the product of two large prime numbers. Calculating the product is a trivial operation, as is calculating one of the original primes if both the product and the other prime are known (by simple division). However, calculating both of the input primes from the output value, while possible, cannot be solved without applying an algorithm that is effectively a brute force search of all the possible pairs of prime numbers (there are some algorithms that are faster than a pure brute force search, but all known factorization techniques still require an amount of time that grows exponentially with the size of the number to be factored).

For very large primes, this is effectively impossible on current computer hardware, because the process of factorization would take millennia to complete. As an example, the factorization of a single 512-bit prime number in a competition run by RSA Laboratories took approximately 35.7 years of CPU time (in total) on a large number of machines running at approximately 300 MHz! Furthermore, each additional bit added to the size of the number increases the required time for factorization exponentially. Thus it is generally accepted that 2048-bit primes will remain unfactorable regardless of the amount of processor power available (within sane bounds), unless a radically more efficient factoring algorithm is found.

While there is no known mathematical proof that such a factoring algorithm does not exist, one has not yet been found. Furthermore, for the purposes of games development, the question is effectively moot: as public key cryptography is increasingly being used to provide security in all manner of computer systems, if a mechanism for factoring very large prime numbers in less than exponential time is found, the possibility of cheating in online games will be the least of our worries!

Public Key Signatures

Public key signature algorithms are based on these trapdoor functions, and this makes them an *asymmetric* cipher: one where the key required for signing is different from the key for signature verification. The keys are generated as a pair, and one is kept secret by the developer and used to sign the game data files. The other is embedded into the game executable itself, and used to verify that the content of the files has not been modified since they were signed. Since the two keys are different, this means that the key embedded in the game (which is, implicitly, available to any attacker sufficiently determined to reverse engineer the binary file) cannot be used to sign a new block of data.

The process of generating a signature for a given block of data can be regarded as being much the same as that for encrypting the same data. Effectively, the encryption process generates a "signature" in the form of the encrypted output, which can then be decrypted and compared to the original data. However, most public key encryption algorithms are quite slow, and encrypting or decrypting such a large block of data is generally not a viable proposition, especially during the loading process of a game.

Cryptographic Hashing

Therefore, instead of the actual data itself being signed, a *cryptographically secure hash* of the data is calculated first. This is a checksum of the contents, but calculated using an algorithm such as MD5 (MD standing for "Message Digest") rather than a traditional CRC system (more information about MD5 can be found at *http://userpages.umbc.edu/~mabzug1/cs/md5/md5.html*). The reason for this is that CRCs are designed for detecting errors introduced by data *corruption*, not malicious modification. Most CRC algorithms can be trivially "broken" in that block of modified data can be altered such that it produces the same checksum value as the genuine block, thereby defeating the integrity verification. Cryptographically secure algorithms, such as MD5, are designed so that it is mathematically unfeasible to generate a block of data that has a hash value matching that of another.

Once this hash value has been calculated, it is then signed instead of the original data. This way, only a very small amount of data (128 bits, in the case of MD5) needs to be signed. Since the MD5 calculation is very fast (and, if even more speed is needed, the faster still MD4 variant can be used), the procedure for both signing and verifying blocks is much more efficient.

Cryptographically Strong Random Numbers

One common element in most signing and encryption algorithms is that they require a source of random numbers that are used as "salt" values (which ensure that the same plaintext will never get encrypted in exactly the same way twice), and to insert padding into blocks of data where required. They are also necessary to pick the initial values for the key generation process.

It is vital that the random numbers used for these purposes are as close to truly "random" as possible. The pseudo random number generators typically used in games actually generate numbers with certain patterns, which can sometimes be exploited as a means to break the cryptographic algorithms. Thus, it is important to have PRNG which is "cryptographically strong"—that is, one that generates a sequence of numbers so that given n numbers from that sequence, it is a mathematically intractable operation to calculate the $n+1$th number without knowing the original seed value. Cryptographically strong PRNGs algorithms can be built in many ways, but a common approach is to make use of a cryptographically secure hash function, giving as input the seed value and an incrementing counter.

The other element in generating cryptographically strong random numbers is the initial seed, which should be derived from a source that is as unpredictable as possible. Typical sources for this are hardware devices, such as the low bits of a microphone input, or a series of recorded (random) mouse movements from the user. While the values these inputs produce may not be particularly random in themselves, hashing them using a secure hash function will result in a (close to) genuinely random number.

Using Cryptography in Games

While the mathematics behind cryptographically secure hashing and public key signature algorithms is not particularly complex for the most part, when building any sort of system for use in a "hostile" environment (that is, for any purpose other than purely academic interest), it is highly recommended simply to use an existing algorithm and, if possible, an existing, reviewed and tested implementation. There are many very subtle errors that can be introduced at both algorithm and implementation levels that can completely destroy the security offered by such a system, and even systems that have been developed and tested by cryptography professionals are frequently proven to contain fatal flaws.

Some of the more commonly used (and generally considered to be secure) algorithms are the RSA algorithm, ElGamal, and DSA, the latter being a technique developed with the intention of allowing high security digital signatures without enabling similarly high-grade encryption. Despite being developed by cryptography experts at the NSA, shortly after it was released for public use DSA was proven to be capable of being used for (albeit very slow) encryption, proving the extreme difficulty of ensuring the properties of cryptographic algorithms. The MD5 algorithm is probably the most frequently used secure hashing algorithm, along with the previous variants MD2 and MD4, and SHA1 (the Secure Hashing Algorithm).

In general, it is unnecessary to use digital signatures to protect all of the content supplied on the game disc, only certain key files and data retrieved from untrusted locations, such as over a network. Also, some console systems already make use of public key encryption and signature algorithms as part of their built-in protection systems, so there may also be library services available to perform these operations.

It is also worth remembering that even the best cryptographic system offers protection only as long as the actual executable's integrity is maintained. For many purposes (such as cheating), an attacker will find it much simpler to disable the verification code entirely. That said, as in many cases (on consoles, for example) altering the game executable is impossible for the vast majority of users, if the aim is to prevent modified content being widely distributed (for example, to prevent unauthorized expansion packs being released), then public key signatures will provide a very high degree of protection.

One final problem with the use of some cryptographic techniques is that the field is littered with patents held on various parts of the algorithms used. Until September 2000, for example, RSA Security Inc (*http://www.rsasecurity.com*) held a patent on the core algorithm used by the RSA encryption scheme. If you are planning on using any encryption technology in your game, it is essential to take the effort to properly research the legal status of all the algorithms (and implementations, if third-party code is used) involved.

ENCRYPTION

While digital signatures provide a "provably secure" means of verifying the origin of content, there is no equivalent technology for encryption. Any encryption system employed by a game to protect data files can be broken by a sufficiently determined attacker.

The reason for this is very simple: in order for the encryption to be useful, the game itself must be able to decrypt the files. Thus, the game executable must include all of the algorithms and data required to do this. All an attacker has to do is disassemble the binary file and extract it (or, even more simply, run the game until it decrypts the file he wants to view, and then examine the decrypted copy in the machine's memory).

This fact effectively renders the protection offered to any game content encryption as merely "security by obscurity": the system can be made marginally harder to break by making it more complex (and hence harder to understand), but as soon as the attacker has figured out how the system works he will be able to decrypt any file encrypted with it.

As a result, there is little mileage in implementing complex encryption schemes for game data, as the attacker will simply ignore the encryption algorithm itself and attack the weakest link by ripping the decryption routines wholesale from the game executable. The only security offered comes not from the mathematical properties of the algorithm, but how well it is concealed within the code.

As such, almost any cipher will do; the implementation is more important than the actual algorithm. Commonly used choices are repeating pad ciphers (where each byte of the file is XORed with a byte from a repeating block of random numbers), or PRNG-based ciphers (which are similar, but use a pseudo random number generator to construct a predictable stream of values to encrypt against). Neither of these stand up to even relatively simplistic cryptanalysis techniques, but they are still strong enough to make attacking them pointless—and they are fast enough that their use will not cause a significant performance hit during loading.

What to Encrypt

As with digital signatures, there is generally little mileage in encrypting all of the data files a game uses (although if a simple cipher is used, it is somewhat more feasible). The key thing is to identify files that an attacker is likely to want to examine the contents of, and encrypt those (possibly signing them as well to detect modifications).

The most common candidates for this treatment are files containing executable code for the game, or key assets such as map data or player character models that the game cannot be played without. In many ways, encrypting fewer files is actually the better choice, as the less frequently the decryption routines are used, the harder they will be for the attacker to locate and analyze.

Decryption Code

The actual implementation of the decryption algorithm should be as obfuscated as possible to improve the difficulty of finding and disassembling it. Typical tricks for doing this include utilizing self-modifying code, spreading parts of the routine throughout often-called functions in the main game code, performing some of the processing from interrupt routines or other processors, and even encrypting the decryption routine itself, and only decrypting sections of it as required. Another common anti-piracy technique is to encrypt key game files, and store the decryption key in an "unreadable" section of the disc, thereby causing a copied disc to be useless as the game cannot decrypt the data it needs without the key. However, the actual details of most of these techniques are largely a "black art" (not to mention being closely guarded secrets, as they would offer no protection if they were widely known), and outside the scope of this book.

COMPRESSION

Compressing game data serves two purposes. The first is the most obvious: by reducing the size of the data, more can fit onto the media. This can be significant when working with smaller formats such as CD-ROMs or cartridge systems, although it is less so in general when targeting DVD-based consoles or PCs, as generating enough compressible asset data to fill a DVD disc is fairly rare (in general, the majority of the space is used by FMV or audio data, both of which tend to be already compressed).

The second reason for compressing data is more subtle, however, and applies mainly to CD or DVD games. For more simple compression algorithms, the decompression process can actually be performed faster than the data is read from the disc. This means that by compressing the data, the effective transfer rate of the drive is increased, speeding up the loading process. This latter case can be quite useful in improving performance, although adding compression to files generally places more restrictions on their use.

What Can Be Compressed?

When compressing game assets, some care has to be taken about what is actually worth compressing. Data that is already in a compressed format such as FMV or audio generally will not compress well, neither will data that has been encrypted (although compressing data *before* encryption is a valid approach). It is also rarely worthwhile to compress very small files, as the performance and space gains for doing so are far outweighed by the setup costs of performing the decompression.

In addition to the content, the usage of the files needs to be considered as well. In most cases, files need to be compressed as a single block (otherwise the compression achieved is negligible), and decompressed in their entirety. Therefore, compressing files that will have small blocks loaded from them, or files that are to be streamed, is not viable.

Compression Schemes

There are a vast number of different compression schemes that have been developed, all of which offer different trade-offs between compression levels, processing time, memory overheads, and other factors. The choice of which algorithm to use is a difficult one, and in fact it may be desirable to implement more than one, and choose between them based on which one achieves the best compression or performance for a given asset.

RLE

One of the simplest algorithms to implement is RLE, or "run-length encoding." This works simply by detecting long strings of bytes in the input data, and instead of storing the byte many times, storing it once, along with the number of repetitions. RLE decompression can be made exceptionally fast—there are some games that actually make use of it at runtime on a frame-by-frame basis, as it can be more efficient than copying large blocks of decompressed data. The main disadvantage of RLE is that the compression it achieves is marginal at best. It is mainly suited to compressing textures with large blocks of solid color (it is excellent for compressing shadow maps, for example), or other similar structures.

LZW

LZW stands for Lempel-Ziv-Welch, so named after its creators, Abraham Lempel, Jacob Ziv, and Terry Welch. The LZW algorithm is very widely used, and forms the basis for many common data formats such as ZIP files and GIF images. LZW works by using a *dictionary*, or table of byte sequences. When a sequence of bytes occurs several times in the input data, it can be compressed by inserting a pointer to the entry in the dictionary instead.

LZW builds its dictionary as it reads the input file, simply by adding every new byte sequence it sees. As a result, the compressed data does not need to explicitly contain the dictionary; the decompressor can construct it in the same way the compressor did, as it reads through the file. The LZW dictionary is a fixed size and is typically quite small (typically around 16 k for a 13-bit dictionary implementation). When it becomes full, the compressor inserts a flag into the data to clear it and the compression process effectively starts again from a clean slate.

This fixed memory overhead and the fact that decompression occurs in a strictly linear fashion makes LZW a good choice for using in runtime implementations, especially as the dictionary will typically fit into cache RAM, speeding up decompression massively. The compression achieved is also typically very good, especially if the encoder can test several different dictionary sizes and distributions, and pick the one that produces the best results.

Huffman Encoding

Huffman encoding is another dictionary-based system, but it uses rather different principles to LZW. Huffman encoding works by assigning bit sequences, or codes, to different input bytes (or sequences of bytes). These codes are of variable length, and a frequency distribution is used to decide how to allocate them; more frequently occurring sequences are allocated shorter codes.

The dictionary for Huffman encoding takes the form not of a linear list, but of a binary tree. This tree is built based on the frequency data from the input, and the leaf nodes represent the byte sequences in the file. Each nonleaf node of this tree represents one bit in the input file, and the two children are the states reached if that bit is 0 or 1 respectively. Therefore, the process of decoding a Huffman-encoded file is simply one of walking down the tree from the root node, reading each bit from the input, and moving to the appropriate child node. Every time a leaf node is reached, that byte sequence is written into the output buffer and the process returns to the root node.

Unlike in LZW compression, where the dictionary is implicitly stored in the compressed data, the tree must be stored in the file alongside the compressed bit-stream. This adds some overhead to the file and tends to make Huffman encoding less efficient for small files.

There is also an often used variant on Huffman encoding known as "Adaptive Huffman encoding," which adds the ability for the tree to change according to the shifting probabilities of certain sequences appearing in the input. The tree is also built dynamically as the data is processed, removing the need for the tree to be included in the file (in much the same way LZW does). Adaptive Huffman encoding is more efficient for large files or files that contain several different types of data, as it is not tied to producing a single frequency table for the entire scope of the input.

Huffman decoding can be very fast, although Adaptive Huffman is slower due to the need to maintain the tree as decompression progresses. The compression achieved by Huffman encoding is not generally as good as LZW on arbitrary data, but it is often used as a post process to further compress data from other compression systems. For example, LZW-compressed data can often be compressed further using Huffman encoding. This does add significantly to the complexity of and time required for decompression, however.

Other Compression Issues

On-the-fly decompression of data can speed up the loading process for assets, but it is generally not advisable to use it for data that is streamed or even simply loaded in the background during gameplay, as the decompression process will then have to "steal" processor time from the game itself (the exception to this, as noted previously, is RLE compression, which can often be faster than simply copying the data).

Another point to be wary of is that like encryption, there are patents on various techniques in the field. For example, Unisys held patents in several countries, including Canada, the U.K., and Japan, on the LZW algorithm, most of which expired in June 2004. A corresponding U.S. patent on the algorithm expired in June 2003.

As always, doing research into the legal implications of using any algorithm is strongly advised.

DISTRIBUTION MEDIA

There are many ways in which the distribution media for a game affects the assets it uses, the most obvious being the space available for storage. However, there are various other media-specific factors that can influence the asset- and disc-building process. What follows are descriptions of some of the more commonly encountered requirements and limitations of each type of media.

CD-ROMs

CD-ROMs are arguably the most ubiquitous distribution media, only recently being overtaken (slowly) by DVDs, mainly on games consoles. Compared to some media, CDs hold a comparatively large amount of data, typically 650 MB, although 700+MB can be crammed onto a disc using "overburning" techniques, where data is deliberately written closer than usual to the edge of the disc. With the increasing use of high-quality FMV and audio in games, however, CDs seem increasingly restrictive, and it is not uncommon for games to be supplied on several discs.

As mentioned previously, the bane of CDs is the time needed for the laser head to move across the disc surface when seeking to a new location on the disc. This access delay is the main factor in determining how long it takes data to be read from the disc. Most modern CD drives also feature an on-board cache, which reads a number of sectors ahead of the current location, enabling quick sequential reads of data. Again, performing long-distance seeks across the disc will tend to negate this benefit.

One subtle feature of CDs is that they are a CAV, or Constant Angular Velocity, technology. This means that the disc spins at the same speed at all times, regardless of the position of the laser head (as compared to CLV, or Constant Linear Velocity media such as Laserdiscs, which change rotational speed so as to keep the laser moving across the disc surface at the same velocity). As a result, the transfer rate of CDs is actually faster near the outer edge of the disc, where the head is moving across the surface more quickly.

Since data is burned onto CDs in concentric rings from the center outwards, this means that the *last* data placed on the disc will be read more quickly than the first. It is therefore beneficial to place data that must be read quickly as close as possible to the outside. In addition, if the volume of data on the disc is less than the full capacity, then adding a "padding file" to the start of the disc will effectively push all of the data outwards, boosting the reading speeds for everything.

DVDs

DVDs behave much like their predecessor CDs in many respects; they are also a CAV technology, so the same rules about read speeds being faster near the edge of the disc apply. They are also largely bound by the laser head seek times, which have not changed much since CD drives, although as the density of DVD discs is much higher, seeking over the same amount of data moves a significantly smaller distance on a DVD.

DVD discs can either be single-layer or double-layer (there are also some double-sided DVD discs, but these were mostly a commercial failure and are extremely rare). Each layer of the disc holds approximately 4.5 GB of data, and in a dual-layer disc the two layers are sandwiched together and so the laser must refocus to move from one to the other. This refocusing operation can take a very long time; 500 ms or longer is not unusual on some drives. Therefore, seeking between layers on a regular basis is generally not a good idea.

Cartridges

Cartridge formats are radically different from virtually every distribution media, as they are effectively just ROM chips attached to the main processor of the machine, and mapped into the address space as with any other memory. Cartridge capacities tend to be an order of magnitude lower than those of other media as well, due to the sheer cost of the mask ROM chips used: a typical cartridge game may only have 4–8 MB of space available.

Unlike CD or DVD formats, cartridges have no seek time performance problems at all, although the actual speed of access to data on them is generally somewhat slower than access to the main RAM of the system, due to cheaper, slower ROM chips being used. Some consoles allow several different cartridge memory bus speeds, with faster cartridge ROMs being available to publishers at a higher price!

As a cartridge appears as memory, cartridge-based systems typically have relatively little RAM because the majority of assets are expected to be used directly from the cartridge. As such, memory ready data formats are absolutely vital. Compression can be very useful in helping to fit all of the data into the limited space available, but again the shortage of RAM to decompress data *into* can be a major limiting factor.

Hard Discs

Hard drives are not generally a distribution media, strictly speaking, but most PC games install themselves to the machine's hard drive and store the majority of their assets there rather on the source discs, and some consoles (notably the Microsoft Xbox) feature an internal hard drive to which data can be copied for fast access.

Hard drives have very fast seek times and high data transfer rates, although for reading large numbers of files the seek times can sometimes become a serious issue. The high performance of these drives is often enhanced further by large quantities of cache RAM (8 MB caches on PC drives are not uncommon), both on the drive itself and sometimes the controller, which can have a large impact on performance.

As a result, hard drives are ideal for streaming operations, and can generally maintain quite a large number of separate streams before the data rate suffers unduly. Also, hard drive sizes are large enough that storing uncompressed copies of data for streaming is frequently a viable option.

One feature of hard drives that is less appealing, however, is that they often suffer from fragmentation, where the process of creating and deleting files has led to the free space being broken up into many small chunks, rather than being contiguous. Because of this, the act of reading a single file may involve many seek operations, and the performance characteristics of a heavily fragmented drive can become very unpredictable indeed. There is no good solution to this problem, unfortunately, beyond attempting to educate users as to why using a "disc defragmenter" to rearrange the files on their drive back into contiguous blocks is a good idea.

Unlike every other media discussed here, hard drives are also writable, which allows for some useful tricks, such as caching highly-compressed data in uncompressed form, and even using hard drive space as virtual memory, by swapping pages from RAM onto the disc as required.

Internet Distribution

Internet distribution is not really a distribution media, per se, but the basic concepts involved in preparing a game for downloading over the Internet are similar to those for other media.

Typically, Internet distribution places fairly strict limitations on the size of files so heavy duty compression is advisable wherever possible. Even though Internet access speeds are increasing, many users still have slow connections, and larger files will increase the server bandwidth required to distribute them. Fortunately, Internet distributed games are currently almost exclusively the domain of the computer, rather than console systems (although there are some Xbox games that allow for expanded content to be downloaded, and upcoming systems such as the Phantom® are designed to offer fully downloadable games), with the result that a lengthy decompression and installation process to the user's hard drive is perfectly acceptable.

Streaming over the Internet is possible, although few games have attempted this due to the wide variation in connection speeds and quality. Streaming in this manner must be several times more robust than that designed from streaming data from a disc, and the time delays involved are significantly larger, too: streaming a room from DVD may take five or six seconds, while streaming the same data over the Internet could easily take over a minute.

Handling downloaded content also requires fairly careful consideration of the security issues, too; content signing is almost certainly necessary to avoid maliciously modified data being used, and all code that could possibly read from an untrusted source needs to be carefully checked to ensure that it does not contain any bugs that could lead to a compromise of the software (for example, by allowing a maliciously crafted fake game file to overwrite the stack or executing code).

AFTER SHIPPING

Although in most cases the role of the asset pipeline ends when the final game disc is mastered, there are still some important tasks that need to be performed after this point. Some types of games (particularly PC multiplayer games) often have patches and content upgrades released after the game has hit the shops, and even on projects where there is no possibility of this (most console titles, for example), there is still a strong need to ensure that all of the data and tools for the game are preserved so that they can be used again in the future.

Data Archival

One of the most frequently overlooked asset management problems is that of archiving all of the source assets, so that they are available for other projects (a sequel, for example), and if the need arises the original game data itself can be reconstructed. There are two distinct sides to this problem: archiving the assets themselves, and archiving the pipeline itself.

Asset Storage

The simplest method for archiving the source assets is simply to archive the entire asset database. Most database and asset management systems provide functionality that allows the entire database content to be dumped to a file, which can then be stored on suitable backup media. This approach has the advantage that all of the contents of the database are preserved: the structure, past revisions of files, history, and other metadata. Reconstructing the database is also simply a matter of reloading the contents into the original application.

Even this type of archive does not represent the entire set of asset data from the project, however; the balance of probability is that there already exists a number of archives containing past revisions of assets from the database that were removed when they became too old or more space was required. Fortunately, by archiving the entire database, references to these will remain intact, so those archives can simply be stored alongside the full copy of the database, and their contents retrieved as normal when required.

The disadvantage of this, however, is that the amount of space required for the archive is very large, and a lot of the stored data will likely be redundant; for example, nonfinal revisions of assets are generally useless, unless radical changes in art style or construction occurred during the project. Even then, unless the changes were made relatively close to the end, the probability is that the old revisions have been removed or already archived.

Another approach, therefore, is to archive only the latest revision of each asset. In virtually all cases, these are the versions that are actually going to be needed in the future. This considerably reduces the amount of space required for the archive, making it easier to create and store. In addition, since only one version of each file is required, it is possible to store all of the files in a normal directory structure rather than the asset database.

This has advantages and disadvantages. On one hand, storing the files in a normal filing system makes retrieval much simpler because there is no need to install the asset database software and re-import the database into it. There is also less chance that if the archive copy becomes corrupt all of the assets will be rendered inaccessible; data errors will probably only affect individual files. On the other hand, none of the metadata associated with the assets is stored (unless this is exported as a separate file in some format), and if the asset pipeline was tightly coupled to the database it can be difficult to reconstruct it.

Archiving the Pipeline

As well as archiving the actual source asset *data*, it is also important to archive the asset pipeline itself as well. There are two reasons for this: first, it may not be easy to recover the correct versions of the various tools used in the pipeline to perform the processing, and changes to data formats or functionality may have rendered more recent versions of applications useless for integrating with older pipeline components. Second, there is usually a considerable amount of implicit information about the assets stored in the pipeline setup itself, such as processing settings, input and output directory structures, and dependency information, for example.

Without this, it can be very difficult to get the pipeline into a state where it is functional again, and it is even harder to ensure that everything is being processed in the same way as it was originally. Subtle errors in assets can very easily be introduced during this process.

One particularly awkward problem when archiving the pipeline setup occurs if the processing system interacts with the network or asset management systems to perform tasks. It may be necessary to (either when archiving or restoring the setup) change the addresses of servers, network drives, and so on so that the tools can find the data they require. Ideally, prior to being archived, the entire pipeline and asset database should be moved onto a single machine and tested thoroughly without a network connection. This ensures that all of the data required is available locally, and no tools are attempting to retrieve information from sources that have been overlooked.

Patching Data

As mentioned previously, while many types of games are "set in stone" once the master disc has been burned, in some cases it is necessary to issue patches or updates after the game has been shipped. In many cases, these will simply be fixes for bugs or incompatibility problems, which only require an update to the game executable itself, but in other cases assets will need to be patched or added as well. In particular, large multiplayer games often feature major changes to both game code and content as part of their regular update process, and some also offer "expansion packs" that add large quantities of new content, and are often distributed online as well.

While adding assets is relatively "simple," there are two different ways in which modified assets can be updated: either the entire new version of the asset file can be supplied with the patch, and used to simply overwrite the previous one, or a *delta*, or difference file, can be created, which records only the data that differs between the two. Supplying the entire file is the easiest option, but it can be awkward if a large file must be patched, particularly if the bandwidth or storage available is limited (for example, on a console online service).

Delta files essentially work by taking the updated file, and then removing all of the bytes that are the same as the original, recording the ranges of those bytes that *have* changed. This way, the vast bulk (hopefully) of the file is removed, leaving only the changed part. Some delta schemes are more complex than this—most notably, making allowance for bytes to be removed from or inserted into the file, and automatically moving all of the data after that point forward or backwards to allow the file size to change without having to include all of the data after the modified section again. Since delta files encode only the changes between versions, they allow files of any size to be updated, with the size of the modifications themselves becoming the limiting factor.

These patches can either be applied directly to the source data (if, for example, it is installed on a hard drive), or used to override it at runtime. This latter option is particularly useful if the assets are stored in a package file or other packed format;

in most cases, since the format is designed to be read-only, applying patches to a package is not a trivial process, especially if files need to be added or change size.

Overriding Packaged Data

Overriding assets at runtime is simple enough in theory; all that is required is that when the game looks for a given asset, the patch is searched first to see if an updated version is available. In the case of a package file based system, this can be done very simply by allowing the game to load multiple package files and read the file table information from all of them. If the load order is set so that patch packages are loaded first, and the file search routines always return the *first* matching file they find, then any file that is duplicated in a patch will be loaded from there in preference to the original.

Extending this scheme to allow for file deltas to be used instead of complete copies of files is slightly harder, and the simplest method for doing so depends on the system resources available. If the target platform has a hard drive, and the goal of using file deltas is simply to reduce the bandwidth required to download the patch, then the simplest solution is to create a complete package file containing the modified data when the patch is installed, by reading the original files from the package, applying the delta information, and then writing a new package file. This avoids the need for any support in-game for applying the patch delta information.

Using Runtime File Modification

If this is not possible however, due to storage limitations, then it is necessary to apply the delta information to files as they are loaded. This is a lot more involved, but with some care it can be implemented into the file handling system so that the bulk of the game code can remain unaware that a file is being patched. Essentially, what is required is to keep a marker in the file table indicating which files have delta information available, and where it is stored. Then, when one of those files is loaded, the delta information for it is also stored, and after each block of the file is read in, the modifications are applied before (or while) it is copied into the target memory.

Version-Based Patches

In some cases, there may be several different versions of a game in circulation, with different asset files: different releases for different territories, for example, or as the result of a number of previous patches that may or may not have been applied. In these cases, it is generally desirable that after applying the patch, all of the data files are bought up to date with the latest revisions of the assets.

In a scheme where the entirety of each modified file is distributed, this is relatively straightforward; the patch simply needs to contain *all* the files that may have changed since the first revision, and applying it will bring everything into line. However, if the file deltas are being used, then the process becomes much more complicated.

The problem is that applying the file deltas to a different version of the file from the one the delta was created against will, under virtually all circumstances, simply corrupt the file. The immediate solution to this is to include a checksum of the original file in the delta itself, which will allow the application process to check that the file is as expected before continuing.

Unfortunately, though, this merely solves the problem of accidentally corrupting files; it does not actually allow other versions of the file to be patched. There are two possible solutions to this: either create different deltas for each version of the file, and apply whichever has the matching checksum, or create a single delta that encompasses all file versions. The first option is the simpler of the two, but it tends to increase the patch size considerably if more than a handful of files may exist in different states.

Creating a single delta for many files is relatively simple in principle. Rather than simply containing the differences between one original file and the updated one, the delta file contains the differences between *every* original file and the updated one. In other words, any byte that is different between one or more of the versions is stored again in the delta. When the delta file is applied, any of these changes that are unnecessary for the version being patched will simply have no effect, as they will be writing the same data as already exists in the file.

This way, the delta can be used as a "universal patch," bringing any of the known versions of the file up to date. It is generally a good idea to still store the checksums of all the files used to generate the delta anyway, just in case a version was accidentally missed, or the user has a corrupt copy of the original data.

Compressing Patches

Obviously enough, the size of patch data can be reduced further, sometimes quite significantly, by compressing it. If the patch modifies the existing data files as a once-off operation, then the most efficient compression possible can be used, as the decompression process only has to take place once. However, if the patch is to be applied at runtime, then more care must be taken; using a fast decompression system such as those mentioned in the previous chapter is generally advisable. In addition, it is usually necessary to compress each patched file or delta separately, so that they can be extracted without the need to decompress the entire patch. If very large patches are being applied, it may even be necessary to compress the patch in blocks so that the section affecting a particular range of bytes in the original file can be extracted alone.

Patching over a Network

While in the majority of cases the update process works by downloading a patch file to local storage and then applying it (either as an install process or at runtime), there are some cases where it is necessary to apply a "hot-fix" patch at runtime, where the patch is sent to the game over a network and applied immediately. The typical use for this is in online gaming on consoles, where fixes for cheats or bugs must be applied without any local storage being available.

The vast majority of patches applied this way affect the game code, rather than the assets, but in some cases it may be necessary to alter the asset data too. In most cases, the procedure for doing this is much like the one when using a delta file patch from disc, except the delta information must be stored in a memory buffer somewhere. Then, as the affected file is read, the delta can be applied.

Another approach that is occasionally used, generally in games where support for network patching of assets was not implemented prior to shipping, is to allow the affected asset to be loaded normally, but then to patch the in-memory version of it. The difficulty of this depends largely on the type of asset in question, and how it is laid out in memory. Patches to be used this way generally need to be constructed by hand, rather than through an automatic process, although if the data in the asset file is in a memory-ready format, then it may be possible to use a delta of this as a starting point.

CONCLUSION

Arranging the layout of game files on disc to minimize seek times and increase throughput can have a massive effect on the performance of most media (cartridge-based systems being the exception to this rule). In addition, intelligent use of data compression can boost performance even further in some cases.

Verification of data integrity is useful for two reasons: to detect accidental corruption of files due to media faults, and to avoid malicious tampering with data by crackers or cheaters. Encryption can also help in some circumstances, although it is never capable of fully protecting the data on the disc as all of the information required for decryption has to be present somewhere.

Finally, after the game has shipped, the problems of patching and archiving may need to be considered. In particular, the patching process can be made much simpler and more efficient if some consideration is given to it before the final data formats are decided, and for games such as MMORPGs where patching is a frequent occurrence, this may be a very significant factor in the decisions.

Bibliography

[Evans96] Evans, Francine, et al., "Efficiently Generating Triangle Strips for Fast Rendering," available online at *http://www.cs.sunysb.edu/~stripe.*

[O'Rourke98] O'Rourke, Joseph, *Computation Geometry in C,* Second Edition, Cambridge University Press, 1998.

[Teller92] Teller, Seth, et al., "Visibility Computations in Polyhedral Three-Dimensional Environments," available online at *http://graphics.lcs.mit.edu/~seth/pubs/pubs.html.*

[Teller93] Teller, Seth, et al., "Stabbing Oriented Convex Polygons in Randomized $O(n^2)$ Time," available online at *http://graphics.lcs.mit.edu/~seth/pubs/pubs.html.*

Index